THE SUMMER ISLES

Also by Philip Marsden from Granta Books

Rising Ground: A Search for the Spirit of Place

THE SUMMER ISLES

A Voyage of the Imagination

Philip Marsden

GRANTA

Granta Publications, 12 Addison Avenue, London, W11 4QR

First published in Great Britain by Granta Books, 2019

Last printed July 19

A CIP catalogue record is available from the British Library

9 8 7 6 5 4 3 2

ISBN 978 1 78378 299 4
eISBN 978 1 78378 301 4

www.granta.com

Text designed by Lindsay Nash
Typeset by Avon DataSet Ltd, Bidford on Avon, B50 4JH

Printed and bound by CPI Group (UK) Ltd, Croydon, CR0 4YY

For Max, Jake and Tamara

Lí na fairge fora taí,
Gelded mora imme-roi:
Ra sert buidhe & glas
Is talam nad ecomrass.

The shine of the sea on which you sail
The brightness of the ocean over which you voyage:
It is spread with yellow and green;
It is solid earth.

Immram Brain, Voyage of Bran

Droops the heavy-blossom'd bower, hangs the
heavy-fruited tree –
Summer isles of Eden lying in dark-purple spheres of sea.

Alfred Tennyson, Locksley Hall

TRISH: You never said it was a big island, Terry.
TERRY: It's not big, is it?
TRISH: That's a huge island.
TERRY: Is it?
FRANK: Hard to know what size it is – it keeps shimmering.
ANGELA: Has it a name, our destination?
TERRY: Oileán Draíochta. What does that mean, all you
educated people?
TRISH: That rules me out. Where's our barrister?
BERNA: Island of Otherness; Island of Mystery.
TRISH: God, it's not spooky, Terry, is it?
TERRY: Not that kind of mystery. The wonderful – the sacred
– the mysterious – that kind of mystery.

Brian Friel, Wonderful Tennessee

CONTENTS

West Coast of Ireland

Lenan Head
Lough Swilly
Inishdooey
Malin Head
Greencastle
Tory Island
Inishsirrer
Gabhla
Bunbeg
Burtonport
Lough Foyle
Derry
Inishkeel
Malin More Head
Church Cove

Frenchport
Inishglora
Donegal Bay
Sligo
Inishkeas
Achill Island
Clare Island
Inishturk
Inishbofin
Omey Island
High Island
Slyne Head
Cleggan
Clifden
An Cheathrú Rua
Galway
Skerd Rocks
Ros an Mhíl
Galway Bay
Aran Islands
Inis Mór
Inis Meáin
Inis Oírr
Cill Rónáin

N

Carrigaholt
Kilrush
Loop Head
Shannon Estuary
Scattery Island
Kerry Head
Blasket Sound
Fenit
Dún Chaoin
Mount Brandon
Great Blasket Island
Dingle
Cork

Fastnet Rock

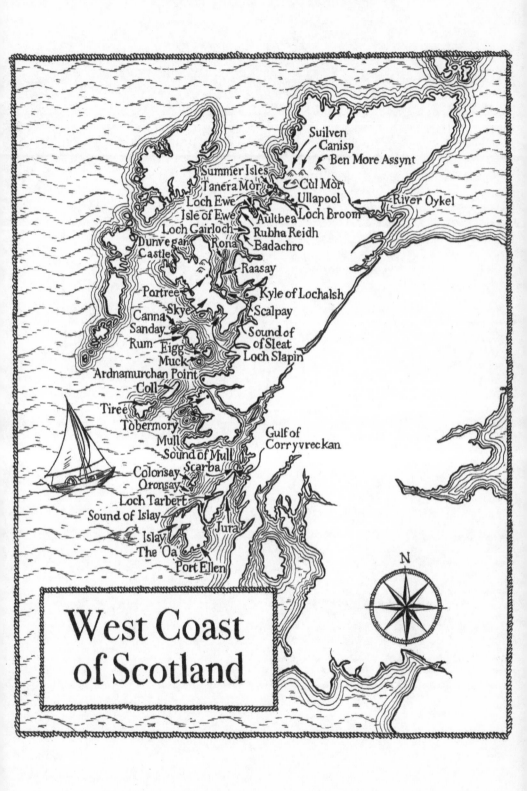

Suilven
Canisp
Ben More Assynt
Cùl Mòr
Ullapool
Loch Broom
River Oykel
Summer Isles
Tanera Mòr
Loch Ewe
Isle of Ewe
Aultbea
Loch Gairloch
Rubha Reidh
Dunvegan
Castle
Rona
Badachro
Raasay
Portree
Kyle of Lochalsh
Skye
Scalpay
Canna
Sanday
Sound of
of Sleat
Rum
Eigg
Loch Slapin
Muck
Ardnamurchan Point
Coll
Tiree
Tobermory
Mull
Gulf of
Corryvreckan
Sound of Mull
Colonsay
Scarba
Oronsay
Loch Tarbert
Sound of Islay
Jura
Islay
The 'Oa
Port Ellen

N

West Coast
of Scotland

1

WE WERE SAILING BACK FROM Fowey. It was late in the year and the October sun lay sharp on the Dodman point. The boat was bowling along in short seas. I squinted up at the sails, at their cream-coloured arcs against the blue of the autumn sky. At the top of the mast, where the rigging converged, the cups of the anemometer spun in a brisk following wind. With me was my friend Mike, skipper of countless passages in the windier corners of the world. I, on the other hand, had never skippered a boat to anywhere I couldn't reach by lunchtime. Come spring, I was due to sail up the Irish coast to the top of Scotland, single-handed, aiming for a small group of islands that, more than twenty years ago, I'd vowed to reach in memory of someone I loved.

Hence the overnight trip to Fowey, so late in the season, grabbing all the tips I could. We'd spent the previous evening going through the electrics and the radio, and the navigation equipment, and looking at a few changes to make to the halyards and sheeting – and I had carefully taken in the details, filling the pages of a notebook with technical information, and all the while thinking to myself: *What, in God's name, have I taken on?*

Now it was morning, and the sails were well set, and the boat was moving with ease, and we were sitting in the sun. I watched the Dodman grow larger off the starboard bow – golden fern and pale grass and the steep snub of the rock. Around its foot was a ruff of white where the seas rose and fell against the cliff. To the south ran a shifting surface of swells, their backs glittering with jewels, and I watched the waves roll on into the distance, becoming smaller as they headed out to the horizon, and thought to myself: *It is for such moments that all the labour of boats is worth it, that everything is worth it.*

Then I saw something strange. Some twenty miles to the west stood three tall shapes. I couldn't make out what they were. Ships' gantries? Masts? Too grey, too bulky. I took my binoculars and looked again. They resembled rocks or skerries, but they were elevated, like sea-stacks. Also, they shouldn't be there. What should be there, on that horizon, in that position, was the Lizard peninsula – the long, flat strip of land leading down towards Britain's most southerly point.

What I was seeing was a trick of the light – atmospheric refraction: the sun's rays are slowed in the earth's atmosphere, causing anything that appears far off to distort; sometimes the light even bends over the horizon to reveal things that are *below* it, beyond the normal line of sight. That afternoon the distant skyline of the Lizard had been altered and broken.

It is not an uncommon occurrence around the coast, and has caused some spectacular effects. In his *Letters in Natural Magic*, addressed to Walter Scott in 1831, David Brewster records all sorts of refractive phenomena – cows suspended in mid-air, ships appearing upside down. It hadn't been many years since the people of Hastings had spilled out onto the town's beach in alarm: the coast of France – generally safe and hidden below the horizon – was suddenly right there, just a few miles away.

Through binoculars, the rocks were altering. They had steepened and narrowed at the base. They now looked like the inverted pinnacles of Phuket. There were more too; they were multiplying to the south. Some of these ones were larger, their bluish shapes suggesting an entire archipelago. I had the explanation: I knew I was looking at an illusion. But something about the sight of new islands, unfamiliar ground in a familiar setting, persuaded me to suspend disbelief. I found myself picturing gull-flecked cliffs. I could hear the cries and see caves beneath, and breaking waves; I could see along the coast to where there were beaches and dunes and small houses pale in the sun, and people in strange dress moving along grass-centred tracks, driving herds of white cattle.

A tiny split had opened in the fabric of the world, and I found myself eagerly passing through it.

Long ago – when the saints had not yet reached these western shores, and heroes were still in possession of superhuman strength, and poets could cut down kings with a single satire, and music could put even the most fearsome warriors to sleep – another region of the earth existed, another layer to the earth's surface. The Celtic, or Brythonic, otherworld was a magical place where there was no sin or labour, no old age. It was a place of beauty and joy and shimmering palaces, where the trees hung heavy with fruit and blossom, fountains burst with cool water, and cauldrons remained full, however much was drawn from them.

In the manuscripts of medieval Irish literature are a group of stories known as *echtrai* – 'outings', or journeys to the otherworld. Only a few have survived, but what they reveal is the extraordinary hold that the otherworld exerts on the imagination. Magical apples, pure love and strange beasts all feature. In *Echtrae Chonnlai*, Connlae, son of Conn, is invited by a woman to visit the otherworld, and her description of it is so enticing that he is overcome by longing (*éolchaire*). He disappears with her in a glass ship, and is never seen

3

again. Cormac was the nephew of Conn, and he too was taken to the otherworld, but returned. He told of two forts surrounded by bronze walls and thatched with the wings of white birds, and a golden cup that shattered if an untruth was ever uttered.

A good deal of scholarly work has been carried out to try and pinpoint the otherworld from the literary sources, to unpick Christian elements that may or may not overlay pagan origins, to trace recurring features and examine possible outside influences. But when dealing with such a subject, conclusions have a habit of sliding like sand between your fingers. Reading the stories, letting their images take shape, is a much better way to understand their significance. They grew from the imagination, and it is the imagination that links us to them across the ages. The otherworld might not be the term we still use, but the ability to believe in places that are invisible, to build stories around them and inhabit them, remains the defining attribute of our species. The great Celtic scholar John Carey, who has studied early Irish literature as rigorously as anyone, concludes: 'I would suggest that the Irish Otherworld's characteristics are, by and large, those of the imagination itself – more specifically, of the imagination as expressed in narrative.'

Natural mounds and hillocks, old castles, ancient burial sites, misty hollows or lakes – these are the sort of places where the passing traveller might encounter the otherworld. But nowhere is more closely associated with its fantastic features than offshore islands. The risks of a sea passage add a certain allure to anywhere across the water, while the coast itself tends to throw up its own visual ambiguities – refractive tricks of the light, land-like fog banks. Add to that the boundlessness of the ocean, the colourful tales of returning sailors, and it is no wonder that the western seas became such a bountiful playground of imaginary places.

In those days, when navigation was little more than cosmic

speculation, the waters to this side of Britain and Ireland had many more islands – Tír na nÓg ('land of the young'), Tír na mBeo ('land of the living'), Tír Tairngire ('land of promise'), Emain Ablach, Avalon, Kilstapheen, Imaire Buidhe, Lyonesse, Heather-Bleather. There were islands that appeared once every seven years, islands that drifted about like giant plankton, populated islands beneath the sea. There were enchanted islands like Inishbofin, and longed-for islands like Hinba and the Green Island of Hebridean lore. There were islands that turned out not to be islands but great sea-monsters when the crews of St Brendan and Máel Dúin lit fires on their scaly shores.

The wider Atlantic was also scattered with otherworld islands. To the Greeks, it was the site of the Isles of the Blessed and Elysium. Plato placed in it the inundated land mass of Atlantis. The Arab geographer Al Idrissi dotted it with 27,000 islands. The spread of Christianity added its own longed-for places. In the eighth century, the island of Antillia was settled by seven Spanish bishops who had fled the Muslim conquest of Spain. The seven bishops founded seven cities and for hundreds of years, hidalgos and conquistadores set sail in search of Antillia, dreaming of its silver and its edifying pieties. But anyone who spotted it on the horizon always said the same thing: when a ship draws close, the island disappears.

Look at the Atlantic charts and portolans of the fourteenth and fifteenth centuries, at the vellum rolls that changed hands in Venice and Genoa and Lagos, and the empty spaces to the west are a potent blend of the factual and the fantastic: the Isle of Demons, Ultima Thule, the Islands of Saint Brendan, the Islands of Eleven Thousand Virgins, Bussland and Frisland all sit alongside the Azores, the West Indies, Greenland.

Most enduring of all the fictitious islands was Hy-Brasil. Some-times it was drawn just off the Irish coast and sometimes far to the south. The Spanish envoy to London noted in 1498 that 'for the last seven years the Bristol people have equipped every year, two, three or four caravels to go in search of Hy-Brasil'. I live in a house in Cornwall once occupied by a family who had lost all their money in the sixteenth century 'looking for an island called Hy-Brasil'. In 1674, a Captain Nesbit of County Donegal managed to land on Hy-Brasil and found a landscape of green hills and woods, but no people. But after his men lit a fire on the beach, a desperate-looking crowd appeared. They had been trapped there for generations and the sailors' fire had broken the spell. The clothes they wore were from a long-past era.

For five hundred years, Hy-Brasil inhabited the shrinking regions of unexplored ocean, in the borderlands between what is seen and what is imagined, a place whose idea long outlived the likelihood of its existence. Its last appearance on a chart was in 1865. But that wasn't quite the end of it. A few years later one of Ireland's greatest folklorists, T. J. Westropp, wrote about seeing Hy-Brasil: 'It was a clear evening, with a fine golden sunset, when, just as the sun went down, a dark island suddenly appeared far out to sea, but not on the horizon. It had two hills, one wooded; between these, from a low plain, rose towers and curls of smoke. My mother, brother, Ralph Hugh Westropp, and several friends saw it at the same time; one person cried that he could "see New York".'

Places are never just places: they are story and myth and belief. Certain types of places attract certain types of myth. Lakes are home to nymphs and deep-water creatures, forests to fauns and satyrs and dark threats, holy rivers wash us clean of our sins, high mountains are the realm of gods and dead heroes, caves are paths to the underworld.

Islands, on the other hand, can be more or less anything. They are where the imagination goes on holiday, ideals in physical form.

Their discrete geography allows a sort of abstract speciation to take place, with its own anatomy of otherworld marvels. They become an earthly fulfilment of all mainland fantasy: perpetual health, unending youth, perfect society, constant happiness, wise men and obliging women. Or they develop into arenas of unfathomable evil, their cliffs echoing with siren cries or the wails of a thousand demons. On land, dramatic hills or enclosing valleys encourage the making-up of stories; at sea the great emptiness takes the process one step further – the topography itself can be made up.

To the literal-minded, such things are pure folly, while those who go off in search of them are quixotic fools, laughable in their delusions. But how much truth is concealed in fantasy? And how often do those fools return not with what they were looking for, but with something of much more value? Alchemy never produced a single grain of gold, but it helped lay the foundations of scientific enquiry. No one really found Hy-Brasil or Antillia, because they never existed, but in looking for them, those medieval explorers discovered an entire new world.

When he left Spain in 1492, Columbus wasn't expecting to find America. He was expecting islands. Thousands of them. He had with him the 1474 chart of Paolo dal Pozzo Toscanelli, with Hy-Brasil and Antillia clearly marked. The entire westward route, from Europe to Japan, showed nothing but islands. It didn't occur to him that some might not be there, because he believed, as a committed millenarian, that all islands were but broken fragments of the ancient paradise, remnants from before the earth's perfect surface was shattered and the sea erupted from below. In rediscovering them, Europe's Christians would be bringing forward the day of Christ's glorious return and that promised time of prelapsarian bliss.

Islands reflect our inner wishes and beliefs – in the twenty-first century as much as in the fifteenth. We may have purged our charts of the imaginary, but that doesn't mean we do not long for mythical places. Our lives are still shaped not by reason but by hope and fear, by narrative, by projection. We seek to give form to such abstractions by attaching them to the shape of the world: hope is a hill, memory a house, fear is a cliff, disappointment an empty field. For all the pinpointing of every ruckle and molehill on the earth's surface, satellite imagery does not even begin to show the planet as we see it. Our maps may tell us where places are, and what they are, but they do nothing to reveal what they mean. Mircea Eliade suggested that mythical geography is 'the only geography man could never be without'. Oscar Wilde put it rather more graphically: 'A map of the world that does not include Utopia is not worth glancing at, for it leaves out the one country at which Humanity is always landing. And when Humanity lands there, it looks out, and, seeing a better country, sets sail.'

The islands of Britain and Ireland were themselves once regarded by Rome as an *alter orbis* – semi-mythical places detached from the three great continents of Africa, Asia and Europe. That they should make their own satellite islands into otherworlds is hardly surprising. 'It would seem that the notion of the otherworld had a very particular resonance for writers in the North Atlantic archipelago,' writes the medievalist Aisling Byrne. 'National landscape shapes national literature, as the multifarious Greek islands gave episodic shape to the *Odyssey*, the unbounded reaches of the North Atlantic informed fantasies of insular travel and discovery.'

The otherworld is more than just a fantasy island, full of strange creatures, magical trees and time-warps. It is all those places that we imagine, that we long for, that sustain our brief span on this earth. Out here in the far west, along the fractured coastline of Britain and Ireland, lies Europe's dreaming frontier, its open horizon, where the solid becomes fluid, the fixed wobbles a little and the cliffs and seas grow their own elaborate mythology. It has always occupied a certain place in the collective consciousness, and drawn a certain type to its shores. I should know. For most of my life, it's where I've chosen to live.

For several summers before I was married, I used to go and write in a cottage in the far north-west of Scotland. The cottage was on the banks of the upper Oykel and adjoined my aunt Bridget's house. Bridget was my mother's younger sister and she and her husband Francis had just moved up there, from a farm in Essex where they'd lived and worked for the previous quarter of a century. Now their children were all grown up, they were relocating to a place they'd chosen for themselves – the wilds of Sutherland.

I remember arriving there the first time. It was a warm June evening. I'd just returned from a year of research in the Middle East and the Soviet Union and needed somewhere quiet to shape my notes into a book. I had ridden up to Scotland from Somerset on an old Kawasaki GPZ550, a journey that had taken the best part of two days. When I turned down the track to the house, set into a bend in the river, with the bare hill beyond and the peak of Ben More grey and distant above it, my heart skipped a few beats. I found Bridget and Francis raking and scything in the evening sun, their forearms bare and scratched, their faces filled with a haymaker's glow, looking for all the world like settlers in a new land.

That summer, I alternated my writing with helping to clear the overgrown spaces around the house. Sometimes, after our work was done, Bridget and I would drive west to walk. We developed a fascination for the strange peaks that rise from the moors of Coigach and Assynt – Cùl Mòr, Cùl Beag, Canisp, Suilven, Quinag. They're not particularly high those peaks, those worn lumps of Torridonian sandstone, but they represent some of the oldest rocks in all Europe. From their tops, in the late afternoon sun, we looked out over the Minch, over the western sea. Its face changed and shifted with the sky above it. Sometimes it was opalesque, sometimes storm-grey, and sometimes it looked less like water than a sheet of beaten silver, and the silhouettes were not islands but glyphs and ciphers tooled into its surface. Those were the Summer Isles.

One of the extracurricular tasks I took on during those months was to sort out Bridget and Francis's books. They had boxes and boxes, many more books than shelves. I started by sifting the old Scottish books, passed down through generations – the topographies, the travelogues, the mountain guides, the bird guides and flower guides, the shooting memoirs. Bridget's interests were represented by her attraction to the more adventurous shores of belief – the works of Christmas Humphreys, Lao Tsu, Thomas Merton, Alan Watts and Arthur Waley. I recognized among them the presents she'd given me as a teenager, her attempts to open my eyes to a world beyond the immediate. And I recalled how much of my own questing urge I owed to her.

One afternoon, a book came out of the boxes with a familiar shape on its cover – the steep-shouldered profile of Cùl Mòr. In the foreground was the arm of a quay, and it took me a while to realize that it was the reverse image of what we'd been looking at from those western peaks. The photograph was taken from the Summer Isles, looking back towards the mountains. The book was Frank Fraser Darling's *Island Farm*.

In the late 1930s, the pioneering naturalist had gone to live on Tanera Mòr, largest of the Summer Isles, with his wife Bobbie and their young son. It was deserted. Their years spent there were an experiment in survival and self-sufficiency, in island crofting. Frank himself was a compelling figure – austere as a rock but with glimpses of a sentient being within: 'There was a time when I shunned humanity and cared little whether I had further contact with it; my heart and interest were with birds and beasts. Now it is different; I love my fellow-men ...' Many years later, in 1969, his Reith Lectures on *Wilderness and Plenty* helped give the science of ecology a new urgency, alerting the wider public to the threat of environmental catastrophe. In some small way, the Summer Isles were the crucible.

Bridget and I were captivated by the book, by its idealism and grit. Frank and Bobbie's fortitude was a studied antidote to the comforts of the urban world. Its extremes, at times, bordered on the comic: the winter night when they struggled in a gale to remoor their launch and Bobbie 'lost all activity: her face was blue and expressionless and her hands hung in front of her belly'; the fall that gave Frank a compound fracture of the leg – he did not think it necessary to go to the mainland but sat it out on the sofa, writing *Island Farm* at a rate of 5,000 words a day.

Rebuilding the courtyard and the quay, restoring the walled garden, the struggle to cultivate poor ground, the sheer force of their conviction – these were the things that impressed us, that we discussed: 'For over three years Bobbie and I have worked alone, sometimes with discouraged monotony, sometimes with doubts as to whether it was worthwhile unless the *idea* went further.'

The islands weren't that easy to reach, but we both agreed on the need to go there. A boat went from Ullapool, when the weather was right. But somehow Ullapool was a long way off and we were both busy, and we didn't have a chance that summer. Nor did we go when I came up for following ones. Then for a couple of years my work took me elsewhere, to eastern Europe and the Caucasus. One day, in mid-September, Bridget rang. She asked when I might be up.

'In the spring? I'll aim for that.'

'And this time, we might make it out to the Summer Isles.'

'Let's try.'

She said she'd been walking a great deal that summer, up the peaks in the west, and around the heights above Corrie Mulzie. She sounded happy. The next day she was planning to climb Ben More Assynt, largest of those far northern peaks – that's why she'd rung. I had been up it once with my cousin, and I told her what I remembered of the route: going in from Inchnadamph, a long steep grassy climb, then the bare rocks of the ridge and that otherworldly place that all true mountains have on top, where everything is suddenly sparse and desert-like and you feel that you've reached a place not entirely of this earth. The weather was as good as it had been all year. High pressure, cloudless skies, endless visibility.

Bridget never returned from Ben More. The mountain rescue team found her body in the early hours next morning. I don't understand her death now any better than I did then. I wanted to know what happened – but there were few details. She was found at the bottom of a steep gully. She'd fallen. That was all.

As the years have passed, narrative of a kind has imposed itself on what was essentially random, an accident. When she lived down south, Bridget used to go on retreat to a convent of Carmelite nuns in Oxford. She once told me that in Scotland walking had absorbed much of her need for contemplative silence. The mountains had become necessary to her. Ben More was the biggest, the one she'd been eyeing from her house, that hovered over her life there like a deity, the one from whose slopes rose the waters of the Oykel. Perhaps she shouldn't have gone alone, perhaps she shouldn't have gone at all. I could have discouraged her – Francis told me he'd tried: 'But it was impossible – you know that.' What matters now is only that she did go, that she is no longer with us, that she failed to live beyond her mid-sixties, that she never saw her grandchildren.

My own regret is that I cannot talk to her, cannot share with her those enigmatic things we both loved, that we never made it to the Summer Isles. When I think of her now, it is with the distinctive elegance of her generation, the selfless sense of duty to her family and her community, and the gaps in her life that such duty left. I think of her too in the convent, reflective and alone, and then on that evening when I first arrived, work-flushed and satisfied, with the cut grass lying all around her. And I think of her on that last September afternoon, high up on the slender ridge, the world spread out beneath her, walking with the gods.

So now when I picture mythical islands, it is the Summer Isles that come to mind, the view of them from the peaks of Assynt, their dark shapes in a sparkling sea, all they've come to mean to me in the years since. This book is about such places – places drawn by longing and memory, places just beyond our reach, places that aren't really there at all – and it's about what happens when you set sail in search of them.

2

It was my grandfather, bridget's father, who taught me to sail. He showed me how to hank on the jib, sweat the halyards, make off the sheets and hoist the main by hauling the throat and the peak together (he taught me too the pleasure, the necessity, of the language). He passed on the art of helming, of *feeling* the boat through the tiller as a rider feels the mouth of a horse; he taught me how to trim the sails, to tie the right knots, to row and to scull. These were the practical lessons. But behind them were also unspoken things that settled far deeper in me – the strange elemental appeal of being on the water, the mystique of boats, the way he spoke about his own, the tenderness he showed every piece of tackle, the winter routine of hanging all the blocks on a lanyard and lovingly varnishing each one, the visceral hurt he felt when anything was damaged.

Later in my teens, I jumped at any opportunity to crew. Friends, friends of friends, anyone who had a boat and wanted an extra pair of hands. I sailed up and down the south coast of England, to Cork and Bantry Bay, back and forth across the Channel to Brittany and Normandy. I loved the footloose rhythm of those trips, arriving in unfamiliar harbours, sailing on the next morning. I gazed out to sea, I read a lot. I enjoyed bad weather, reefed down in heavy seas. It seemed then a perfect existence – contemplation mixed with moments of high adventure. But like all teenage dreams, it was big on ideals and light on responsibility: I was utterly ignorant of the weight those skippers bore.

I bought my first boat with the advance for my first book. It cost £250. It was an imitation of a Laser dinghy. The number 2 on its sail should have been a warning; I suspect there was never a number 3. On Loe beach, I handed over the cash to a man who seemed a touch too keen to accept it. The little boat was massively over-canvassed. Off St Mawes Castle, the nose hit a swell, dug in, and the whole thing somersaulted, throwing me into the water. The fisherman who rescued me grumbled as he hauled my dripping form in over the gunwale: 'You're the only bloody thing I caught all day.'

There were then two other boats. First a 1967 Nordic Folkboat, and a launch that was even older. I never went far in those boats – out into the Fal, up the Helford River and the Carrick Roads, to the coves around St Anthony's Head when the children were young. It was day sailing, in waters I knew well. But the years of coast-hopping had left me with the conviction that longer sea voyages hold in them some hidden capacity for revelation. You leave the land and its familiarities, you operate under a different set of rules, you encounter dangers and wonders, see the world from the side; you return changed, enlightened. It is a technique that combines the extremely practical with the extremely abstract. During years of travel, I had developed a land-based version of it. Now to pursue the original version at sea.

Similar to the otherworld journeys of the *echtrai* are the Irish *immrama*. Literally 'rowings about', *immrama* tell the stories of those who took to the seas in pursuit of some elusive destination – Máel Dúin, the sons of O'Corra, Snegdus and Mac Ríagla, Bran, son of Febal, and Brendan. The stories are classic marvel tales, featuring many of the otherworld elements of the *echtrai*. But the emphasis is on the sea and on islands – islands of joy and hellfire, islands filled with laughter or blood, filled with crystals or apples. In *immrama*, wrote the Celticist Barbara Hilliers, 'the sea connects the real world to the supernatural . . . connects places that seem like heaven, and places that seem like hell'. Of all environments, it is the sea that has the greatest ability to transform – as the crumbler of coastlines or the great driver of the world's climate, as much as the conduit for our own restless hopes. The sea enables and it destroys. It is a constant reminder that we are powerless beside the forces of nature – and that what we feel as firm beneath our feet is not solid. If terrestrial journeys are simple trials of the body, then a sea journey is a passage of the soul.

Some sailors say they will only 'turn left' when they reach the end of the English Channel, heading for the warmer skies of southern Brittany and the non-tidal waters of the Mediterranean. But I had unfinished business to the right. My instinct was to head up to the islands of the west, up to the Summer Isles. Sailing there single-handed, in a boat I didn't have, using skills I'd never acquired, was not the easiest way to reach them. But if I have learned anything from my years of travelling, it is that a journey's trickiness is what makes it most rewarding. Looking for imaginary places isn't meant to be easy.

I began with the boat. I had certain stipulations. It had to be big enough for the whole family to sleep aboard. (Once I'd cracked the problem of hopping along the coast, I naturally planned to impose its pleasures on those dearest to me.) But it must also be small enough to sail on my own. Something longer than thirty feet, but smaller than thirty-five.

My grandfather had left me with his views on what made a vessel worthy. 'Good lines' were essential – form and function fused in the sheer of the hull. Also, a boat should be wooden. In his day, most such boats were. To look for a wooden boat now, in the twenty-first century, when fibreglass offers so much more in terms of comfort and convenience, is mildly eccentric. A yacht-club adage goes: If you don't like someone, leave them a boat in your will; if you really don't like them, leave them a wooden boat.

But there's something about wooden boats. The noises they make, their smell, the subtle curve of their topsides, the way the boards bend to the ribs and frames, to meet at the stem. They have a shape that is unlike anything else made by man, a long evolution of the practical and the aesthetic in which what looks good can generally be held to work well. After spending a good deal of time in recent years planting and tending to 4,000 oak trees on our small farm, I also felt a certain aptness in putting oak between me and the water. Wooden boats have one other advantage: they are often cheaper to buy.

Months of cyber-touring the yards of Britain and Ireland were interspersed with actual visits. I looked at boats in Cornwall and Liverpool and on Lough Swilly in Donegal and on Strangford Lough. In Mersea, I made an offer on a gentleman's yacht designed by one of the great post-war designers, Laurent Giles. She was dignified and ample, fallen on hard times, and had been on the market long enough for me to make a low bid. But the same day, someone walked in, saw the boat, and named a better price. I was cast down for a while – then came a call from a broker about a boat in Salcombe that was coming up for sale. 'I think she's the one for you,' he said. She was smaller, thirty-one feet, but the work of another of the great post-war designers, Alan Buchanan. When a set of pictures pinged into my inbox, my pulse quickened at the sight of her raised bow, the roominess of the cockpit, the saloon with the bowed and varnished timbers overhead. He was right.

On her dodgers was the name *Tsambika*. Exactly what lay behind it had been lost somewhere in the series of six owners she'd had since her launch. All I could glean was that on the island of Rhodes is a monastery where the Virgin of Tsambika, if prayed to correctly, would happily provide a baby to anyone struggling to have one. A Byzantine fertility cult on a far-off Mediterranean island seemed a suitable name for my purposes.

There was a lot to sort out. The boat was in good order, but the jobs list grew. I had writing projects to finish, research to do. The trees I'd planted needed mulching and weeding for the summer. And I was going to be away from my family. I aimed to come back as often as I could, whenever I could leave the boat safely. But nothing could avert the fact of my sustained absence. Charlotte shared in discussions of plans and ideas with her gift for enthusiasm, as if she was going too. But I knew the burden she was being asked to bear – the demands of single parenting, the marshalling of children, the running of the house. And she was worried. I hired a life raft and bought a small PLB (personal location beacon), which would transmit my location if I fell overboard.

The first stage was to sail to south-west Ireland. For that I needed backup. Most people I approached baulked at the idea of crossing the Celtic Sea before May. But a friend put me on to Ian, who jumped at the chance. Ian had skippered boats all over the world, was up for anything, and was a qualified instructor. I could use the passage for training.

By early spring I was ready. *Tsambika* lay a mile or so downstream from our house, in a narrow stretch of the upper Fal where the bottom of the oak woods brushed the top of the tide. The leaves were not yet out, but there were bluebells beneath them and the white stars of stitchwort in the hedgerows. Charlotte and the children came down. We loaded the last bags of food aboard. They'd cooked flapjacks. There were jars of homemade jam and pickle and hand-drawn cards, which I displayed on the bookshelves. The three of them stood at the end of the pontoon as we cast off. The space widened between us. Our black-and-white spaniel leapt into the water and swam after the boat until she realized she would not catch it.

The wooded point began to close on them all, three waving figures and the dog's head below them. I was left with the sailor's doubts, the chill of separation, the guilt of abandonment, and the miles and miles ahead.

Darkness came that evening with a cold that sucked every shred of comfort from the earth. We were somewhere north of the Isles of Scilly. At midnight, Ian went below to sleep. I began my watch, alone for the first time. Settling in the open cockpit with the auto-pilot on, I shoved my hands deep in the fleece-lined pocket of my oilskins. Like a tortoise, I withdrew my head inside the hood. The compass was a dim backlit glow, fluctuating around 245°. The main-sail was a pale presence overhead. Beyond the coachroof, I could see spray flashing in the red of the bow-light. The boat was bucking and racing in twenty-plus knots of wind.

I felt sick. Not seasick, but sick. I had done so, pretty much, since we'd left. Beneath a sunless sky, I'd spent the day staring at the ever-shifting landscape of swells, and it made me feel sick. I put it down to nerves. When I'd told my yachtie friends I was sailing up to Scotland, turning right at Land's End, they said: go up the Irish Sea, don't go up the west coast of Ireland. Mike told me he'd tried the west coast once, but when he rounded Mizen Head, he found such a mountainous swell that he turned back. If he wouldn't do it, with crew, with years of experience behind him, then perhaps it wasn't the place for a novice single-hander.

But things look different when you're in a warm studio, when you're planning, looking at charts and reading books, when the imagination holds sway. Of course I'd go up the west coast! The west coast was the place of islands – real and otherwise. I'd head north from Dingle, weave in and out of shelter, bide my time. I'd be OK.

Now I was in a small boat on an empty ocean, and it was the middle of the night, and I felt sick. I gripped the helm and looked out into the darkness. I could hear rather than see the waves behind my shoulder, mountings of watery bulk that came up and shunted the boat – stern up and forward, then bow up as each one rolled through. Sometimes a crest would thud against the side and there'd be a pause before it slapped down on my back. Once or twice the boat slewed over and the end of the boom clipped the water and dragged, and I was aware – in the hiss of it and the dim white foam – how fast we were going. I heaved in the sheet. For long periods there was nothing to do but watch. Hence the name.

My eyes grew heavy. Shadows played tricks. Shapes appeared in the darkness, thoughts dissolved into dream . . . *railway station* . . . *forest* . . . *childhood bedroom* . . . Then, with a jolt, I woke, twisting round to scan the blackness for ships' lights. I checked my course before settling back against the coaming, against the cold. My nose was rubbing the Velcro chin-flaps of my hood. Eyelids dropping again, shapes forming, reforming . . .

Suddenly, there *was* a shape. A flash, beneath the water, from the side. Like a torpedo. I raised myself up to see better, but it had gone. Had I imagined it? I looked at the dark water. Then there was another, two of them – glittering Vs closing in on the boat, moving fast beneath the surface. Dolphins!

I switched on the autohelm, clipped on my harness, and edged forward. It wasn't their bodies I was seeing but their outlines, traced beneath the surface in trails of sparkling phosphorescence. One skimmed past the bow. Then another two, from the opposite side.

Now there were five, lighting up the water in a display of submarine fireworks. Gripping the shrouds against the tilt of the boat, I tried to follow one at a time, but they'd cross, or swim together, or underneath each other until I was dizzy with watching. I was wide awake now, restored by the circus wonder of it all. I stood there for some time until they flitted off, lights fading back into the seas, into the night.

An hour or so later, I was ready for sleep again. Ian came up for his watch.

'Anything?'

'Few dolphins.'

'Nice.'

The changing of the night watch is no time for chat.

All next day we sailed through empty seas. We sat and talked in the sun. I asked Ian how he'd first got into sailing.

'Growing up in Sheffield didn't exactly lend itself to the maritime life. I was actually thirty-two when I first stepped on a sailing boat.' From then on, progress was swift. Dinghy sailing on a reservoir led to the open sea and soon he'd chucked in his job to sail around the world with a friend in their own boat. He told stories of the Galapagos, of the Red Sea, of fights in Portsmouth pubs and a retired Croatian warlord who wanted help crossing the Pacific in his yacht. 'It was with the Croat that we spotted an island on the Admiralty chart that didn't appear on the electronic chart. We were puzzled. The Croat said that maybe they blew it up. When we reached the place, though, there was a bit of sand with palm trees on it, and he shrugged: "See? Is not so easy to blow up an island."'

We did some drill – running through the outer regions of function on the chart plotter, a few diesel-engine checks, and a man-overboard drill. 'Useful to be able to hove to, even though you'll be single-handed.' Ian threw a fender into the water, and said:

'Now pick it up.' Within moments it was well astern, further by the time I'd brought the boat round, backed the jib, sheeted the main and lashed the helm. I'd tried this before, but even so it was a full ten minutes before the fender was back on board.

I spent downtime that day sitting with my back to the mast, looking out to windward, wave-watching. They came out of the west like shifting mountains, each one different, each one in a state of tension as it offered up its slope and built to break, or not. How many hours of my life have I spent watching waves? Too many to count. What I do know is that whether from a cliff, a surfboard or from the deck of a boat, those hours have been among the happiest. Nothing I've ever seen in the inanimate world comes close to the simple drama of a breaking wave.

In pre-Christian Ireland, waves were more than just waves. They were given names, as if they were fixed features, part of the earth's topography – which in a way they are. 'Beyond the ninth wave' was the phrase used in myth to describe the country's true border, the beginning of alien territory. Rudraige, Clíodhna and Tuath were the Three Waves of Erin, and if the king was in peril, his shield would cry out and all over Ireland the shields of warriors would echo that cry, and the Three Waves of Erin would pick up the sound and spread it on around the coast.

Destructive, unpredictable, beautiful – waves have all the potent caprice of the gods, or of fate itself. They suggested powers of prophecy and counsel. A man once asked St Columba what the meaning was of the strange sound he'd heard coming from a wave, and Columba told him: 'One of your household has died.' The tenth-century Irish text *Colloquy of the Two Sages* recounts how young Néde goes down to the sea because 'poets deemed that on the brink of water was always a place of revelation. He heard a sound in the wave, to wit, a chant of wailing and sadness . . . so the lad cast a spell on the wave, that it might reveal what the matter was.' The surf brought messages from the otherworld, from the place of dead souls and eternal youth, and the mysteries they contained were the mysteries of all those mysterious islands beyond the horizon.

That evening the wind dropped. The seas grew still. The sun laid a yellow track across the water and we headed into it, slightly north of its line. When the moon rose, it was dead astern and the thinner, silvery line it laid was the exact path of our course. Later, on my two-to-four watch, the loom of the Fastnet lighthouse began to sweep across the sky. We raised the Irish coast at dawn.

We were tired now; the weight of sleeplessness slowed us. I felt less sick. I resumed my place against the mast, looking out over the other side, to leeward, not at water but at the waves of the Munster skyline. The day unfolded in a series of rocky headlands and bays and islands – Mizen Head and Dunmanus Bay, Sheep's Head and Bantry Bay, Dursey Island and the Skelligs. Fixed as they are, these features are made a little more fluid, a little more ambiguous, by the stories attached to them. We sailed past the rock of Inis Boí, 'the Cow', where the Cailleach Béara lived – the 'Hag of Béara', with her numberless years and her miraculous eyesight and her feet that never touched the ground. In the mouth of the Kenmare River was Inbhear Scéine, where the wife of Amergin the White-kneed drowned, and the place where Amergin himself landed, placing his right foot upon the shore to begin Irish history with a poem, his famously enigmatic, shape-shifting utterance:

> I am wind on sea,
> I am ocean wave,
> I am roar of sea,
> I am stag of seven tines,
> I am hawk on a cliff . . .

Long before Ireland's interior was mapped, its sites were known in *dinnseanchas*, a body of medieval literature that translates loosely as the 'lore of high places'. If you wanted to be a poet, there were years of rigorous training, and part of the training was to know by heart your *dinnseanchas*, to be able to reach a piece of high ground or marsh or plain or wood and recount what its name meant, what happened there, which incident from the Fenian Cycle it had witnessed. In *Acallam na Senórach* (*Tales of the Elders of Ireland*), St Patrick is taken on a tour of Ireland by the old Fianna warrior Caílte to see the significant places of the heroic age. Only by knowing each site will the Christian faith he brings have any chance of success: 'They set off for the Cataract of the Birds, now called the Cataract of the Oak, thence to the Bridge of the Nine, now called the Bridge of Slaughter, north to the Red Ridge of the *Fián*, now called the Ridge of Baskets, across the Ford of the Grey Stag, to the grave of Caílte, Slaughter of the King . . .'

There are many such passages in *Acallam na Senórach*. I loved that idea: topography as text, a mnemonic for oral lore. My last book had been, in part, about the way certain places, certain natural features in the landscape are made sacred, and how they stimulate the story-telling urge. 'In *dinnseanchas*,' wrote the contemporary poet Nuala Ní Dhomhnaill, 'the land of Ireland is translated into story: each place has history that is being continuously told. The landscape itself . . . contains memory, and can point to the existence of a world beyond this one.' Ireland's writers, from the anonymous scribes of its early tales to Patrick Kavanagh and Seamus Heaney, have made the land itself the ore of their work. *Dinnseanchas* is a variation on otherworld stories, featuring places that are not quite real, but not entirely fantasy either.

We had dolphins all that day. A pod of eight joined us off Mizen Head, ten off Dursey Island, and another dozen near the Skelligs.

Entering Dingle harbour, we spotted three tourist boats circling Ireland's most famous dolphin. Fungie came over and swam in with us for a while, a cetaceous pilot. When Fungie dies, a large part of the local economy will die with him; a bronze statue of him already stands on the quay.

We tied up on the pontoon and ate and drank in the first bar we came to. We slept like soldiers. I saw Ian off in the morning, on a bus to Kerry airport. Passage sailing brings a certain intimacy. I was sad to see him go. He left me with two bits of advice he gave his students: 'Choose your weather – a patient sailor always has good winds. And remember –' he gave me a knowing half-smile – 'the hardest thing is throwing off the lines.'

3

My first visitor on board was Danny Sheehy. Poet, boat-builder, fisherman and farmer, Danny was also a veteran of several epic sea voyages. He had rowed round Ireland and sailed to Iceland in the wake of St Brendan. Now he was part-way through a pilgrimage to Santiago de Compostela, rowing to Corunna from Ireland with three others in a *naomhóg* he had built himself. A *naomhóg* – literally 'little saint' – is what they call a *currach* down in Kerry, and a *currach* is little more than a canvas-hulled dinghy. Danny and his three crew had left Dublin a couple of summers ago, crossed to Wales, and from Wales to Cornwall, to Brittany and down to the Basque region of Spain. They would soon be joining the boat again for the final stretch along the coast to Galicia.

When I introduced myself on the phone, I told Danny I'd just arrived from Cornwall in a wooden boat and I was writing about mythical islands. I'm not sure which of those things persuaded him to drop what he was doing – but within an hour, in navy reefer and Breton cap, he was swinging one leg up over the guardrail, stretching out his hand with a 'How are yer?' and, with the other, presenting me with a bunch of narcissi, a bag of salad, some herbs in a rubber band, and five heads of purple-sprouting broccoli.

'From my own garden. It'll help with the scurvy.' He looked up the mast and then from stem to stern. 'Fine boat. She of oak?'

'Oak frames, yes. Iroko boards.'

'Ah, but I bet she holds the water well!'

Down below, we settled opposite each other in the saloon. I cracked the seal on the ship's whisky and poured out two glasses. The narcissi I put in a third. Danny raised his glass and toasted the boat and my journey, and I toasted his boat and his journey and then he said: 'Cornwall, so?'

He told a story of coming into Padstow one night last summer, rowing round from Bude, and it was late and dark and they hit the sandbar as they came in – had to jump out and scramble over it.

'There's not a soul about in the town when we get there. So I tell the boys, I'll be sleeping here in the doorway. But one of them goes off and comes back with a suite in the hotel!'

He pushed up his cap, scratched his forehead, and smiled. In fact, he was smiling already. His face was set in a permanent half-smile, as if behind the surface of everything was one big joke.

Sixty-five years ago, Danny had been born in west Kerry to a family of storytellers and artists. Until he was thirteen, he spoke only Irish. He had always loved the sea, and good company and music. For the Compostela *immram* he had all three.

'We're not very good, but we're always keen to make a noise. When we get to a port, we make sure to take our instruments straight into the middle of town. *Muna bhfuil agat ach gabhar, bí i lár an aonaigh leis* – "If all you have is a goat, go to the centre of the fair."'

One of the oarsman had dropped out, and for the last leg Danny had just recruited the Oscar-winning musician Glen Hansard ('like getting Shergar to plough a field' was the comment of one of the other crew I met later).

I asked him about building the *naomhóg*.

'I did it in the traditional way – I used tarred canvas on a frame of willow laths. Very important, the tar. Sets the canvas to the frame.'

But it just made me think how flimsy the whole thing is. The little vessels are designed without a keel and without ballast; they do not take the seas in the way that a boat like *Tsambika* does, but bob over them like a cork. Danny had been with boats long enough to know the dangers. 'We only have three rules on our boat. There'll be no captain, there'll be no complaining, and there'll be no anger.'

It was early evening when we went back out on deck. The wind had freshened.

'Good luck to you!' said Danny.

From across the harbour a halyard was slapping hard against a mast, rising in pitch. 'And to you,' I said, adding: 'Do you ever get nervous?'

'*Lagachar corp agus lagachar aigne, / Agus lagachar eile a bheith dian ar an bhfarraige.* "Weakness of body and weakness of mind, / And another weakness is to have no fear of the sea." It's part of being alive. Only those who don't know the sea are not afraid.' He smiled. 'What would you say is the toughest thing at sea?'

'Bad weather?'

'No! I tell you, it's the snoring of your fellows!'

'One advantage of single-handed sailing.'

He rested the flat of his hand against the mast, as if in blessing. 'There's a couple of lines I say every morning when I'm at sea.' He then bowed his head and, with the reverence of one who believes in the power of prayer, recited:

> 'As I cross the deep ocean,
> O king of patience, take me by the hand.
> And if the seas grow too steep,
> Holy Mary, look down upon me, do not leave me.'

Then he touched his cap and was gone. His strides rang out on the floating pontoon, growing fainter as he climbed the walkway back to dry land.

I cooked up his broccoli and his sage. I scattered it with his parsley, and poured melted butter on it all. I ate it standing up in the cockpit, looking out at the harbour and the town, and above the houses, at the grey bulk of the mountains. The fruits of Corca Dhuibne! Danny's vegetables, his herbs and flowers, and his words, still resonating in the boat's timbers.

In the morning, I checked the engine and saw behind it, where the propeller shaft pushed out through the deadwood – *drip, drip, drip, drip* . . . Two bolts were hanging out and the bracket was loose and there was water coming in. It must have worked free on the passage over. For a moment, I just looked at it. I was too shocked to do anything, pulled up hard by my deep-down vulnerability.

The bilge pump could deal with it for now. I tracked down an engineer and he came and fixed the bracket. But there was still the question of how to stop it happening again. I didn't want to go to sea with the thought of it spinning off and ripping a hole in the stern. The engineer recommended fitting a plate to absorb the engine's vibration. I ordered the plate but it would take several days to arrive. Several days! Several days being unable to get going, to start jumping along the coast. In fact, I found I was relieved to defer the moment of leaving – *the hardest thing is throwing off the lines.* And it gave me some time.

Danny had talked about a collection of books in Dingle library, making it sound like a hoard of hidden treasure. 'Go through to the back of the library and you'll see a door and through that you'll come to some narrow stairs there and at the top of the stairs is a

30

room. In that room you will find the best books in the whole world. Ask Bernard for the key. Mention my name.'

I followed his instructions. I climbed the stairs. I unlocked the door on a space which had not been disturbed for a while. The air was stale with book-smell. Utility shelving covered the walls and formed a cramped archipelago of shelf-islands in the middle. There were Celtic studies from Wales to Western Scotland, archaeology, religious history, journals from the Royal Irish Academy, and bound sets of *Ériu* and *Béaloideas* and *Revue Celtique*, and fifty volumes of reprinted manuscripts from the Irish Texts Society, containing *dinnseanchas* and *immrama* and *echtrai*. Irish, English, Welsh, Scottish Gaelic, French, Magyar and Russian. Six thousand books, and all the collection of one man – Celtic scholar and monk, Monsignor Pádraig Ó Fiannachta.

Many years ago, I was going to write a book about all this, about the Celts. I signed a contract with my publishers, amassed a shed-load of research and did a summer course in the Irish language at the University of Galway. I even had a mock-serious title – *Combing the Celtic Fringe*. Then I got cold feet. Too much gift-shop Celtic, too many Celtic mugs and Celtic knotwork. There was also the weight that the name 'Celt' still bears from the mid-nineteenth century. It was then that cultural historians like Ernest Renan and Matthew Arnold identified the Celtic type – that poetic soul, flighty and feminine, much given to music and mysticism but also sadly inclined to defeat in the real world of wars and politics.

'The Celtic race,' wrote Renan in his 1854 essay *La poésie des races celtiques*, 'has worn itself out by taking dreams for realities and in pursuing its splendid visions. The essential element in the Celt's poetic life is the adventure – that is to say, the pursuit of the unknown, an endless quest after an object ever flying from desire.' However true that may be for those who live along this coastline, or by the imagination, it is certainly not confined to 'the Celt'.

Even before the end of the nineteenth century, even in the heady years of the Celtic Twilight, W. B. Yeats became sceptical of such ethno-determinism. He was as interested in folk dreams and splendid visions as everyone else (much more so, in fact). But, in a way that stepped outside his racially obsessed times, he saw the tendency not as distinctly Irish or Celtic but as a glimpse of something that was once universal. What is 'thought wholly or almost wholly Celtic', he wrote in 1898, 'is of the substance of the minds of the ancient farmers and herdsmen. One comes to think of the Celt as an ancient farmer or herdsman who sits bowed with the dreams of his unnumbered years, in the gates of the rich races, talking of forgotten things.' Yeats wasn't always convinced of the cultural nationalism that he himself had helped ignite. Of the Irish tradition of elaborating the land with story, which created the literature of *dinnseanchas,* he wrote: 'Have not all races had their first unity from a mythology that marries them to rock and hill?'

The 'Celtic Fringe' is now largely discredited, obsolete. It says as much about the nostalgic yearning of the industrialized classes who created it as about the far west itself. But in 2015, a hugely thorough genetic study suggested that, during the Bronze Age, there was a large-scale migration of people from the Pontic-Caspian steppe into Europe, bringing with them a proto-Celtic language. The idea of a surviving fringe on the Atlantic coasts, where traces of Celtic languages remain, begins to look a little less tenuous.

In amongst the shelves of that upper room was also an assorted collection of Blasket Island books. It was a library within a library – the canon of a dozen or so memoirs, plus numerous editions of commentary and photographs, poetry, criticism and social study, and each one of those volumes concerning a single island which, in the 1920s and 1930s, when the original books were written, had no more than twenty-two households.

It was a couple of decades earlier when the people of the Great Blasket noticed that learned gentlemen were coming to the island to study the way they lived and the language they spoke. When he saw these men arrive, the king of the island made sure to direct them to the house of Tomás Ó Crohan, who was known to be a great talker. Carl Marstrander, from Norway, was among the first of the scholars, and he impressed the islanders by sharing their manual work and also by taking a paddle from a *naomhóg* and pole-vaulting over Tomás's roof.

Tomás was the first to write a memoir. When he was shown Maxim Gorky's *My University* and Pierre Loti's *Pêcheur d'Islande*, he was persuaded to try his hand. Written in Blasket Irish, *The Islandman* was then translated into English. It became a bestseller. After that, pretty much everyone on the Blasket had a go – Maurice O'Sullivan; Peig Sayers; Méiní Dunlevy, the nurse; Gearáid Cheaist O'Cathain; Tomás Ó Crohan's son Sean; and Peig Sayers's son Michael Ó Guiheen. The books established them as probably the most recorded rural community in Europe.

Being British and not Irish, I have been spared having to study the books in school. So I've grown to love their tales of sudden joy, the nonchalance in hardship, the relish in storytelling and language, the heartiness, the courage and resilience, and the overall impression of lives so alien they seem separated not by a narrow sound but by an ocean. Nor has their charm been punctured by frequent reading of Flann O'Brien's biting parody of them in *An Béal Bocht*, *The Poor Mouth*.

The books made a mythic island of the Blasket. The writer Seán Ó Faoláin said that going there 'was like taking off one's clothes for a swim naked in some mountain-pool'. It was Tír na nÓg, the island where no one grows old; on the Blasket, Ó Faoláin found 'that world of the lost childhood of my race where I, too, became for a while eternally young.'

33

Real life on the Blasket was harsh, isolated and punctuated by premature death. Of Tomás's ten children, only two survived him. The world outside was changing even as it celebrated the life of the islanders. Within two decades of the books' publication, the islands were deserted.

The next day I hired a bicycle and headed out to the far end of the peninsula. At Dún Chaoin quay, I took the small boat that crossed Blasket Sound when conditions allowed. It looked a nasty piece of water. The seas came from several directions at once, and the surface was further disturbed by tidal currents. It gave the impression of deep and violent turbulence. I had toyed for about two minutes with the idea of visiting the islands from *Tsambika*, but I'd need millpond conditions to leave her unattended on an anchor. That morning even the thought of sailing up the sound filled me with dread.

The white ruins of the old island houses dotted the slope like sheep. I had tracked down and photocopied a hand-drawn map showing who lived where. Walking up from the landing slip, I used it to find the cottages of Maurice O'Sullivan and Peig Sayers. Out to the north was Tomás Ó Crohan's, a thick-walled house built and roofed entirely by Tomás himself.

'Nobody handed me so much as a stone or a lump of turf,' he recalled. 'If King George were to spend a month's holiday in it, it isn't from the ugliness of the house that he'd take his death.' (Which slightly begs the question – from what would he have taken his death?)

I ducked below the lintel. The floor was thick with nettles and short-grazed turf; from the crevices of the walls grew delicate bunches of polypody fern and pennywort. Across the roof, clouds drifted in an oblong of blue sky.

A frequent visitor to the island was Robin Flower, a scholar of Irish who translated *The Islandman* into English. The islanders called him Bláthín, or 'little flower'. One evening he came to this house and found Tomás with a group of men. As he entered, Flower sensed there was a tense and important debate going on.

'Here was Caisht saying that there were no such thing as fairies and there never were.'

'No,' said Caisht, 'I am not saying that, maybe, there weren't fairies in the old time, but it is long since the priest got the upper hand of them, and there are no fairies in the world to-day, nor for a long while now. What do you say, Blaheen?'

I was just collecting my words to answer when Peats Sheámuis broke in. 'Maybe there are fairies and maybe not,' he cried with an excited air, 'but everybody knows that there are things outside of this world and they do things that no power in this world could do.'

I was thinking of that scene, and its view of the unexplained and why it is that these coasts sustained notions of the otherworld – was it distance from the centre, or living with the ocean at your door, or simply keeping alive something killed off elsewhere? – when I became aware of a smell. I looked in the room behind the chimney and at once jammed a sleeve to my nose. Strands of wool were scattered beside the half-eaten carcass of a sheep. Its stomach was a crow-pecked void; the head was thrown back, the eye sockets gazed up and its lipless mouth was grinning.

I left the house and left the village, heading out along one of the most westerly tracks in all Europe. It was cut into the steep side of the island and the slope rose at my shoulder and dropped at my feet to rocks and surf below. The ground was soft underfoot, clotted in places by black soil where the water seeped from the hill. I had the sense that I could simply carry on, striding that road to the end of the island and into the ocean beyond, towards whatever shoreline might meet the setting sun. For those who left the Blasket in the mid-twentieth century, that was pretty much what they did, settling en masse in the next parish to the west – which was Springfield, Massachusetts.

Crossing over the ridge, I flopped down in the heather. Far to the south, small clouds were dotting the sea-surface with their shadows. I could see the places we'd passed in *Tsambika* a few days earlier – the mitre of Skellig Michael and then Bolus Head and Valentia Island and the shower-smudged peaks of Iveragh.

'Very often I'd throw myself back in the green heather, resting,' said Peig Sayers. 'It wasn't for bone-laziness I'd do it, but for the beauty of the hills and the rumble of the waves.'

Peig's account of her life on the island is shot through with such moments of joy. But the general direction is down. 'My sorrow, isn't it many a twist life does!' she wrote. 'Isn't Youth fine – but alas! She cannot be held always!' Her own life saw the gradual accretion of tragedy. Her husband died young, and five of her ten children. When one of them was killed falling from the cliffs, he needed preparing for burial. It was Peig herself who 'with motherly hands stroked and coaxed the damaged skull into shape'.

Like the devil, loss has all the best tunes, and the Blasket story is pure lament. Peig Sayers and Tomás Ó Crohan were the last of a folk tradition of Irish storytellers and poets, whose words were a spell, conjuring up a time more solid than their own, when poets were heroes – like Pierce Ferriter, who cocked a snook at the English and hid from their forces in the Blasket caves (before being hanged). But Ferriter's own verse also looked backwards, an elegy for what Hugh O'Neill and the earls from Ulster took with them when they fled in 1607, for the bardic tradition, for a thousand years of literature which began with monks setting down in ink the feats of the Fenian warriors, in an act which ensured such heroes would never be forgotten, but which also wrapped them forever in the shroud of a vanished age. Each generation loses something of the old.

'The young people is no use,' the playwright J. M. Synge was told by a Blasket islander. 'I am not as good a man as my father was and my son is growing up worse than I am.'

Out here in the west, and in the islands beyond, it's always the end of something. Peig Sayers's youngest child was Michael Ó Guiheen, and, like all her other surviving children, he went to America. But he didn't like it. He returned to the Blasket in the mid-1930s to find everyone was leaving. The last twenty years of his life he spent on the mainland, in Dún Chaoin, facing the deserted island. He was known to all as An File, 'the poet', and he really was the last of the poets.

In Dún Chaoin's Blasket Centre, they have his passport. One of the curators brought it out for me and I gently turned its age-stained pages. Each one was circle-stamped with SAORSTAT EIREANN – IRISH FREE STATE, and each was covered in the same dense handwriting. On his return from America, Michael had no more use for the passport, but he did need paper. Some of the watermarked pages had been split, to free more space, and these were covered too, line after line after line. The document which could have opened the world to An File became a notebook to record what remained of the past.

Later, he answered an official request to set down those of the old stories that he knew. Professor Bo Almqvist said: 'One can scarcely find it credible that one single man could have possessed such a rich store of oral lore.' It is lodged in the Dublin archive of the Folklore Commission, a monument to the Blasket islanders – 8,500 pages of An File's handwritten stories.

*

It was late afternoon when, on the edge of Dún Chaoin village, I propped my bicycle against a high escallonia hedge, and went in behind it to meet Maria Simonds-Gooding, one of Ireland's foremost landscape painters.

'Come in – come in!' she greeted me at the door. 'I am going to show you *treasures*.'

The Blasket Islands have been the mainstay of Maria's life and her work. For fifty years, she's lived here in a house built by a man from the Blaskets when the islands were abandoned. He reproduced the exact dimensions of his island cottage. With the walls finished, he rowed back and fetched his old roof. Maria's hearth, in which purred glowing sods of turf, is painted grass-green and came from the house of Peig Sayers. The 'crane' beside it, for suspending pans and kettles over the heat, was also Peig's (presented to her, in a gesture of great significance, by Peig's son, An File).

Maria's studio is a light-filled space appended to the old cottage. In her years of painting, she has travelled widely – to the Sahara, the Himalayas, the Caucasus, Sinai, India, New Mexico, wherever the landscape was large and the people lived lives shaped by it. The journeys have all been variations on the presiding theme of her work – human existence out here on the periphery, in the liminal west. 'You won't see a single person in any of my works, but every picture is about them.' Scattered around her studio were minimalist images of bare slopes, field patterns, single-line watercourses – pure and beautiful and intensely felt.

Maria spent much of her childhood in Kerry and when she returned in the 1960s, straight from art college, she came to live at the end of the Dingle peninsula. She showed me a photo of herself at that time, the decade when anyone under twenty-five seemed to have come from Tír na nÓg. She is wearing a light summer dress, with big hair and the same wide eyes. She sits head and shoulders above the Blasket islanders beside her. The abandonment of the islands was only a decade or so before.

In those early years, she used to go down to the quay at Dún Chaoin and ask the men to row her out to the island. She'd stay there alone for days, weeks sometimes. Her face brightened at the memory. 'I've always loved isolation, *loved* it.' In conversation, she had the habit of modulating her voice, declaring something with force, then dropping it to a conspiratorial hush.

'I lived off limpets and periwinkles. The islanders taught me how to snare rabbits, where to put the snares, how to do it all without cruelty. Couldn't possibly have survived otherwise. I slept on the floor of an old cottage. I remember when they came to pick me up the first time –' stage whisper – 'I was wild as a coot!'

We went back into the cottage. On the wall of the main room, framed and mounted, were a large number of pictures. They were all by An File.

Maria met him soon after moving out to Dún Chaoin. She used to pass his house on her daily walks. 'I had no idea who he was. But we struck up a rapport.' He was then in his sixties. She recalled a man adrift and alienated. 'He had this great *loneliness* about him.'

Within a few days of meeting him, Maria went to his house when he was out and placed on his table a gift of paper and paints and brushes. 'He never *said* he wanted to paint. I thought he'd just use it all to light the fire! He never actually mentioned it – but soon he was bringing me pictures.'

The first one he did was of his late mother and her cat.

Maria showed me that painting. Peig is sitting on a stool in her shawl and her cat is beside her, but the interior is the very opposite of the cramped island cottage. It is a hoped-for version of it – vast and full of light. Maria pointed on her walls to other pictures of An File's – a seal hunt, and fishing trips, and pictures of seabirds, and an underwater scene of lobsters approaching a creel. There was a *naomhóg* with a loose-footed sail; a large man sat at the helm and a much smaller one on the thwart beneath the sail.

'That's An Rí, King of the Blaskets, bringing the Frenchman across. They all loved the Frenchman – he'd bring oilskins and wine and olive oil. And buy lobsters from them for a shilling a piece – a *fortune!*'

The pictures were naïve but each had an expressive energy – in the simple pose of his mother, in the sweeping angle of the king's boat. A drawer in her studio, said Maria, held another 188 of An File's paintings.

Outside the cottage, in the green shade of her escallonia hedge, stood a granite bench. We went to see it. 'The "wishing seat". Go on – sit on it! *Wish.*'

I made my wish.

'It's always cast a spell, that bench. When I saw it in Buckleys in Dublin, just after moving here, I knew I *had* to have it. Everything about it has always been quite *magical*. When it arrived here in a van, there was no road to the cottage, but they were filming *Ryan's Daughter* at the time. The engineers dropped the set-building to build the track, just to get it up here. When An File first saw it, he just stood and stared. He loved that bench. He was *enchanted* by it. He called it the "coronation seat" and wrote a long poem about it, a story that took it way back – back to the time of the Flood, weaving in all sorts of folklore and stories. It went on and on!'

In the poem, he calls the bench *an liag fáil* – referring to An Lia Fáil, 'the stone of destiny', or coronation stone, at Tara. It was a similar piece of granite, but upended, and had the power to restore the king's energy, and would cry out in joy at his touch.

Back inside, Maria showed me one more of An File's paintings. Two figures, both wearing black. They are sitting together on the bench. Above them is not the hedge but a triangular structure, like the doorway of a tent, and its apex forces their heads to lean together. The man is somehow hunched up and small. She is smiling, while he looks towards the ground, pensive and priestly. An File has written some lines of verse beneath the picture which translate as:

> This pair are smitten, in a bind
> Light in heart, calm of mind;
> In all the time from Flood to Doom
> No other pair shall know their tune.

It's clear that the picture is of An File and Maria, and it's clear that the two of them are somehow united by the mythical bench, on which all things are possible. And it's clear too that An File painted the picture not from life but from some wishful place in his heart, where his people still lived on the Blasket and his mother was in her cottage with her cat, and he and Maria were sitting forever on that rough granite bench.

4

BACK IN DINGLE, TSAMBIKA WAS in a sorry state. The boards of the cockpit were all up. The battery boxes lay on the side-deck. Everywhere there were tools and oily bits of steel. Rain was driving in from the south and I'd rigged up a cover from the boom to allow us to work beneath it. By 'us', I mean mainly Richard, who had contorted himself into a space in the bottom of the boat with a skill that is as much a part of marine engineering as testing fuel injectors.

Richard was a lobster fisherman as well as a marine engineer. He put out creels along the coast, and his favourite spots were tucked in around the Great Blasket. 'Don't know what it is about the Blasket waters, but the place crawls with shellfish.'

He was the first call for yachts and trawlers who limped into Dingle with faulty engines, and he also spent a good deal of time travelling up and down the coast on tugs and ships. He had a lot of stories.

'Yacht comes in last summer – don't know where the fuck from, Baltimore or Cork. *You have that 17?*' I handed down the large spanner. 'Engine stalled as they entered the harbour and I go on board and the boat's a bloody mess – electrics, rigging, everything all over the fucking place. *The mole grip?*' I handed it down to him. 'So – the repair itself's pretty simple, impeller or something, and I say, looking around the boat, You boys must have had a fair bit of weather. And they say, Weather? We only just started . . . *These nuts – are – solid.*'

There was a blowtorch in his bag. I rummaged around and handed it down to him.

'So I said to them, Where you headed? Greenland, they tell me. *Greenland*, for fuck's sake!'

He wriggled round to free his other hand and light the torch, then he turned it down to a roaring blue. I watched him work it up and down the bolts until they glowed.

Suddenly he turned it down. 'You have got a fire extinguisher, I take it?'

My fingers were already curled around it.

The roar again. 'And they say, We're going straight up from here. Straight across to Greenland on that pile of shit! I tell you, I couldn't get off that boat fast enough.'

He tried the nuts again with the spanner. Nothing. 'Have to cut the heads off.'

I passed him a grinder and it screamed in the bottom of the boat, sending showers of sparks bouncing off the stringers and down into the bilge. I gripped the fire extinguisher more tightly.

Richard managed to cut the bolts and pull them out. He slotted in the vibration plate between engine and shaft and reassembled it with new bolts. We put the batteries and boards back in and tested the engine and everything was fine. We tidied up. Then we sat below, drinking beer.

'Where are you off to?'

'Fenit.'

'Up the sound?'

I was still undecided. Going outside the Blasket Islands would add half a day to the passage but I hadn't liked the look of Blasket Sound. The pilot book was not encouraging: 'Passage through Blasket Sound can be bedevilled by dangerous mid-channel rocks, fast tidal streams, overfalls, magnetic anomalies and poor visibility.' It required 'diligent planning' and 'rigorous seamanship'. I wasn't sure it sounded the best place for my first single-handed sail.

'Here, I'll show you. Got the chart?'

I spread it out on the table. Richard took a cable tie and ran it over the water. 'You come in past Slea Head and there's a rock out here, and that's visible. But then there's one just here that isn't. Stand well out towards the island before cutting up into the sound.'

'Are there any navigation buoys?'

He emitted a noise that was somewhere between a snort and a chuckle.

So, no buoys.

'Don't even think about turning in before you're well over halfway across.'

I nodded.

'Ah, you'll be all right! Long as you follow those leading marks, and you have good weather, and the tide's with you.'

But he couldn't help telling a story about a local trawler. 'Those guys knew the waters like the back of their hand. They're coming down the sound one night – everything on the computer and the helmsman's just moving the boat on a mouse-pad and that's fine. But then he goes off for a fag, the ship rolls and the fucking mouse slides off the table.' He took a final draught of his beer. 'Straight on the rocks. Sunk in minutes.'

The morning dawned cold and clear. I was lying in my bunk. I was looking up through the hatch and listening for the wind. Just the faintest of breezes. OK – I'll go.

I had breakfast, cleared up, stowed and wiped everything with extra diligence. I went into town to buy food. By the time I came back, the wind had freshened. I got the engine going, checked the prop bolts, took off the sail covers. The wind was now gusting twenty knots, and rising. I could always leave it, try again tomorrow.

The hardest thing is throwing off the lines.

The harbour master came down the pontoon. 'Are you off?'

Decision. 'Yes!'

He freed the bowline and coiled it up. 'Ready?'

'Ready!'

He threw it aboard; with a sharp flop it fell on the foredeck. One hand on the helm, I leaned down and pressed the throttle forward.

From the inner harbour, a corridor of buoys led out towards the entrance – red, green, red, green, red . . . I passed between them, pointing the bows towards the gap in the cliffs, towards the ruffled water of the open sea. High up, in a field of pasture so green it glowed, I saw a man with a dog. He was throwing a stick and I thought: land life, normal life, the ground hard beneath their feet. I felt a flash of envy.

Fungie came over. He gave a couple of glistening back-arches as he followed me out. Maria told me she'd swum with him when he first appeared, and that he cured her of a mystery illness. I found myself calling out: 'Goodbye, Fungie – long life to you!' Then he peeled off, and the first swell came up under *Tsambika*.

The bow rose. When there was enough sea room, I brought her up into the wind and freed off the main halyard. The mainsail edged up the mast, a triangle of white growing against the blue of the sky. It thrashed back and forth and I pushed down the helm and the boat came off the wind and the sail filled and calmed. The genoa was next. I took the outhaul off its cleat, checked it was running clear, then put two turns on the winch and pulled. The gears of the winch made a metallic ringing as it spun. Up forward, like a butterfly hatching, fumbling and flapping into life, the sail pulled itself out.

Another turn on the winch, and I heaved the sheet in tight. The boat surged forward. Tugging the engine-stop, there was a double cough, then silence. Just the wind, and the faint swish of the bows. For an hour or so I sailed west across a sparkling sea, out to the end of the Dingle peninsula. There was no one else about. One by one the worries fell away and I looked out at the water and the islands, the last fragments of Europe breaking away from the mainland, and was gripped by a sense of freedom so intense that I felt I really could control the eight tons of wood and iron beneath me.

I looked for An Seanduine, the 'old man', the rock that the Blasket Islanders would use as an indicator of sea state. If the water was white around its base, then the old man was shaving and when he shaved he was bad-tempered – best to stay ashore. There was a little white water today but I told myself it was harmless foam.

Passing the rock and Slea Head, I could see Blasket Sound opening up to the north: *Stand out towards the island, don't turn in too soon.* I kept the Great Blasket off my starboard bow. The island's form has been likened to the roof of a church. Looking at it now, the scale was something larger, grander – more like a Gothic cathedral. The geology was all vertical, the bedding planes tilted heavenwards in broken arches and finials of Old Red Sandstone. Below the surface was the rock I was trying to avoid, and I pictured it in the same style, as a submerged steeple. In the nineteenth century, it had ripped open the hull of the English gunboat *Stromboli*, after which it is named. It had done the same, three hundred years earlier, to the *Santa Maria de la Rosa*, which had left Spain with the Armada but ended up rounding Scotland, limping down the west coast of Ireland to founder here.

Now I could see up the full length of Blasket Sound. I tried to pick out the transits. Simple enough on the chart, when Richard was explaining, but I was struggling now to make out what was what. I checked the pilot book for the third time: 'The primary leading

47

line through the sound is the summit of Sybil Point in alignment with Clogher Rock on 015°/195°T.' I could see Sybil Point some five miles off, but not Clogher Rock. 'A newcomer to the area would need very sharp eyes to readily identify the transit . . .' No kidding. For further encouragement, it suggested 'treating compass bearings with caution' – magnetic readings were sent awry by the geology.

Few things are more uncomfortable on a boat than being in a tight bit of water and not being sure of the way out. I could sense the tide shifting beneath me. Through binoculars, I scanned the distant cliffs – back and forth along their grey facade. Then I spotted a bit of cliff that was not cliff. An off-lying rock – Clogher Rock. Lining it up with the top of the headland, I brought the boat up into the sound. The compass and the chart plotter were giving different readings. I busied myself – heaving at the mainsheet, winching in the genoa. The boat heeled, the sheets creaked and the boat quickened. It took some time before my doubts had eased, before the compasses had settled, and the course was set.

Passing the end of the Great Blasket and Beginish, I squinted out to the west. The sun was warm on my neck but the cool of the breeze offset it. I gazed out at the rocks and, in my state of alertness, each one was suggestive of something else: there was a clenched fist, a cock's comb, a couple of grotesque heads (twisted mouths and squinting eyes), and a tortoise. Lying on his back was the famous sleeping giant of Inishtooskert.

Beyond Smerwick Bay was the bulk of Mount Brandon. I looked up at a thousand feet of slab and shadow and above that the high green world of heathery slopes and streams. The mountains were doing strange things to the wind. It would drop away to nothing, then come fluking down hard and knock the boat to the gunwales. A mile or so ahead, I could see darker water where the squalls fused into something continuous.

Suddenly four dolphins, breeching, some fifty yards to windward. Their fins sliced through the water towards me. Soon they surrounded the hull, seven or eight now, diving, arching up out of the water three at a time, their pale flanks gleaming. I felt thrilled at their company in the vastness of my surroundings. I took them as talismans, and while they were there felt that no harm could come to me. Traditionally dolphins were seen as signs of good luck. They were believed to help bring the dead to the Fortunate Islands, to guide ships from difficulty or sailors ashore from wrecks. 'Full of fine spirits, they invariably come from the breezy billows to windward,' wrote Herman Melville with typical exuberance. 'They are the lads that always live before the wind. *They are always accounted a lucky omen.*'

But they were ill portents too. The leaping of dolphins and porpoises was thought to imitate a coming gale. 'When porpoises sport and chase one another about ships,' wrote Plutarch, 'expect then some stormy weather.' What the discrepancy really shows is the prevalence of mariners' superstitions, that out at sea – with its blank face and constant threat – all things signify something, or several different things.

The dolphins weren't going away. When they surfaced they looked close enough to touch. Observing fauna usually involves stealth, but in a boat, on these coasts, you just wait and the dolphins come to you; it is unusual for a wild animal actively to seek out human beings, unless it's to attack them. Sound is the dolphins' hypersense and it is said that they can detect the tiniest variation in sonic bounce, able to distinguish between a sheet of aluminium and a sheet of steel. I liked to think that they were attracted by *Tsambika*'s wooden hull. When the wind dropped and the boat stalled, I thought they'd become bored. But there they were, changing down a gear to match the speed of the boat.

I looked at my phone and found two bars of signal. I called Charlotte. We chatted, about things at home, the children, the vegetable garden, about the newly planted trees and the shelducklings that had appeared in the creek. And it seemed strange to be back there, picturing the daily advance of spring. Then came a big squall, and the boat stumbled. 'Hang on. I'll call later.'

I was passing the mountain and the wind was fierce as I came out of its lee, shunting the boat over. The toe-rail dropped, and I could see foam rushing past it. In the cockpit, the loose sheets slid across the seats. From down below came a heavy shifting, and a thud. I couldn't check what it was. I was needed up here. The sea was now a mass of white and dark tousled water. I looked at it all and felt the wind fierce on my face, and its weight and thought: *Here is menace.*

Brandon Bay opened out to starboard. The wind was steady now – but no less strong.

I kept thinking it would drop with the sun. It didn't, it increased. It reached twenty-five knots, then thirty, then thirty-five. It whipped up ranks of short seas. The bows reared and plunged, throwing out gallons of spray – wings spreading from each side – which then blew straight back into the cockpit. I was soaked before I had time to get my waterproofs. I couldn't get below anyway. I'd tried the autopilot, but in this wind it wouldn't hold the course for longer than thirty seconds. I was stuck at the helm.

Up, down, thump, duck . . . up, down, thump . . . mile after mile, hour after hour. I felt I'd come up against a burly aggressor, committing random acts of violence against anyone in its path. I braced my legs for each lurch. I watched the ridges for the larger seas, to steer off them. But they still got me, still doused the cockpit. At one point I heard my own voice raised above the wind: 'Fuck off! Just – *fuck off!*'

Beyond Brandon Bay were the Magharee Islands. The normal course was around them, pushing right up to the north. The pilot book had advised that the inside passage 'should only be used in settled conditions such as those depicted in the aerial photo'. The photo showed a mirror-calm sea. It went into detail about the passage through the islands. I recalled none of it. There was no way I could get to the book to check, nor the paper chart. I was already on the edge of the islands. I figured that with the wind coming off the land, at least I would not have breaking seas to contend with. But I was only trying to justify taking the short cut, to shave off a couple of hours. Poor seamanship. I still had the chart plotter clamped to the bulkhead in front of me. I used it to find a route south of Gurrig Island and on to the largest of the group, Illauntannig Island.

As the island slid past, I could see on its treeless surface the traces of beehive huts: a monastic settlement. Just for a moment, amidst the wild flinging of the boat, I thought of those devotees, out here for months on end, with their prayer routines and vigils, lives of night and day, winter and summer, lives less burdened by choice.

The harbour at Fenit was still an hour or more away. The wind was dashing down the valley from Tralee. I steered for the white dot of the lighthouse on Little Samphire Island. The dot became a stick. The stick became a post. The seas became a little smaller.

I needed fenders and lines. In brief bursts away from the helm, I did what needed to be done: finding a bowline, tying it to the samson-post, running it out under the guardrail, back outside the shrouds. Fixing a sternline. Tying on fenders. I came round into the harbour. There was a wharf to one side with its shipping. The small marina was opposite. Someone was pointing to a berth. I aimed for it. The wind was still strong and I'd have only one stab at it. (Why had I not carried out my own intention to practise this, this coming into a pontoon? It was the first time I'd done it single-handed). I cut the throttle, threw the bowline to my shoreside pilot, and waited to jump down with the sternline. We slowed the boat, brought her to a standstill. I thanked him, leaned down to adjust the line with an inch or two of slack, and as I made it off again with quick loops around the cleat, I noticed for the first time how much my hand was shaking.

A couple of men came over as I was clearing up. They were on a boat a few berths along and we started one of those dockside chats that moves from routes to boat-gear to weather, before returning to routes and boat-gear and weather – because that's what's on every-one's mind. They were doing a course in coastal navigation and had arrived from the north earlier that day, before the wind had fresh-ened. They said, Come and have a drink when you're done.

They were in an old motor yacht and we sat inside its spacious wheelhouse – in semi-darkness, because of some problem with the electrics. The arc-light from the marina leaked through the windows and gave our little group a piratical glow. Their instructor swivelled, boss-like, in the helmsman's chair. He had a Hemingway beard and the squarish bulk to go with it. On the chart table beside him was a bottle of Sea Dog rum. I felt as if I was in a scene from *Tintin*.

He took the bottle and filled four plastic beakers. He handed one to me. 'Bit breezy out there this afternoon.'

'A little bit.' Understatement was clearly the mode of speech in that wheelhouse.

'Me and the boys, we got in early. We saw that one coming.' He was claiming victory – over me, over the elements.

'You were lucky.'

'Not luck, my friend, not luck.' He twisted a little in his chair, then fixed me with a tutelary gaze. 'Be afraid of her and she'll treat you right. Take her for granted and you'll end up dead.' He threw back his drink, wiped his beard and reached for the bottle.

The sea was written all over him: the sea as adversary, the sea as combatant, the whole business of seafaring a contest in which his own prowess was proven by the sea-miles he'd put in, his years of coast-hopping and passage-making, and by the fact he was still alive.

I admitted my mistake today. 'I sailed in too close to the cliffs. The winds were all over the place.'

'Always best to stand out. High ground makes the winds lethal. And remember – ' he wagged a finger at me – 'the shore is your enemy. Rather die in deep water than be battered to a corpse on the rocks.'

I wasn't sure I could face more of his death-filled advice, so I asked: 'Where did you come in from?'

'Kilrush today, Aran before that.'

We talked about the Aran Islands and Galway hookers, the traditional turf-carrying sailing boats. There had been something of a revival of hookers in recent decades. I told him I'd gone out in one years earlier, when studying Irish up in An Cheathrú Rua. 'I remember we filled the bilges with rocks from the beach before leaving. Then when we were going downwind, we just tossed them overboard!'

He knew all about that. 'Used those rocks for return ballast. Now the geologists look at those rocks on the mainland shore and they can't work it out. They know that the glaciers moved everything south – but here are these boulders moving north. Drives them crazy!'

He slopped another couple of inches of Sea Dog into my beaker. 'Where you headed?'

'Aran as well, then up to Mayo and Donegal, to Scotland eventually.' Just saying it out loud gave me the heebie-jeebies. 'That's the plan, anyway.'

'Mice and men,' he mused. 'Mice and men. Few plans survive long at sea.'

'Originally, I'd planned to go up the Irish Sea, up the east coast.'

'The east coast?' He threw back his drink with a theatrical scoff. 'The east coast is for pussies.'

The next day was bright and windless. I took stock, washed clothes, read books. I raised the cockpit floor, took out the batteries and checked the engine: the bolts had held. I varnished a patch of the tiller where it was damaged. My shoulders were stiff from yesterday. In the afternoon, I walked out to the end of Fenit Island. The long beach stretched out northwards, fringed by dunes. It had been the scene of the great horse race when Fionn mac Cumhaill brought all his people here and won a famous black steed; there are old middens in the dunes known as *fulacht fiansa*, 'cooking place of the Fianna'.

On the way back, I stopped to sit on the beach. I took off my boots and pressed my bare feet into the sand. I looked out at the sea and the small clouds above it, at the water and the glitter-track of the sun. All was west here – the thinning of the land, the widening of the sea, the end of what is solid, the beginning of what is not. I remembered an afternoon from decades ago. I was in my mid-twenties. I'd taken a few days off from my desk job to ride down to Cornwall on my motorbike. Before returning to London, I went out to the cliff. The low sun and the water lay before me, like this, and I was filled with the sense of what was out there, and that a life that did not go off and examine it was not worth living. Maybe it was that moment or maybe not, but within weeks I'd handed in my notice, to seek out what was extraordinary in the world, try my hand at writing about it. I'm still trying.

Small groups from the town had come down to the beach. A few yards off, a boy was busy digging a hole with a spade. He looked at his hole and was satisfied with it but now he needed something else to do. He started to wander down to the water's edge. It was a long way but as the beach grew steeper, his legs worked faster. Soon he was running, and his wide-stepped dash was not entirely controlled, but he had the spade in his hand and the wind on his face, and all is well with the world when you're five and you're running towards the water and you have a spade.

'Be careful there, Jake!' called his mother.

Being careful was not what Jake was doing that afternoon. What he wanted was to carry on running down the beach with his spade. Before him everything was flat and shiny and he came to a halt in front of the water and stood looking.

'Go down for your brother, will you, Tom.'

Far down at the water, Jake had spotted a jackdaw. Hop-hop, went the jackdaw. He started to run towards it. The bird flew off. Jake's spade flopped down at his side and he watched the bird glide along above the beach. He took a few steps into the water and made splashes with his spade. Then he stood looking into the sun.

A hand slipped into his. He was being turned away from the water. He was being led back up the beach. The going was slower and harder and he was stumbling. His spade was dragging behind him, making a wavy line in the sand. The boys reached their mother.

'Here, Jake,' she said. 'Have a juice.'

He sucked at the carton, and looked back down the beach. What had just happened?

Late in the fifth century a boy was born near here, and a number of things coincided to point at the path of greatness that lay ahead for him. Thirty calves were delivered to thirty heifers, the bishop saw a blazing light, and a white mist – *broen finn* – spread over the Fenit district. The boy was named Brendan after the mist.

His father was Finnlugh and his mother was Cara; his family were of the Alltraige, people of the shore, and they were known in all Ireland for their skill with boats, as the coast around Fenit was so hazardous. Brendan grew up and chose a life dedicated to worship. He became a virtuous and able cleric and in time a widely respected abbot. Three thousand monks were in his charge. One day he was given a book of stories. They were strange and beautiful stories that told of places beyond the horizon, stories that stretched credulity so far that the good Brendan felt obliged to throw the book in the fire.

Such scepticism! God could not allow a worthy like Brendan to remain ignorant of all that He had created and hidden in the furthest parts of the earth. So He bade him go out and climb a high mountain – the mountain that ever since has been named Mount Brandon. For many days Brendan sat on the mountain. He looked out upon the empty water and a vision came to him of an island of such marvels that he knew he would not be able to rest until he'd found it.

He came down from the mountain and began to prepare. He recruited fourteen monks and they built three boats, and from a creek below Mount Brandon they set sail.

For seven years they ran 'over the loud-voiced waves of the rough-crested sea, and over the billows of the greenish tide, and over the abysses of the wonderful, terrible, relentless ocean'. They saw the promised sights. They came to an island of plenty, where the sheep had grown to a huge size, and an island that was not an island but the back of a large fish, and an island where there was a tree covered in birds. When he saw the tree, Brendan was overcome with grief, because he knew that each of those birds was a fallen soul. But one bird rose from the tree and came to him and told him not to worry: they'd been released. They were now peregrines, wanderers like him, free to fly.

The monks set sail again. For three months they sailed on, finding nowhere to land. They reached the island of St Ailbe, but it offered no shelter. For many days they ran along the coast until an inlet was spotted with two fountains at its head. They rested, replenished their supplies, restored their strength. When they left St Ailbe, they encountered water that was thick and heavy like a bog. They visited many nameless places. They witnessed a battle between two great beasts. They suffered storms, and came to an island where there was continuous singing, and one where grapes grew to the size of apples. They saw a column in the water that rose to the sky. The column was made of blue jacinth and a curtain of gold hung from it and they sailed in behind the curtain and found an altar made of pure emerald supported above the water on a beam of gold. All was lit with lamps of beryl and there was a chalice of pure crystal.

For three days, the monks worshipped there before setting off again through a gap in the column. When they came out into the sunlight they found themselves in a sea as still and flat as glass. Beyond that they soon saw an island strangely shadowed and although they steered away from it, the wind brought them ever nearer. The sun vanished from the sky and they saw valleys full of flames and giant demons hammering rings for torture, and they knew they were looking at Hell.

Their course brought them close to the island but they escaped and sailed on. They sailed past a rock in the ocean and on the rock was a man clinging to a pole, wounded and bloody from being dragged about by the surf. The man explained that this bare rock was actually a respite – it was the place he was brought to after being tortured in one of two separate hells. The monks wondered what sin he had committed to deserve such torment, and he said: I am Judas. As they watched, the monks saw a thousand demons approach, crossing the sea to take him. Brendan prayed hard and for one night the demons stayed away from Judas, but in the morning they came again, and the ships sailed on.

Next they reached an island dominated by a tall mountain. Brendan went on alone to climb the mountain and there he found a hermit. For ninety years the hermit had lived on the island, supplied with fish by an otter. His beard was whiter than snow and he told Brendan that now their voyage was nearly complete – soon they would reach their destination, they would arrive in Paradise.

And then when they left, the motion of the boats felt different. They had the sensation of being guided by an invisible presence. They came to a bank of thick fog. The fog opened up to form a corridor. For three days they followed that passage through the fog and when it cleared they saw before them a wall. Gems and gold flashed from that wall – chrysolites and topaz and jasper and amethyst. They saw a gate guarded by dragons and a sword in front of it which was spinning. A beautiful youth appeared and greeted them each by name. He led them towards the gate. The dragons lay down and the sword stopped spinning and they stepped into a green land full of flowers perpetually in bloom and fruits which were always ripe and woods full of game and rivers full of fish. No cloud ever entered the sky of that country and no wind troubled the trees. It was never too hot and never too cold. No one living there ever wanted for anything.

The youth took them up a mountain and they looked around and marvelled at all that was there. Away in the distance, almost out of sight, they could just see the shape of another land. The young man explained to Brendan and his monks: There is a place beyond this which is a hundred thousand times more glorious. You have come in body, but you will only reach that other place when you come in spirit.

*

High up on the end of Great Samphire Island, where I was moored, stands St Brendan. His bronze limbs are blue-green with patina, his bronze hair is blown back, and he is larger than life. Under one arm he clutches a bound sheaf of scripture, while his left hand points with mighty conviction towards the open sea. Time has not been kind to St Brendan. Below him, on the docks, the Liebherr crane works have expanded, slicing half the rock away beneath him, shunting its roof towards him, robbing him of the full drama of his pose.

But there was a period in medieval Europe when Brendan's voyage was one of the best-loved of all stories. Versions existed not only in Irish and Welsh and Breton but in German, Flemish, Italian, Catalan, French, Norse and Anglo-Norman. One hundred and twenty manuscripts survive in Latin. What can be read into its popularity? The perennial appeal of sea voyages and otherworlds has a lot to do with it, helping to explain why translations are still being published, music is being written and journeys still made in Brendan's name.

The search for paradise is also a narrative staple. Tradition in Christian Europe held that the Garden of Eden lay to the east, but since the rise of Islam, the east was closed off. St Brendan's account suggested that it lay in the western ocean, helping to swivel Europe's gaze away from the Holy Land towards the west and the Atlantic. As the years passed, the island found by St Brendan appeared in cartographic form. It is marked on the Ebstorf World Map of 1235, the Hereford Map of 1275, the portolan of Angelinus Dulcert in 1339 and that of the Pizigani brothers of 1367, and on numerous charts throughout the fifteenth century. In 1526, Fernando Alvarez led a small fleet out from Gran Canaria to search for the isle of St Brendan; a generation later an official inquiry was held to ascertain the co-ordinates of St Brendan's paradise. It was named in the treaty of

1494 that divided the territories of the world between Spain and Portugal.

Details from St Brendan's voyage have been picked over for clues to his route. The Island of Sheep was the Faroes, the fiery mountain of hell was Mount Hekla in Iceland, the turbidity he encountered was either the weed of the Sargasso Sea or frazil ice in the waters off Greenland. The column of crystal was an iceberg. More recently, the case has been made for his discovery of America. In 1976, Tim Severin built a craft using forty-nine ox-hides and followed Brendan's route from Iceland to Greenland and Newfoundland.

That's one way of responding. But it wasn't what spread Brendan's *Navigatio* so widely so many centuries ago. Brendan's voyage is a story, and, like all good stories, its strength comes from a mythic fundament. It's a quest, an allegory. It's the *Odyssey, Pilgrim's Progress, Moby Dick*. The Christian elements are added to a narrative frame that goes back to the very origins of storytelling. Something enigmatic, something true comes from making one thing into another, from making the passage of our earthly life a sea journey, giving perspective to its obstacles by showing them in extremis. The voyage of St Brendan is instructive without being didactic. Take up your stick, it says. Go forth, be bold, keep looking. Trust to fate, or to God's will or to luck (or whatever your chosen belief). Remain innocent, always open to the world's marvels. And don't go throwing books of wonder on the fire.

5

I LEFT FENIT, DROPPED THE LINES, motored out of the harbour. Coming round into Tralee Bay, I headed first south, then west before my bows settled just shy of north. There the sea and sky were sucked into the same hazy void. Some sixty or seventy miles inside it were the Aran Islands, which give even the Blaskets a good run in the myth-making stakes. I planned to break passage to them with a stop in the Shannon estuary.

Flicking on the autohelm, I went forward to sort out the cordage. In the gentle swell, I leaned against the mast, coiling and tidying, checking the sheets and a wear-mark that had appeared on the main halyard. The Kerry mountains filled the sky astern. For the next two hours, they grew no smaller. Their rocky contours softened and turned a paler blue, but their presence remained on the parapet of the horizon – Beenoskee, Stradbally and, largest of all, Mount Brandon.

Just inland were the Slieve Mish peaks. In the early Christian period, St Patrick came here with the warrior Caílte to bless the region and learn its *dinnseanchas*. At that time, the fields were being stripped bare by flocks of birds and Caílte put a curse on those birds: 'Rise up by the strength of this charm and spell, away onto the choice, blue-crested sea, so that each of you may kill the other and dust and ashes be made of you.' And the two of them watched those birds rise from the fields and fly away to the west, out over the water where the rock on the shore is called the Rock of the Flock of Birds.

I passed close to another rock, the evil-looking Mucklaghmore, and it made me think of Judas in the Brendan story, clinging to his pole. In this light on this coast, through the hours of the morning, everything started to suggest something else. Staring at it, steering into it, did strange things to my perception. White without depth or edge, a white emptiness which dissolved the earth's surface and its atmosphere, and tempered the hard borders of reason. I remembered a story told to Robin Flower on the Blaskets, of a church and churchyard floating up into the air and drifting off to look for a new site. In medieval Ireland, ships were often seen crossing the sky. At Clonmacnoise on the Shannon, a vessel once passed overhead and the monks spilled out of church to grab at its hanging anchor. High above them, they watched a sailor jump overboard and swim down to free it. The monks held the sailor. 'For God's sake,' he cried, 'let me go! You are drowning me.'

St Barra of Cork was once out at sea in a ship when he spotted St Scoithin having a walk. 'How is it that you're walking on the sea?' Barra asked. 'Because it is not the sea,' explained Scoithin. 'It's a field.' And he bent to pick a crimson flower. Barra, for his part, leaned down, scooped up a dripping salmon, and lobbed it to Scoithin. A similar story is told in the *Immram Brain*, the *Voyage of Bran*. Two days into his ocean passage to the otherworld, Bran spots a chariot coming towards him over the waves. It is driven by Manannán Mac Lir, God of the Sea, and he calls out in verse to Bran and his sailors:

> What is a clear sea
> For Bran's skiff
> Is a happy plain thick with flowers
> To me in my wheeled chariot . . .
> Speckled salmon leap from the womb

Of the white sea, on which you look
They are calves, they are coloured lambs.

Such stories are more than just picturesque. They're subversions. They undermine those rules which appear to be most fixed – that what is heavy shall drop, what is land is solid, and what is sea is liquid. In political terms, they are the hopeful musings of people denied agency by a stifling priesthood and a harsh occupation. More universally, the tellings and retellings depend on the agreed nature of the otherworld, a place behind the surface of this one, where earthly constraints fall away. 'Here all things are possible,' wrote the Celtic scholar John Carey, 'opposites can exist without conflict, essences and attributes can be isolated and transferred.'

In our empirical age, we have no more use for such notions. The otherworld doesn't exist. Ships do not sail across the sky. Buildings tend to stick to their sites. If an island is not on the map, it isn't anywhere. But such stories retain an appeal which is not merely aesthetic. They are a reminder that the way to understanding is not always linear, that the most improbable of paths can lead to the most rewarding of places, that the imagination is the oddest of human faculties, and also perhaps the greatest.

Morning slid into afternoon. The wind was a steady force three. A milky sunlight glimmered on the swells. Water trickled past the hull. I watched the drowsy outline of Kerry Head take form off the bows. Approaching it, I could see grass-covered slopes give way to cliff and a series of long steps that sloped down into the water. I watched the waves push up the rock, bursting against the risers in slow fountains of spray. High up on the headland was a single farm. What would it be like to live there, to work there in the wilder months, ambushed by wind at the end of the barns, balanced right on the edge of Europe?

The scale of the Shannon estuary itself seemed out of place. Its ten-mile-wide mouth should lead in to rainforests and tropical basins; instead it drains the soggy interior of Ireland. I met a man who'd been exploring its waterways in a boat not much smaller than *Tsambika*; it had taken him a whole summer, and still there were more. Here at the seaward end, Loop Head was a faint line to the north. Turning into the estuary, I freed off the sheets and headed north-east. For some time, the two shorelines hardly converged. I pictured my tiny sail from above, a lone piece of zooplankton flowing into the mouth of a whale.

Somewhere here is believed to be a submarine province called Little Limerick. From time to time, reports have been made about the tide shoaling around submerged church towers and steeples. The sounds of tolling bells, of cattle and sheep were sometimes heard from deep underwater, also the smell of wild flowers. But for anyone who noticed them, it was a great misfortune. In 1823, Little Limerick was spotted from a boat, a thing of wonder beneath the waves. All fifteen people on board saw it, were amazed by the subaqueous shimmer of its buildings, and all fifteen people died. They were last seen solemnly filing up from the shoreline and into church. While imaginary places out at sea tend to be places of plenty, blessed or filled with fruit and happiness, those closer to land are more dangerous. Wonders lie in the distance, threats are closer to shore. So it is with the sea itself.

I needed to concentrate now, to come into harbour. I left the main estuary and followed a tight channel which dog-legged to the east and ended up at a lock-gate. A lock! As I approached, the outer doors swung open. I nosed in between them, and cut the throttle.

'You're all right there!' From the window of the control tower leaned the head of the lock-keeper.

64

I jumped onto the platform, secured the stern, then went forward to fix the bow.

'You come from the south?' he called.

'From the south, yes! Fenit.'

'What you make, three hours from Kerry Head?' He'd begun to close the gate behind me.

'About that!' I was watching the boat, trying to work out what was going to move against what.

A final whirring and *clunk* . . . The seaward doors closed. The lock-keeper began to activate the inner set, and their jaws parted. A vertical trickle of water appeared first; then, as the gap widened, came a silent surging of eddies and mounding water. The hull rose, and the platform too, clanking up its piles. The new water was the colour of milkless tea. It gave off a smell that was unfamiliar – not the salty tang of the harbours I'd been in, but something softer. It was the vegetable smell of compost and peat, the smell of the land.

The lock-keeper was pointing to the inner harbour. 'Go past the first ope there – take one of the finger pontoons. Any of them's fine.'

'How should I pay?'

'Don't worry – I'll find you.' There was a heavy sound as the gates creaked shut. 'You're my prisoner now!'

In the Buggles pub, a man was standing at the bar: pale suit, dark burgundy tie, thinning hair slicked back over his head. His suit was a lot broader than he was and it gave him a solid look, square and important. He'd been to a funeral.

'Eighty-six.' He had tiny deltas of blood vessels in his eyes. 'Not a bad age.'

'Not bad.'

He lowered his lips to the rim of the glass. 'I been drinking all day.'

There was a certain composure about him, as if drinking all day was a place he knew his way round pretty well. 'He was a great man, you know. A great man . . . my father was the first influence on me, but Bernard there, he was the second. He helped everyone he met – where he worked, he helped all of them. He helped the women on the council. He helped my daughter Marie – she's gone to Australia now, married a trumpet player. He liked the horses sure enough. He once bought an old horse from a priest, just as a kindness. But then that horse went on and won the strand race.'

He had slumped a little as he spoke. He put a hand to his shoulder, bunching the pad and the grey cloth of his suit. 'I shouldered him.' His eyes were shiny with tears. 'I shouldered him into the cemetery, here . . .'

I ordered another drink for us both. As he talked, about an old friend who was a singer in America, and the Romans, who could never rule Ireland, and the funeral again and all the people there who had been helped by Bernard, I couldn't help noticing on the wall behind his head a picture. It was a mirror with a logo of *Guinness Extra Stout* in the shape of Ireland. I followed my own passage up its left-hand edge, around the south-west corner, up to Dingle, up to the indent at Fenit and the indent here at Kilrush and the Shannon. Above it, the coastline stretched high up the mirror. I had sailed just *inches*.

'Suppose that's all it is in the end,' he said. 'The good we do for others.'

I stayed a few days in Kilrush. The skies were clear and the winds were northerly. Passage to the Aran Islands would only be eased when they passed. I spent a good deal of time ashore. The ground feels different when you come off a boat, when your balance is used to movement and your mind is filled with maritime matters.

It had been with me for a while now, since before leaving Cornwall; it had skulked around like a harbour scamp as I prepared the boat; it had snuck aboard for the passage to Ireland; now it was with me the whole time, this sea-anxiety. There were occasions when I appreciated the alertness it brought, when I was grateful for the nagging – to write down the details of each course, the calculations for each tide, to be diligent with the boat, to check everything, to scrub and fix and clean. But at other times, frankly, I found it a little wearing. It was there with me when I woke, when I went ashore, when I visited people. It had made me leave at home the leather wallet that I'd bought some years ago at the Vasa museum in Stockholm (the *Vasa* was the hubristic statement of King Gustavus Adolphus, a huge ship which had sunk in 1628 on its maiden voyage). I heard less from it when I was actually out on the water, and found it most chatty when I was doing the simplest of things – like shopping in the Kilrush Supervalu. No to quadrefiore pasta – looks like waves. And granola was out for its resemblance to reefs and rocks in the water. A muesli called Ancient Legends was OK (fits my subject), but I wished I hadn't spotted that toy boat, mast broken, sail torn, upside down in a roadside skip.

In *The Golden Bough*, James Frazer collates examples of such thinking under the heading of 'homoeopathic magic' or the 'Law of Similarity'. If you want something to happen (or not to happen), imitate it (or avoid imitating it). Sailors are particularly prone to such suggestion, as they are so little in control of the forces that play on them. 'There is,' wrote the explorer Thomas Gibbons, 'but a plank between a sailor and eternity and perhaps the occasional realization of that fact may have had something to do with the broad grain of superstition in his nature.' Not just the threat of it, but the sheer scale of the sea allows space for a good seepage of speculative thought. The entire enterprise of seafaring, and the unimaginable expanse of water in which it is pursued, stretches logic. Novelist James Fenimore Cooper wrote that 'there is a majesty in the might of the great deep that has a tendency to keep open the avenues of that dependent credulity which more or less besets the mind of every man.'

I was looking at the next stretch of coastline, spread across the chart table. It was exposed – sixty miles from Loop Head up to Galway and not a shadow of a harbour anywhere along it. I traced it up the edge of County Clare, past the seaside resort of Kilkee, Spanish Point (another of the Armada's graveyards), to the Cliffs of Moher and the surfing centre of Lahinch. In town, the tourist signs invited you to take the Wild Atlantic Way. I'd picked up a leaflet: 'Visit the famous Cliffs of Moher! Europe's second tallest sea cliffs! Famous for spectacular views!'

Havenless coastline, cliffs, wrecks, beaches, surf. None of these was appealing, and it certainly brought out the loquacious nature of my sea-anxiety.

'The western world contains not a more hallowed island.'

So said an angel to Scattery Island's saint, St Senan, when he established a monastery there in the sixth century. Lying just offshore from Kilrush, the island has always had a powerful mystique. On the day I was due to leave, I spent the morning ambling its daisy-speckled paths. I looked at the waters of the Shannon, spreading outward, the twin shores diverging and opening to the Atlantic, thinking of my coming passage and wondering how much of the island's sanctity could be explained by that view, that striking sense of standing on a threshold.

A tenth-century poem, *Amra Senáin*, tells a story about Scattery. Narach the artisan was on one side of the Shannon estuary. He needed to take his household to the other side and he was worried about the sea-monster. Everyone at the time was worried about the sea-monster. But on Scattery Island, St Senan said he would guarantee Narach's safety and that of his kin. Narach was a man of faith and he was reassured. He set off. Halfway across, the monster came up out of the water. He swam over to Narach's boat and swallowed him up, along with all his family. Senan then killed the monster and brought Narach and his people safely out of its belly.

Several things appealed to me about the poem. The initial fallibility of the saint, and the message that the course of good is not always a straight one. Then there was the saint himself, the same saint who made his way to Cornwall and left his name in Sennen, most westerly of its villages, filled with happy associations for me of camping and surfing and walking. There was also the exuberance of the poem itself, a panegyric in Old Irish, with its playful sibilance – *Senan soer, sídathair silem soailche, sainemail suib amra* – and effusive praise: 'Senan, noble father of peace, sower of virtues, unique, beautiful, marvellously arranged, a fine sage, a sheltering head, a goblet of wine.'

But in my current state of mind, I saw it as a parable. You have a challenge, you prepare, but misfortune will still occur. The point is what happens then: have faith and even misfortune can be turned around. Then the rewards are inestimable.

I'd been reading Danny Sheehy's *In the Wake of St Brendan*, a wonderful account of his sailing up to Iceland some years ago. He knew well the transformative potential of such sea passages, as well as their dangers. He'd had the urge to take as talisman a number of small stones – in his case, from the beach below Mount Brandon. An artist had made a little leather pouch for each one. For good luck, he tied it with a leather thong – according to Frazer's Law of Similarity – like the timbers of Brendan's ships. On the leather the artist had inscribed images from Brendan's *Navigatio,* and inside each pouch was a piece of paper with some of the magical lines from the *Song of Amergin:*

> *Is loch I maigh*
> *Is briathar aindeithe*
> *Is focal eigse*
> I am a lake in a plain
> I am pagan words
> I am the word of poetry.

I reached the place where the turf gave way to beach. The shingle gave off a hollow chinking sound as I crossed it. To those leaving the Shannon estuary for the open sea, a stone from Scattery was regarded as lucky. Taking my cue from Danny Sheehy, and urged on by my superstitious voice, I selected one the size and shape of a new potato and took it back on board.

6

WAITING UNTIL LATE AFTERNOON TO catch the tide, I motored back down to the lock. In its doored-off chamber, I secured the lines to the platform and watched. The water dropped and the boat dropped and a deep shadow crossed the decks. Then the doors began to swing open, the light spilled in and ahead lay the sparkling plains of the Atlantic.

'She's all yours now!' The lock-keeper was leaning out of his window. 'God bless you!'

It was hot. The northern shoreline of the Shannon slid past in an early-summer vision of pale fields and vigorous growth. The bungalows above the sandy cliff moved in transit against the slopes behind, as if they themselves were on a raft, untethered to the land, moving off with me downstream.

Some ten miles west was the bay of Carrigaholt, the last shelter before Loop Head. Those ten miles gained a couple of hours for the passage up to Aran. With the sun low, I picked up an old mooring for the night. Huge skirts of kelp hung down from the buoy. There were no other boats. I scrubbed the decks, phoned home (Arthur had been surfing, the dog had buried a pheasant in the bath, all was well). I watched as the sky dimmed and the land below it turned black. It was late when I lay in my bunk, looking up through the forehatch at the square of night sky. A jet appeared far overhead, and shining on its side, like a ghost of the day, was the sun.

The wallow of contemplation gave way, as such on-board wallows usually did, to the press of the practical. *Fuel* – tank full, twenty litres in two reserve cans, fifty-five litres in all. I still had to calculate: five and a half knots, two and a quarter litres an hour – ten litres about every four hours, fifty-five litres enough for some twenty or twenty-five hours cruising if the wind failed – plenty. *Tides* – a little ebb from five a.m. or so, further up the coast, negligible. *Weather* – force four to five, easterly, due to fall away later. So – leave at six, pick up the tide, arrive on Aran after about nine hours. Cill Rónáin, on Inis Mór . . . good harbour, good holding . . . Cliffs of Moher . . . must check the seacocks, check the reefing lines . . . check engine oil . . . check, check . . . check . . .

Hours later. *Thuk! Thuk! Thuk-thu-huk!*

Inches from my side, something hard against the hull – *Thuk-kh!*

I stuck my head up through the hatch. The land was where I'd left it. Up the estuary I could see the first glow of dawn. *Thuk-thuk!*

I hauled myself out on deck, looked over the bow. The raised ring of the mooring buoy was swinging back and forth. The tide was pushing the boat against the buoy and the ring was striking the woodwork with its jagged edges. I lay flat and stretched to hold it off, managed to free a few metres of mooring line with my other hand. But the tide was pushing the boat against the buoy again.

I was in a bit of a bind, a single-hander's bind. I could hold the shaft off the boat by stretching down like this. But as soon as I let go, it drove in again. *Thuk – thu-uk!* There were already dark patches where it had gouged into the timber.

I did the only thing I could: I untied the line. Loose, it pulled swiftly through the ring. As the boat found itself free, it started to spin in wind and tide, heading for the edge of the bay. I dropped down through the hatch, threw on some clothes, hurried back through the saloon. I reached into the bilges to open the seacock, flicked on the nav lights, instruments and radio. Starting the engine, clipping on my life jacket and PLB, I grabbed the helm and pointed the bows towards open water. The headland was just visible in the half-darkness, the glow of day was spreading astern. I checked my phone: 4.36 a.m. Not the sort of departure I'd planned.

It was fully light by the time I reached Loop Head with its sheer-sided, wind-polished top. The tower of the lighthouse shone toothpaste-white in the early sun and the squared-off point of rock, reaching into the Atlantic, looked like the setting for some dramatic story. And so it was: Cú Chulainn was here. Great hero of the Ulster Cycle, wiliest of warriors, strongest of men, Cú Chulainn was accustomed to attracting the lustful stares of women and the jealousy of men wherever he went. It was a woman who had chased him out to Loop Heap, along the narrowing peninsula to the edge of the ocean. But Loop Head isn't quite the end. A rock lies just sixty feet from it. Cú Chulainn leapt across to it. She leapt too. He leapt back, but when she did the same, she fell. As I passed it, the gap opened up and, just for a moment a slit of light flashed through it, before closing again to solid rock.

Rounding Loop Head, I hardened sheets and picked up my course – just off north, 020°. The wind was easterly. It dashed out from the shore, full of the land's dryness, kicking up brisk little seas as it came. The boat leaned away from it, the lee deck dipping and hissing through the water which burst against the stanchions in puffs of spray.

The morning unfolded. I kept busy, filling in the hourly log, marking off my position against the rhumb line, putting in a reef, shaking it out, checking this, adjusting that. I watched guillemots and petrels, saw a few dolphins. The hours rolled past. Hours pass more swiftly at sea. Something to do with constant looking, the looking and listening. Such attentiveness should drag out time, but it does the opposite.

I kept one eye on the northern horizon. There was nothing to see. Sailing blind is an act of faith – faith in your compass and charts. You have to believe that your destination is there in the haze, but it might not be. It might just be haze, for ever. I stared at the blue-grey of the sea and the blue-grey of the sky and could see no boundary between them. I stared so hard that dots danced before my eyes.

Then – soon after midday – a distant piece of sea-sky that was imperceptibly darker, a faint outline. Aran! The shape of Inis Mór or Inis Meáin or Inis Oírr– hard to tell. The name Aran anyway covers them all, used not just for the largest island but as a generic name for all three: *Aran*, like an abstract noun, a state of mind, what the islands' great modern chronicler Tim Robinson calls 'the unsummable totality of human perspectives'. Fanciful stabs at the name's derivation link it to the Irish *ard-thuinn*, 'height above the waves', and to Aaron, brother of Moses. The actual origin is more prosaic: it comes from the Irish *ara* or 'kidney' and the word's usage for a ridge of land – the shape of the islands as seen from the mainland.

I took a bearing – 040°. I checked the chart. The shapes were not Aran. They were the Cliffs of Moher. Unconsciously I'd already edged my bows towards them. I reverted to the compass course.

It wasn't long before another faint shadow took form in the mist, and that *was* Aran.

By the time I approached the islands, three hours later, the wind had gone. The water was oily and unruffled. When a cormorant dived beside the boat, I followed its submarine passage through a trail of rising bubbles. The waves themselves were slow and dead-looking, conceding their undulations in flashes of sheen and shadow. The glare was blinding, the whole world awash with light. I had to squint to see the coast a mile or so ahead. The low shoreline of Inis Mór ran away to the left. On the other side were the cliffs of Inis Meáin, high and cut-off, like the profile of a bison. Between them was Gregory's Sound, named after St Gregory of the Golden-mouth, a hermit on

Inis Meáin who chewed off his lower lip at the thought of his own sins. A golden lip grew back.

The instruments were showing forty metres below the hull. As I passed between the two cliffs on that light-drenched afternoon, I had the sensation that the hazy islands were not islands at all but mountains, that I was no longer on water but poised over a chasm, following a narrow path around the cliffs, towards an unseen fortress.

Into its limestone fissures and sea caves, and in among its 1,500 miles of drystone wall and 14,000 fields, along its winding *boreens*, Aran has been luring the imaginations of outsiders for well over two millennia. As much as anywhere along the Atlantic coast, the Aran Islands show how the chance arrangement of geology – in this case, three fragments of limestone broken away from the mainland Burren – can accommodate the loftiest and most otherworldly of notions.

In earlier centuries, that meant holiness. The islands may well have been used as a ritual centre in prehistory, the ruined *cashels* built not for defence but for worship and rite. The early Christians found the islands equally conducive to faith. Ára na Naomh, it was called then: 'Aran of the saints'. 'No one even knows but God the number of saints buried there,' boasted one twelfth-century scribe. St Enda, credited with establishing monasticism in Ireland, had his cell on Inis Mór and is buried in its shallow soil alongside a hundred other saints. Before St Brendan set off on his voyage, he went to Aran to consult with St Enda.

'The Isles of Aran are fameous,' wrote Connemara's early chronicler, Roderic O'Flaherty, in 1684, 'for the numerous multitude of saints there living of old and interred ... frequently visited by Christians in pilgrimage for devotion, acts of penance, and miraculous virtues there wrought.'

By the late nineteenth century, Aran's spell was acting on less pious spirits. W. B. Yeats visited Aran in August 1896. He set a large part of his unfinished novel *The Speckled Bird* there: 'Everything about the island, even the gulls rising and falling as they fed, had that unreal look, that look of being beyond the ramparts of the world.' With him on that visit, in a similar state of transcendent rapture, was the poet Arthur Symons. 'More than anything I have ever seen,' he announced, 'this seashore gave me the sensation of the mystery and the calm of all the islands one has ever dreamed of, all the fortunate islands that have ever been saved out of the disturbing sea.'

A few years later, Yeats met the young J. M. Synge in Paris: 'Go to the Aran Islands,' he urged the aspiring writer. 'Live there as if you were one of the people themselves. Express a life that has never found expression.' Synge took his advice – but unfortunately the folklorist Lady Gregory was already there doing the same thing. The two of them wandered about on Inis Mór, busily jotting in their notebooks and ignoring the other one.

On Aran, as on the Blaskets, Gaelic revivalists discovered what they took to be the essence of pre-conquest Ireland. When Patrick Pearse helped establish a branch of the Gaelic League on Inis Meáin, he predicted that 'Aran will again be a university and a torch of knowledge for all the people of Ireland as she was in the old times.' In the 1890s, the travel-guide writer Mary Banim recorded her impressions in rather simpler terms. She was drawn to Aran by the expectation of 'a people the most genuinely Irish, in language and customs, of our race still left in the West of Ireland: a simple, primitive, but highly intelligent people.' (Genetic studies have revealed that in fact the presence of English soldiers in the seventeenth century make Aran's population less Irish than any equivalent area on the mainland.) James Joyce was told by an islander that Aran was 'the strangest place in the world'.

In 1937, Antonin Artaud – French surrealist, wounded visionary – came to Ireland with a stick. The stick was the *Bachall Isu*, once used by Christ to ward off evil spirits in the Judean desert, then taken up by St Patrick. Until the late Middle Ages, the stick was kept in Dublin, a sacred relic, a part of Irish ritual, but it disappeared in an iconoclastic purge during the reign of Henry VIII. Four centuries later, a friend of Artaud happened to find it in a Belgian flea market. He gave it to Artaud, who was already in a somewhat credulous state. The previous year in Mexico, he had taken a lot of peyote and had since become prone to 'terrifying moments of hallucination and overwhelming lucidity'. Artaud knew what he must do. He must take the stick to the heirs of the Druids, who would use it to rekindle the lost spirit of Europe. Ireland was where he'd find the Druids, more specifically on the islands of the west coast, and most specifically on Aran. He stayed two weeks there, found no Druids, fled with unpaid bills, and left his stick behind in Dublin when he was deported. On arrival at Le Havre, he was put in a straitjacket.

Even Tim Robinson, whose two magnificent Aran books – *Pilgrimage* and *Labyrinth* – are rooted in the real, and who confessed that 'the deep truths of myth act on me less than their deep falsities', admits to the islands' strange capacity for prompting the imagination. They certainly prompted his own. A casual visit in 1972 changed the course of his life. He and his wife moved to Aran from London and remained in the west of Ireland for the next forty years. Robinson's own response to the islands has been as devoted as any of his predecessors. He learned Irish to understand its names and its stories. He mapped the islands and researched their past – not in a standard century-by-century account of landlords and garrisons, of population rises and falls, but in an intricate unravelling of every field and cove, every boundary and traveller's tale, every toponymic curio, every dwelling and monastic cell.

The human lot, Robinson explains at the beginning of the 800-page project, is a state of inflamed awareness, a response to place in which each 'step carries us across geologies, biologies, myths, histories, politics etcetera, and trips us with the trailing *Rosa spinosissima* of personal associations'. He conceived of a work of art that would contain it all, and identified Aran as '*the* exemplary terrain upon which to dream of that work'. His own books are a gallant attempt, a wonderful exposition on the imaginative power of place. But it's impossible to achieve, he admits, even on this tiny patch of the earth's surface. No one's life is long enough.

In Inis Mór's harbour, Cill Rónáin, I picked up a mooring and unfolded the Zodiac dinghy on the foredeck. With each press of the foot-pump, the air sighed into the tubes; with each press, they rose a little. Then – *ping!* – the stopper shot out from the pump, described an impressive arc over the water, and disappeared. The pump was now useless. I was aware again of my fragility – how one little thing breaking can halt the whole show. I whittled a cork. That too popped out. It took several corks and some duct tape before I could get a piece to stick. I dropped the dinghy into the water, fixed the outboard to the transom and motored in, to pit my own credulity against the stones of Aran.

Cill Rónáin was in a high-season fever, bustling with bicyclists and backpackers, alive with assorted accents and languages. Amidst the sweater shops, the ponies and traps, the crowds off the ferry, I found a man on the quay tying up his boat, and I checked with him about the mooring.

'Ah, you'll be all right there,' he said, 'unless it blows nor'east. And you can be sure it won't do that.'

Rory Doneely had spent twenty years fishing off the islands, netting prawns in sixty fathoms of water. He still put out a few pots, but mainly he did island tours in a minibus. We indulged in a bit of bonding boat-talk, and the following afternoon, I joined him in his bus with a small party of elderly Germans and Americans. We drove out west to the cliff-top fort of Dún Aonghasa.

Nowhere contains Aran's mysteries better than Dún Aonghasa. The questions begin outside – in the field surrounding the perimeter walls: a large area of densely packed limestone slabs slotted in the ground with their edges and points upstanding. It is known as the *chevaux-de-frise* – but was it ever used as such, as a deterrent against cavalry attack, way out here? Inside the fort, the semicircle of limestone wall is equally puzzling. Half of the cliff-edge structure appears to have been ripped away by a giant hand. Yet the cliff was old when the fort was built, and the semicircle was all there ever was – with the sheer drop beyond, hundreds of feet, down to the surf. Entering the fort, you forget any notion of defence or security offered by the concentric walls and the *chevaux-de-frise* behind you. Instead you are aware of only one thing: the dizzying space. The structure is oriented, designed for that purpose, to frame that drop. A natural platform of limestone stands in the middle, bordering the cliff, known as An Bord, 'The Table'. The whole place feels faintly creepy, with its hint of killings and sacrifice and dark deeds. It made me think of the execution of Aesop, thrown from a cliff at Delphi.

Stepping to the edge, I was struck by the neat slicing of the limestone, the precise and sudden transition from the flat to the vertical – and the abyss. The *cashel* is positioned at the highest point of the highest cliff on Aran, and height is the sensation it projects, reverence and awe the intended response – a framing of the ocean, the cosmic vastness beyond.

One afternoon, in September 1857, a banquet took place here in Dún Aonghasa. Seventy learned gentlemen entered and arranged themselves on the rocks. Hampers of food and drink were unpacked on An Bord. Curious islanders sat against the walls and watched them. The gentlemen had travelled from Dublin to Galway by train, then they had travelled out to Aran on the Trinity House steam yacht *Vestal*. For several days, they'd been touring the islands, inspecting Aran's antiquities. 'The Aran Excursion,' concluded the tour's report, 'has been the most memorable and the most important exploration of Ireland's historical monuments that has ever yet taken place.'

In terms of its long-term effect, it is tempting to read even more into it than that. Assembled here for the banquet were many of the pioneers of the Irish renaissance – John O'Donovan, Eugene O'Curry, George Petrie, Samuel Ferguson, Charles Graves, among others. At Dún Aonghasa that day, the seed of an idea took root, an awareness that the traces of Irish antiquity, the foundations of a renewed and revitalized nation, remained out here in the far west. It was a mystical idea, one that drew a good deal from the spectacular site, and one that over the coming decades would help produce the Gaelic League and the Gaelic Revival, the *Athbheochan na Gaeilge*. In his essay 'Certain Set Apart: The Western Island in the Irish Renaissance', John Wilson Foster discusses the importance of islands like Aran and the Blaskets in that process: 'the entire Revival fashioned the western island once again into an Otherworld, but one you could actually see and land upon as well as one that afforded the spiritual and psychological nourishment of living myth'.

The afternoon was hot, 'the sun almost too warm'. Glasses of sherry were handed out and, under the gaze of the islanders, the 'hungry savants' settled down to eat. The entire expedition had been organized by Dr William Wilde, surgeon, polymath, antiquarian, folklorist, father of Oscar Wilde. He was well aware of the power of the islands, and of this place in particular, and the speech he rose to make after the meal was suitably grandiose: 'Why have I brought you here, and more particularly to the spot where I stand at this moment to address you? It is because I believe I now point to the stronghold prepared as the last standing place of the Firbolg aborigines of Ireland, here to fight their last battle if driven to the western surge, or to take a fearful and eternal departure from the rocks ... Perhaps, the sentinel on Dun Aengus, two thousand years ago, casting his glance on a summer eve over that vast expanse of Atlantic water that now rolls between us and America, brought up in fancy on the western horizon that far-famed island of O'Brazil, the tradition of which still lingers among those peasants now grouped around us.'

Others rose and spoke, and were not sparing in their many thoughts about the auspiciousness of the occasion and the magnificence of the place, and there was much cheering at the rising of each speaker. Men from Cambridge spoke, from Belfast, from Edinburgh and Paris, as well as from Dublin.

The islanders listened to the long speeches in the English tongue and were pleased when the linguist Professor Eugene O'Curry turned to address them in their own Connacht Irish. 'There are gentlemen here in the midst of [us] with true Irish hearts, and who love everything that belongs to their dear old country – gentlemen of great learning, who devote their time for many a year to study and to write about Ireland.'

'Musha, musha!' called the islanders. 'They're welcome!'

O'Curry then said there was, however, one matter for the islanders to address. Rabbit hunting. How wrong it is, he explained, to destroy these ancient walls for the sake of hunting rabbits. The rabbit skins are worth little and, in hunting them, great damage is being done to the ancient walls.

Others from the party stood and made speeches. There was nothing mean in the number of speeches that afternoon, nor in the amount of words those men uttered. Fulsome was their praise for the site, for the food and their praise for Dr Wilde's hard work in arranging it all. And they each repeated the message to the islanders, to desist from hunting rabbits.

Dancing followed: 'a musician, with a bagpipes, then played some merry tunes and the banquet of Dun Aengus terminated with an Irish jig, in which the French Consul joined *con amore*.'

In the early evening, Rory drove our party out to the far west of the island, and we all spilled out of his minibus and on to the slip below Bun Gabhla. The swells broke on the slip, licking up over the concrete in wide tongues of water.

'You have a fine view there, out to the west,' explained Rory.

They followed his gaze.

'A fine view,' he repeated.

They took photos of the orb of the sun.

'Look out there very hard and you might be lucky. You might just see the island of Hy-Brasil.' He pronounced it '*bra*-sil', with the emphasis on the first syllable.

'Please,' asked one German man, his fingers curled over a pair of Leica binoculars. 'Which direction?'

'It's only a story,' explained an American. 'It's not real.'

'No one knows that for sure,' said Rory. He paused, letting possibility seep into the silence. 'I tell you, a couple of times out there fishing, I seen it myself.'

Some of the heads turned seawards again.

He then gestured to me with an ambiguous smile. 'Philip here has been sailing up the coast. I imagine that from your boat, you too have seen the island out there?'

7

Twenty years ago, i'd spent some time on Inis Meáin –
the 'middle island' – while studying Irish on the mainland at An
Cheathrú Rua.

Inis Meáin has always been seen as the most remote of the Aran
islands, with its spoken Irish the truest, its limestone fields the
rockiest and its drystone walls the highest. When I was there last,
a new harbour was about to be built. There was a lot of muttering
about how it would be the death of the island and make it a tourist
trap like Inis Mór. EU-sponsored concrete was poured into a site
on the northern shore. But somehow it was never quite completed,
and while it has decent landing for the ferry, there was nowhere to
leave *Tsambika*. She remained at Cill Rónáin. I took the scheduled
crossing to Inis Meáin, filled with curiosity for a place I recalled
so intensely.

A couple of cars and a hotel minibus met the boat – to pick up
just four passengers. I walked up from the shore into the island. The
vehicles pressed on ahead of me, looking outsize as they squeezed
between walls and patchwork fields. They were astonishing, those
fields, in their summer brilliance. I peered into them as I passed.
Each presented a world in itself. Some were bare rock, pavements
of pale limestone without a grain of soil, narrow cracks across them,
and in their shadowy trenches tiny fronds of spleenwort – like
miniature soldiers waiting to go over the top. In others, there was

enough soil to support a sward, and the grass glowed in the sun with a luminous green. Others were yellow – thick with kidney vetch and bird's foot trefoil and flag-iris. Another was a galaxy of daisies.

I carried on past the island's settlement, the thatched cottage where J. M. Synge stayed, the fields where an islander told him he'd watched a rabbit playing a flute. The southern side of the island, beyond the ridge, is unpeopled, a vast labyrinth of walls and fields falling away to the sea. As it opened out, I shielded my eyes, looking out over the stone walls to Gregory's Sound, where I'd sailed in a couple of days before, and to the rocky coast of County Clare and then the endless blue of the west, overcome by a feeling of joy so powerful that I had to sit down for a moment.

The whole day was like that. I spent it wandering, light-footed in that hallowed place. I walked out towards the southern shore, entering fields thick with orchids and gentians where I hardly dared tread. I followed the lanes down towards the cliffs, where the walls were well over head-height. Beyond them was a bare rock platform and streams which flooded out of the turf. They followed an ordered course over the limestone to the cliff-edge – then scattered into spray like so many well-made plans. I lay on a patch of dry, stuck my head over the edge and watched the swells on the rocks below – rising high and falling back in brief white cascades. The sun was high and bright, but there was weather coming. The seas were building. I found myself picturing *Tsambika* in Cill Rónáin harbour, and the mooring line and the single knot that held it to the samson post.

Along the eastern shoreline, I reached the old quay. That was where I'd landed on previous visits. In the grass was an abandoned *currach*. It looked like a beached sea-creature, long and black, with its articulated bow pointing up like a mandible. The bottom boards were painted an old-looking red. In the crutch of the frames, tiny weeds had taken root and the timber of the thwarts and the paddles were sun-bleached to the colour of old bone. The tarred canvas of the hull was warm to the touch.

In the shape of the *currach* is contained hundreds of years, hundreds of generations. Reference to hide-covered craft appears in the earliest records of these coasts – from the accounts of St Columba and St Brendan to the twelfth-century Giraldus Cambrensis. Canvas has replaced hide, and laths are now used instead of wicker frames, but the hull shape is unchanged. These coastal communities were hardly isolated from other mariners, but, like an endemic species, their boats somehow lost the ability to breed with outsiders, to adapt, to evolve.

To islanders, the boats were always more than just functional. They were life itself – passage to fishing grounds, kelp-carriers, cattle-carriers, bringers of priests and doctors, conduits for marriage and for social contact. The *naomhóg* of the southern coast, the 'little holy one', suggests the way these boats were regarded. To change the design would be to alter the unalterable, like tinkering with the liturgy. For visitors, the boats were carriage to a mythical place, casting the initial spell under which the entire islands were experienced. When Synge arrived on Inis Meáin, he recalled: 'It gave me a moment of exquisite satisfaction to find myself moving away from civilization in this rude canvas canoe.' Robin Flower was a regular visitor to the Blaskets and he wrote: 'There is no greater pleasure on earth than to lie in the stern of a *naomhóg*, almost in the embrace of the water as the strong rowers snatch the boat over the waves.'

Up in the village, I called in on Ruari Roscommon, the island's *currach*-builder. He was watching his goat. An ash tree spread out above his yard and the goat had its front hooves in the branches and was nibbling at the leaves. 'Will you look at her!' he said with affection. 'She just had two children.'

He had a lean-to shed round the back, full of sawdust and off-cuts and an electric lathe in the middle. He trotted off the details of construction. 'Oak ribs, white deal frames. Nineteen and a half feet long, fifty-one feet across.'

'You mean inches?'

'Inches, yes.' He smiled. 'What they say about me is I'm a little absent-minded.' He told a story about delivering a new boat to a customer, and he'd forgotten to put in anywhere for the rowlocks. 'That's Ruari, they said! Makes beautiful boats, but he's a bit absent-minded.'

Demand for new *currachs* had pretty much dried up. Ruari now made small wooden coasters on the lathe for sale to visitors. I picked one up. It had an image of a *currach* carved into it, detailed with his boatbuilder's knowledge of sheer and rig. On the underside was a sticker saying: LÁMHDHÉANTA IN INIS MEÁIN – 'Handmade in Inis Meáin'.

'You start at the machine and you can't leave it alone. You'll be at it for hours.'

I thanked him and said goodbye. But he was already bent over the spinning lathe, and didn't hear.

A little way on, I fell into conversation with another islander. He was coming up from the fields with a black Labrador. He'd been checking on his cattle. When I said I'd been out to the end of the island, he said: 'Did you hear the corncrake out there? No? The corncrake, like? We haven't had him here a good few years. He's up at Inishbofin now, but they have no cuckoo, no cuck . . .' His voice was modulated, like the cuckoo's call itself. 'She was here two weeks ago, the cuckoo, all right. That'll be two weeks ago this Wednesday. Stays until the first week of July. Last year it was the ninth, the ninth of July, all right.'

His speech flowed from him, a stream of sounds that was two parts words and one part music. 'Yes, Inis Meáin, it's good for the birds, all right, it's good for the birds.' Then he tilted his head. 'Can you see the lark up there?'

I peered up; it was too high. His eyes had been in shadow but now with his face raised I could see them. They were clouded over; he was blind.

I booked into a B & B and woke to rain beating on the lean-to roof. Heaving on my oilskins and sea-boots, I walked off to catch the ferry. It was half-dark, like dawn, but the sun had been up for a couple of hours. I passed the airstrip, and the orange windsock fat with gale. No one else was on the quay yet. I stood at the end and listened to the rain patter my hood. The seas outside the harbour were long and heavy, and I watched them press on towards the mainland. The ferry was running, but it was not a day to be on the water. The warm rain ran down my hands. At my feet, swells were pushing in round the edge of the wall, rising up its concrete side to flop and surge into the inner harbour.

Then suddenly, from long ago: a morning like this, in Cornwall. I was five or six. A gale was coming in and we'd risen early to move the boat and I was with my grandfather on the quay, and he was pulling in the dinghy and his black oilskin coat was shiny with rain. I could see the seas outside, long and heavy, peeling in around the harbour wall to rise up the stonework. The rain was pattering on my hood; it was running warm over my hands.

'I wonder more as I grow older how great the influence of nostalgia is on the course of our lives. How far does it make a man creative or does it become a token of his defeat?'

The opening sentences of Frank Fraser Darling's *Island Farm*, his memoir of the Summer Isles, are the most striking of the whole book. When Bridget and I read them all those years ago, no amount

87

of discussion quite resolved his question; we often found ourselves asking about someone, or something read, or in the news: creative nostalgia or defeated nostalgia? Fraser Darling's first chapter is titled 'Nostalgia' and it is the frame for his own decision to take his young family from a comfortable dairy farm in Buckinghamshire to live on a group of deserted Scottish islands. Now I thought: how much of all this is just nostalgia – the draw of the Aran Islands, the west coast, this sailing, this wooden boat, the Summer Isles?

In general, nostalgia gets a pretty bad press. It's reactionary and escapist. It's the comforting solidity of the past preferred to the alarming fluidity of the present, passive reminiscing to active improvement, the irrelevance of what's gone to the responsibility for what's to come, the primitivist appeal of a place like Inis Meáin to the progressive context of the urban, the modern. The word 'nostalgia' itself is now a catch-all term, spanning not only a soft longing for the past but also the narrative of entire nations.

It was first used in 1688 to describe a condition identified in Swiss mercenaries fighting in the French lowlands. They would take to their beds and weep, lying around in a state of useless torpor. Some physicians said they knew the cause – it was cowbells. Constant exposure to the sound of Swiss cowbells had clearly damaged these young men's minds. One doctor suggested that the increase in atmospheric pressure caused a corresponding increase in blood to the skull. But it was a junior medical officer, Johannes Hofer, who proposed that the condition was a form of homesickness, arising from 'continuous vibration of animal spirits through those fibres of the middle brain in which traces of ideas of the Fatherland still cling'. He called it 'nostalgia' – from *nostos*, 'home', and *algia*, 'pain.

Since then, nostalgia has gone through its own odyssey of meanings and emphasis. In the nineteenth century, it was understood to be a form of melancholia, sometimes with violent consequences, causing 'incendiarism, infanticide, and suicide'. The rise of psycho-analysis in the twentieth century led to a new understanding. It was still seen as 'a variant of depression' but, according to the neuropsy-chologist H. A. Kaplan, it represented 'an acute yearning for a union with the preoedipal mother, a saddening farewell to childhood, a defense against mourning, or a longing for a past forever lost.'

More recently, a number of psychologists – often in response to personal feelings of homesickness – have started to think that nostalgia might in fact constitute an important part of mental health, a processing technique to restore or maintain balance. 'In difficult situations, it appears that nostalgia grounds you,' proposes Dr Sedikides, one of the fathers of contemporary 'nostalgia studies': 'It gives you a base on which to evaluate the present as a temporary state, and in doing so it perhaps builds resilience.' When subjected to analysis, nostalgia reveals itself not as damaging or regressive but as beneficial, an essential part of our psychological well-being. Krystine Batcho, professor of psychology at Le Moyne College, New York, highlights its capacity to embed our stabilizing percep-tions: 'Nostalgic yearning may promote the sense of ownership of thoughts, actions, and feelings across time and change.'

Nostalgia studies are a growing part of academic psychology. The University of Southampton in particular is a centre for the subject, and the 'Southampton Nostalgia Index' is an internation-ally accepted measure of nostalgic feeling. Experiments are carried out in clinical conditions. Sad music is played, or individuals are encouraged to dwell on Christmases past or family weddings, in a technique known as 'vivid autobiographical recall methodology'. Against a control group, the nostalgic subjects have been shown to display a range of positive tendencies – greater altruism, less anxiety about money or death; they are more likely to engage with strangers, and show enhanced social tendencies; couples who reminisce report greater intimacy. In one experiment, a group was asked to arrange chairs for a meeting; those in a nostalgic state of mind consistently placed them closer together. Inducing nostalgia is being trialled in the treatment of dementia and depression, as well as in nursing homes and among those recovering from major surgery.

Feelings of nostalgia have been found to be pretty much universal. Data sets gathered from around the world reveal a remarkable consistency, though there is some regional variation in its prevalence, the Chinese being particularly given to it. Air temperature appears to make a difference – colder days are better for inducing nostalgia, and sixty-eight degrees has been discovered as the optimal temperature for nostalgic feelings. One of the observed effects of nostalgia is that it raises body temperature. It is easy to see how it might have offered an evolutionary advantage: sharing memories not only reinforces group cohesion but keeps the cold at bay.

Nostalgia has its collective realm. Many mythologies are driven by the notion of an idealized past, which builds over generations. The Judaeo-Christian tradition has the Garden of Eden, ancient Greece hankered for the pastoral harmony of the Golden Age. As early as the eighth century BC, Hesiod describes life for his forebears: 'And they lived like gods without sorrow of heart, remote and free from toil and grief: miserable age rested not on them; but with legs and arms never failing they made merry with feasting beyond the reach of all evils.' Much of the Irish otherworld echoes such paradisiacal traditions.

Almost all belief systems retain a vision of lost perfection, an ideal against which the flawed present is measured. The Egyptians had *Tep Zepi*, the 'first time', the Australian Aborigines their Dreamtime. The Caribs of Surinam believed in a primordial era when 'the trees were forever in fruit, the animals lived in perfect harmony and the little agouti played fearlessly with the beard of the jaguar'.

Similarities in paradise myths have suggested to some ethnographers a common root, a proto-myth. More convincing is the idea that the stories are an aggregate of personal experience, that their narrative arc is that of all individual lives – a patterning of transition from innocent childhood to burdensome adulthood. Common to them too is their emphasis on location, on particular or imaginary places. The topography of paradise provides an entire parallel study in landscape aesthetics – holy mountains, sacred trees, fertile plains, luminous green gardens. An uncanny number of primal sites feature four rivers – from the mythology of the Kalmyks to that of the Navajo, from Genesis to the Scandinavian *Edda* and the Hindu *Vishnu Purana*. Islands also feature a good deal. Plato's Atlantis was wonderfully rich and abundant: 'whatever fragrant things there are in the earth, whether roots, or herbage, or woods, or distilling drops of flowers or fruits, grew and thrived in that land'. Among the Polynesians of the Pacific there is a tradition of lost islands and the joyous lives once lived there. They speak of a place called Hava-Iki, which gave the name to Hawaii, while on Hawaii itself is found the creation myth of a perfect garden on Kahiki-honua-kele, 'the land that moved off'.

St Brendan's Isle, Hy-Brasil, Atlantis, Antillia – the mythical islands of the Atlantic all offered hints of a vanished and noble past. The Aran Islands and the Blaskets do something similar. J. M. Synge's travel accounts are filled with a longing that embraces not just the plain elevation of an old way of life but something universal, a pattern of thinking felt by his subjects as much as by him: 'an emotion that is partly local and patriotic, and partly a share of the desolation that is mixed everywhere with the supreme beauty of the world'.

We can't help being nostalgic. We are creatures afflicted from birth with an awareness that something is missing, that something has already passed. We are *homo nostalgicus* and all our greatest achievements, our greatest art, owe a little to that capacity for longing, for trying to reach a place that no longer exists, that possibly never did, to recapture a mood that we were never even aware of at the time.

At its most basic, nostalgia is an elevation of the past, a browsing of merchandise in museum shops, a preference for heritage. But the nostalgia that is most powerful is the version that struck that morning on the quay at Inis Meáin – the sudden transcendence, the piercing of the present to reach a season long gone. It is not just a moment of recall but carries with it the exhilarating sense that all time exists behind the screen of the physical world. Once glimpsed it is hard to forget, and we spend half our lives trying to see it again. Music might initiate it, and it comes usually in a state of reflective peace. So it is with many stories of visiting the otherworld, the random and contemplative scene when the journey begins: Thomas the Rhymer lying by a tree, Bran son of Febal idly wandering near his father's castle.

So Fraser Darling's question has no clear answer. Nostalgia can be creative, but it can also be regressive. Good and bad – like most things. In my notes from that first summer up in Sutherland with Bridget, I found a scribbled-down quote from Cyril Connolly: 'Imagination = nostalgia for the past, the absent; it's the liquid solution in which art develops the snapshot of reality. The artist secretes nostalgia round life, as a worm plasters its tunnel, a caterpillar spins a cocoon or as a sea-swallow masticates her nest. Art without imagination is as life without hope.'

I did not return at once to Inis Mór and *Tsambika*. I took the ferry from Inis Meáin to the mainland, to Ros an Mhil and An Cheathrú Rua, which retains a piece of personal nostalgia.

It was two decades ago, another century. I was in my mid-thirties. I'd been travelling and writing for ten years, going wherever books and articles took me. Winters were spent in Cornwall – the last one trying to finish a story about Poland. I'd come to Ireland that June via research in Belarus and Cyprus. I was struggling to find a form for the book about the Celts. Studying Irish was a part of that, and it had brought me here, to an outpost of the University of Galway in the Connemara Gaeltacht. But in truth my heart was in Russia, from where, three years after the end of the Soviet Union, stories were spilling like doves from a long-closed dovecote. I'd met someone – and she was in Russia. By November, I'd abandoned the Celts and was living in a flat off Kutuzovsky Prospekt in Moscow, committed to a book about the fringes of Russian belief and to Charlotte, whom a few years later I married.

But here, now – I didn't recognize any of this. Memory had twisted it. The main road and the islands of scattered bungalows were all a different shape. The college building did not look the same. The sign was new: ACADAMH NA HOLLSCOLAÍOCHTA GAEILGE under the banner of National University of Ireland, Galway. Then – a patch of grass, a small patch of grass in front of the building and a crowd of us lounging around between lessons, in the sun – Donna and Ross and Steve and Martine and the others, and Debbie on the steps playing the penny-whistle. We were all foreigners on the course. About half were American; most from Boston. There was also a Czech, three Germans, an Italian, two Australians. There was a Japanese woman wanting to translate poetry from Irish, and a Russian called Dasha from the town of Borodino. Dasha told me she had had a dream in which she was told to learn Irish. She'd never heard of Ireland, but she began studying and arrived in An Cheathrú Rua speaking it perfectly. I was the only Englishman.

I made friends with the college driver, a local man named John.

One evening we swam his horses across to a small islet, following them in a *currach*. On the island was an abandoned cottage where John had been born and brought up with his twelve brothers and sisters. He went there sometimes with his own children: 'Just to camp nowadays.'

On another afternoon, we sailed across Galway Bay to Kinvara in his *púcán* – like a Galway hooker, only smaller. We were becalmed, it rained for three hours and we arrived long after dark. The next day John and some others came into class for conversation. The idea was that we students would use our limited Irish to talk with him. When it came to my turn, I had an advantage. I knew something about him.

'*An bfhuil bád agat?*' I asked John. 'Do you have a boat?'

'*Tá.*'

'*Is bád álainn í – bád mór.* It's a beautiful boat – a big boat.' I was confident now. '*Bhí mé uirthi inné. Bhí am breá againn.* I went on it yesterday. We had a fine time.'

The tutor was struggling not to laugh.

'Next?' he spluttered.

Afterwards he took me aside to explain: the Irish *bád* is 'boat', but *bod* – the way I pronounced it – is slang for 'penis'.

When I reached Cill Rónáin again, the wind had gone through and a stillness had settled over the harbour, the sort of deep stillness that follows violent weather. I heaved the Zodiac down the slip and motored out to *Tsambika*. Climbing aboard, I flicked the puddled rain from the mainsail cover, pumped the bilges, tapped the barometer, checked the batteries. I opened the PassageWeather app on my phone and let the wind charts play out through the next day or two – blue and pale blue and white, west backing southwest; nothing to worry about. Then on day three, a great blob of green sliding in from the Atlantic, with a yellow and red core following behind. I'd need to be well sheltered by then.

I took the pilot book, the almanac for the tides and my own logbook into the cockpit, and spread out the paper chart. Now the coast was getting interesting. Moving northwards, it frayed first into inlets and islands, then the islands themselves frayed into a hundred rocks and shoals. With the Portland plotter I worked out a route around all the dangers (Namackan Rocks . . . Fools Shoal . . . Big Breaker . . .) and drew three bearings – 290°, 315°, and 043° – towards the corridor of Clifden harbour. Eight hours or so. I turned to the tides and jotted down a lot of numbers in the logbook – dates and heights and adjusted timings. I calculated the streams and added their vectors to my course. Soon the log page looked like my children's maths homework.

Course-planning done, I took the Zodiac over to the beach. The evening was as bright as steel. Walking up over the back of Cill Éinne, I came to the island's opposite slope, the less peopled one, where the land falls away to the sea and a line of sheer cliffs runs out to the west for six miles or more. Below them, the water looked flat. But as I watched, there appeared a continuous flashing, silent bursts of spray that every few seconds detonated somewhere along that limestone wall. It was the 'western surge', the ceaseless Atlantic swell that hour after hour, century after century, picks away at the fortress of those islands.

8

I WOKE TO SUN AND NO wind. The sea was all shine and glitter. Another boat lay a little way off in the harbour and its mooring rope dropped rod-straight from the bow. Beside it, an inverted image of itself stretched out across the water in a scribble of broken spars and rigging. When I motored out of the bay, my bow left a clean *v* of wash on the surface. A shag swam off at my approach, then took flight, full of indignation, as if it was frankly impertinent for anyone to be moving about on such a morning.

For an hour or more I followed the treeless coast of Inis Mór. The regularity of the limestone scarp made it look like a flat-pack island just pulled from the box (vegetation not included). On the other side, way off to the north, the skyline of Connemara was more fulsome, bulbous with the granite peaks of the Twelve Bens.

A mile or so in front of me, dead on my course, were Na Sceirdí, the Skerd Rocks. The name comes from the Irish *sceird*, a 'bleak, windswept place'. The largest of them rose more than sixty feet from the water, and there was threat in its height and blackness. Even today, it was surrounded by skirts of surf. I'd read of the nine women dropped off on Sceird Mór years ago to collect dulse. The weather came in and they could not be picked up. For nine days and nine nights they were stranded there. But they were tough, those Connemara women, and the only ill effects were swollen jaws from chewing the dulse – although, according to one of their husbands, they 'weren't as good as they used to be until a fortnight after coming home'. In October 2000, a large trawler – the *Arosa* – was driven on to the Skerd Rocks: just one man from a crew of thirteen was recovered alive.

I adjusted my course. I wanted those rocks well to the north. I didn't trust them. Sure enough, after going below for a few minutes, I found that they'd sneaked nearer on the tide. Close up, their presence was more animate, with sculpted brows and haunches. Every now and then, waves rose up their fringe, ghostly arms stretching out to try and get a hold.

The Skerd archipelago is also visible from the north, from the mainland. The rocks lie far enough offshore to have become part of that hazy and suggestive territory, the cartography of the not-quite-real, the wished-for, the possible. Roderic O'Flaherty wrote of them in the 1680s: 'These rocks sometimes appear to be a city far off, full of houses, castles, towers, chimneys, sometimes full of blasing flames, smoke and people running to and fro.'

From the cockpit, I watched them closely as they passed, shape-shifting with each glance. They slid past my beam, then my quarter. Then they were astern and shrinking.

The hours melted one into the next. Overhead the sun remained half-hidden behind a film of high cloud. It added to the strange suspension of that morning. The sea surface was so colourless and smooth that I felt I was flying – like the sky-ships of medieval Ireland. Having cleared the end of Inis Mór, I picked up a swell from yesterday's blow. The waves were long enough not to trouble the boat, but each time I was in a trough, the rise of water was deep enough to hide the land.

Towards Slyne Head, a breeze came out of the south. I pulled up the sails and cut the engine. The quiet came as a shock. My ears rang with relief; their only stimulus now the gentle slop of water past the gunwale. I looked ahead to where the land tapered to a point, breaking into a dot-dot-dot of islands and rocks. My internal chatter was toying with names. Slyne Head: *slyne . . . skerd*; down in Kerry, there'd been *Slea* Head and *Sybil* Point. I wondered about the snakey sibilance, whether there was a link to their threat. I couldn't think of any other examples so I dropped the theory and focused on getting past the headland.

Around such points is often great agitation. Blocks of tide-driven water pour along the coast at different rates, at different levels; where they meet, there's usually some reckoning to be done. The swells become confused and steep. Overfalls can add to the chaos. The charts mark these places with a couple of discreet wave symbols, while the pilot books advise that they are 'best given a wide offing'.

But they move around, these tide races. Sometimes they're close in, sometimes further out; the winds affect them, and the state of tide. Now on the skyline, just a few hundred yards off, I could see upturned wedges of water. I was trying to work out a course to avoid them when the sea became oddly flat. Sooner than expected. I pushed down the helm and headed back towards the head. There was often an inside passage of calmer water close to the land. But now disturbed water lay in all directions.

Suddenly the boat dropped away to port. I stumbled. My shoulder knocked hard against a winch. My arm was in water. As the boat righted, I picked myself up. At once the stern lifted and we were being driven forward, fast, with another train-size flood. I turned on the engine, stowed the genoa. The wind was too light: I needed power for steerage.

I looked around. All was angles, formless slopes and dips, shapes that water couldn't hold for long, and didn't, collapsing in violent patches of froth that now dotted the seascape. It made me think of the field of *chevaux-de-frise* outside Dún Aonghasa. This was a liquid version.

In a large and regular sea, you develop a rhythm at the helm. No two waves are ever the same but they follow a pattern, like a piece of music. This was just noise. Great stands of water would come surging out of the mess. All I could do was grip the tiller against them. Hoisted for a moment on a mound of sea, I took in my surroundings: acres and acres of turbulence, a fluid plain of jut and rupture. It was hard to tell what progress the engine was making through the water – four or five knots on the instruments. But with the shifting of the water itself, that meant little against the land.

In fact, it was working in my favour. I could see the headland and its lighthouse moving south. And now ahead, a hundred yards or so, all was smooth again. One more shove from the sea, one more yank of the helm. The movement began to settle. Soon *Tsambika* had found her feet again, and we were free, following the line of a different coast, pushing north.

In there somewhere, amidst the mess of reef and rock and low cliff, was the entrance to Clifden harbour.

I jumped down to the chart table and found the sheet marked up with the approach. I'd been given it in Kilrush by Adrian O'Connell, traditional boatbuilder, Commodore of the Royal Western Yacht Club, and descendant of the liberator of Irish Catholics, Daniel O'Connell. Adrian was also the man behind protecting a large stretch of this coast with two RNLI stations (yacht clubs and lifeboats have kept their 'royal' handles in Ireland). He had helped install lifeboats not just at Kilrush but at Clifden, where he'd done his seafaring for many years. When he heard I was sailing there, he made a copy of the Admiralty chart, marked it up, laminated it and brought it to the boat. Watching his finger slide across the sea, explaining passage and entry to Clifden, I realized his enthusiasm was driven not just by the desire to help, but – like all such giving of directions – by a love of the known place and the vicarious pleasure in going there.

$080°$ – he'd written the bearing on the chart and drawn a bold transit line which ran from deep water through the end of Fishing Point to the ruins of Clifden Castle – giving a clear run into the harbour mouth. It all looked simple on paper – but which was Fishing Point? I scanned the shore with binoculars. I could see breaking water on rocks – rocks on the land and rocks offshore. I imagined others below the surface. There – a beacon, white stub of a building. And there – a ruin. And between them – that looked like a channel opening. *Right.* I turned in and prepared to line them up, watching the two slide together, watching the compass – but the bearing wasn't right.

I headed back away from the shore. As more of the slope came into view behind it, so there appeared a much larger ruin. A castle, definitely, with its skull-like facade of hollow windows and towers and castellations. Clifden Castle. Now the bearings matched.

Turning in towards the channel, I dropped the mainsail, took the mooring line forward and motored in. I was entering a long harbour. On one side, the slopes rose steep and fern-covered. On the other was the face of Connacht, the face of the congested districts, the hard-to-work muddle of turf and rock.

I found a mooring, pumped up the Zodiac and, with another bumpy passage behind me, went ashore to find a drink.

Clifden Boat Club is a building all on its own, cut back into the hill and shaped like a piece of Toblerone. A short jetty pushes out into the harbour below it. It is a modest club as such clubs go, but over the next couple of days, I found it a hub for a certain sort of adventurer, a certain sort of man (almost always men) for whom the sea's challenges help make life worth living. Peter Vine had helped set it up. He had worked with Adrian O'Connell to install the lifeboat. I met him in the clubhouse that evening and he sketched out a maritime life launched by early exposure to the films of Jacques Cousteau and Hans Hass. No one in his family had ever been to university, but Peter went on to take a PhD in marine science. Tube worms were his specialty. He'd pioneered fish farming in the Persian Gulf and the Red Sea and once spent ten days in a Sudanese jail. His own boat was being repaired, having hit a rock in Joyce's Pass, an impossibly narrow channel through the islets off Slyne Head.

'If there's anything at all I can do to help you, let me know.' He was a member of the *Frères de la côte* – the worldwide fraternity committed to the support of mariners. Just the offer was reassuring.

That night the gale arrived. In the early hours, I could hear the banshee scream of the wind in the stays, the rain tap-dancing on the decks. *More rain, more rest*, goes the yachting adage, *fine weather is not always best*. I spent the day in the clubhouse, chatting with those from two other boats sheltering in the harbour. Steve and Malcolm had sailed from London and were toying with the idea of going 'round the top', down the east coast of Scotland and England.

The other boat was the base for a round-Ireland swim. Maghners was the swimmer, and he astonished me with his story. He'd decided on the challenge after cycling from Cape Town back to Limerick, and from Istanbul to Shanghai, running a 'couple of marathons' on the Tibetan plateau and kayaking down the Yangtze. The current round-Ireland trip was a surprising venture to him – as, 'when I decided to do it, I had no idea how to swim'. Later a deaf American dropped in and explained that he was preparing his steel ketch for a trip to Greenland. He had no instruments and no radio. 'What's the point?' He tapped his earlobe. No one in Clifden would sail with him and he had used the internet to recruit crew; they were due to arrive tomorrow from France and Germany.

The forecast made for poor viewing. The current gale was followed by another depression clipping the top of Ireland, and behind it days of bunched-together isobars. I took the chance to return home, to reconnect with my land life, lest I turn up at some later stage and get taken for some bearded stranger. A bus to Galway, to Dublin and a small prop plane back to Cornwall: school runs, trips to the beach, extended talks, reconnecting, house maintenance, tree maintenance and a couple of long-promised articles to write, then the return journey, the thought of rocky shores ahead and – a pulling on of an old coat – the re-acquaintance with all the frailties of my boat world.

The first morning back on board, hardly awake, my ears reached for weather sounds. Finding none, they settled on creaks, *Tsambika*'s whispered intimacies. I prepared to leave the shelter of Clifden harbour for Inishbofin. It was no more than a few hours away, but I busied myself with stowing and fiddling, tide-checking, chart-gazing, course-confirming, halyard freeing and fuel-filling – finding my place on the boat again and recognizing as I did so the familiar dovetailing of nerves and excitement.

9

HEADING OUT OF THE CLOUD and shadows of Clifden harbour,
I could see sunlight ahead, pooling across an expanse of open water.
Not exactly open, more a dense mash-up of land and sea and surf.
It wasn't easy to work out what joined up with what, to translate
the god-like perspective of the chart into the sailor's view from the
cockpit. Down here, headlands coalesced, rocks separated, islands
closed and drew apart. Steering south of west, I found a course that
pushed round the whole lot, to where there was only the roll of
the sea to deal with. When I could make out High Island and Friar
Island, and when the narrow sound opened up between them about
six miles off, I came round to head pretty much due north.

High Island (Ard Oileán means the same in Irish): steep sides
and, on top, a cap of green that covered a ridge and low peak. Landing on the island is rarely easy and, with large seas, there was no
chance today. Perhaps as a result, that tiny patch of unreachable
grass created in me such an ache that I found myself binocular-
scanning each of its cracks and hollows, its cushions of thrift, its
hidden areas above, bouncing the question back and forth: what's a
place like that *for*?

The monks of the early Christian centuries knew what it was for
– contemplation and extreme penitence. They built a chapel and
stone huts. A community grew up around the elderly St Féichín,
who liked to 'lay his wretched body in the stony cell without

raiment'. In the nineteenth century, the island was bought by a man who thought it was for mining and brought miners from Cornwall to extract its copper. But there wasn't enough of it. There was always grazing, though, once you got the sheep there, and shepherds used it until the 1960s, when the poet Richard Murphy acquired it and re-established the purpose for which it was first used by monks – contemplation, dreaming. 'I wrote continuously,' recalled Murphy, 'sometimes in the dark, with nowhere to sleep except on the ground.' The dedication of those who had lived here before him haunted the island: 'a stone altar seen through the door of the oratory . . . a sign of order surviving in ruin, of an idea outliving not only the builder but the building.'

As well as High Island, Murphy bought an old Galway fishing boat – a hooker, the *Ave Maria*, and for years ran her for charter out of Inishbofin and Cleggan. She was a couple of feet longer than *Tsambika*, and another fifty years older. Like me, Murphy had had no experience of skippering such a boat. 'To make our tourists feel they were in safe hands, I wore a yachtsman's cap with a shiny black peak, a white plastic cover and a gold-threaded anchor-badge.' He bluffed his way through a few tricky episodes, and he had good local crew who knew the waters well. Everything Murphy did, he did with a certain *chutzpah*, and soon he was taking the *Ave Maria* out with passengers, navigating the labyrinth of rocks and islands for pollack.

If I couldn't land, at least I could show the island a respectable spread of canvas. I'd been motoring all morning, in light airs, but now, in honour of Murphy, I set about putting up the sails. A formidable swell was running and I crept forward along the deck, keeping my centre of gravity low. The seas were throwing the boat from side to side. High Island was close now. I needed to be quick; the tide was working swiftly. I leaned hard against the mast, tied the bowline at the head of the sail, and edged back to the cockpit. Hand over hand, I hauled it up, watching its creamy shape unfold against the cloudless blue.

Then it stuck. The halyard had swung the wrong side of the crosstrees. I crept forward again to free it. With one eye shut against the sun, I peered up the mast, tried to flick it free. Again and again it swung out, then back to the same place. I tried using the swells – if I gave the rope slack at the right moment, the drop of the boat would free it. With the first swell, the rope looped out and fell back, still behind the crosstrees. Likewise the second. I watched the mast metronome across the sky, waiting for it to drop away. I could hardly see.

Then the sky was suddenly black – the island's cliff. I was closer in than I thought. I slacked off a wide loop and watched it arc away and drop back again. The cliffs were coming nearer. I let out more rope and watched it squiggle and swing. I was aware of the rock face as it swung back. But now it was clear. I raced back to the cockpit to winch it in.

Cutting the engine, I let the breeze fill the sails. We moved away from the cliffs, and, with something like control, pushed into the corridor of water between the two islands. It was full of eddies and flat patches. Little waves kicked up in the rushing tide. A lobster-pot buoy was half-submerged by the pull of the current, the warp taut below it, as if being dragged along by some bottom-dwelling monster. In the end it was the water more than the wind that took the boat through the sound.

I could now see clearly the long ridge of Inishbofin, an hour to the north. Its blue-grey form was bulky in the middle and at the western end, tapering eastwards to rocky edges. From a distance, in the hazy afternoon sun, it was possible to imagine that what was visible was all there was, that there was nothing of the island beneath the sea-surface, that the whole thing was simply floating.

Along this Atlantic coast are invented islands like Hy-Brasil, Tír Tairngire and Kilstapheen, and real islands like Aran that themselves are crucibles of invention. Inishbofin has been both. For centuries, it drifted untethered in the vastness of the ocean. It would sometimes pop up on the skyline, and then be gone. Those who managed to reach the place where they thought they'd seen it found only empty water. The more elusive it was, the more people wanted to get there. Then one day a couple of fishermen, lost in fog, spotted its grey outline. As they approached, they were surprised to see that it did not move away. They landed on its shore, lit a fire – and in that moment the island's wanderings ceased.

Sweden's largest island, Gotland, showed similar impermanence. It used to be invisible by day; only at night would it rise above the surface of the water. It took the local hero Tjelvar to put a stop to its daily caprice – again, with fire. In the twelfth century, Giraldus Cambrensis recorded an island off the north coast of Ireland which became topography by means of a forge-hot arrow piercing its side. In the voyage tales, the *immrama*, of St Brendan and Máel Dúin, the opposite happens: the sailors reach an island and light a fire on it, and the fire reveals it to be the scaly back of a fish, which then begins to move away.

Fire has always been the way we bring to heel the chaos of creation, to put it to use. We have cleared woodland with it, kept warm with it, cooked with it, used it for making metals and for locomotion. 'Combustion,' wrote W. G. Sebald, 'is the hidden principle behind all we create.' Why should it not also prove useful in that most tricky of earthly tasks, to make the imaginary real?

An island that has been tamed by fire is an island that man has dominion over, that can be settled and grazed. But something is lost too. Sliding in and out of view, Inishbofin was a magical thing, suggestive of powers that exist beyond the physical. The alteration of such places has a tinge of post-Edenic shame about it, of nostalgia, the nagging suspicion of the terrible truth: that fire has bought us control at the cost of enchantment.

The harbour of Inishbofin is one of the safest places on Ireland's west coast. But entry is tight. The channel runs between barriers of reef and rocks on one side and Gun Island on the other. You have to line up two pepper-pot towers and keep close to that line, passing within a boat's length of Gun Island. Once in the harbour, the protection is total. In the seventeenth century, under Cromwell's Commonwealth, the English feared such harbours and what they offered rebels and invaders. They promised a reward to anyone who could block up the entrance to Inishbofin. When that failed, they built a castle, whose dark ruin still stands at the entrance. The castle was used to imprison Catholic priests who, simply by being priests, were deemed guilty of high treason. Before being deported, they were brought here. Many were 'tortured with great cruelty'.

I moored up in the pool just to the castle's east. That evening, I took the Zodiac ashore to Day's Bar, where much of Inishbofin's magic has been dispensed in recent times. It was Saturday night and a group of smokers stood outside. Their red faces were a gauntlet of high spirits.

'He's off a boat!'

'Where d'you come from?'

'The UK – Cornwall.'

'You're very welcome.'

I pushed open the door on a hubbub of talk and music. A man

was shouldering through the crowd, hands wrapped around three pints: 'Brion! Will you take these?'

Hanging up lifejacket and oilskins, I made my way to the bar. In the far corner was a group sitting and standing around three pulled-together tables. They were of all ages, each of them engaged in the struggle to be heard. When a woman in their midst rose to her feet, they stopped talking one by one.

She raised her chin. She straightened her pullover and closed her eyes.

> 'I – skimmed across black water
> with-out once submerging
> on to the banks of an urban mor-ning –'

'That's a beautiful song,' said the man next to me.
'Christy Moore?' I said.
'It is.'
'It is not!' said the woman beside him. 'That's Mary Black's.'
'It's not Mary's,' said someone else. 'It's by Jimmy MacCarthy.'

> 'And she – like a ghost beside me
> Goes down with the ease of a dolphin . . .
> For she is the perfect creature, natural in every feature'

When she finished, there was clapping and cheering. A couple of women were standing with their backs to the bar, and one of them leaned in close to be heard. 'We're only from Galway. We all like to come out here to Bofin, for the craic.' She introduced her friend as related to the republican martyr John MacBride.

A large man with a small voice then sang 'Star of the County Down'. Now there was a guitar and a bodhrán, and someone was playing the spoons. A couple in their seventies rose to dance but, finding no space, just held each other, and swayed.

I wallowed in the fug of it all and made my way back around the bar. I chatted to several people there. Then Tommy Burke arrived. I'd been given Tommy's name in Clifden. He was an islander, a dark, thick-set man with a velvety way of speaking. He had an extraordinary interest in, and command of, the island's past. And not just the island. While we talked of St Colman's monastery and the Irish and Saxon monks he brought here to reconcile them after the Synod of Whitby, Tommy dropped in casual references to Bede and Adomnán, to the Anglo-Saxon Chronicles and Irish history, and asides about modern Egypt and Tibet and Iraq.

He had to leave; I said I'd ring and went over to inspect a bronze plaque pinned to the wall: *Theodore Roethke 1908–1963*. It was because of Richard Murphy that Roethke came to Inishbofin. When he heard Roethke was visiting Ireland, Murphy wrote to invite him out here to the west. He headed the letter with his current address, enjoying its 'erotic' ambiguities: 'Hooker *Ave Maria*, Inishbofin, nr Cleggan, County Galway'.

A few weeks later, Roethke and his wife Beatrice were standing on the quay at Cleggan. For Murphy, the first sight of the great poet was a disappointment. He looked 'like a defeated prize-fighter, growing bald, groggy and fat, clumsy on his feet, wrapped in silence'. In his New York suit, Roethke seemed less prepared for sailing to Inishbofin than for 'lunch with T. S. Eliot at the Athenaeum . . . his high forehead creased with anxiety, sweating alcohol.'

But the island worked its spell on Roethke. He began to relax. He and Beatrice had planned to stay a couple of days; it was two months before they left. Theodore livened up the bar here at Day's with his stories and his money. If it was Murphy who had brought him to the island, then it was the 'copious hospitality' of Day's Bar that persuaded him to remain. The bar was run by Margaret and Michael Day, said to have been 'one of the handsomest couples in the world'. Michael opened the bar when he wanted, and during all-nighters would lie down on the floor to sleep, relying on customers' honesty to serve themselves.

In Day's Bar, Roethke found what he'd been hoping for when he first planned a trip to Ireland – life stripped of its metropolitan gloss, the flow of language, a poetic force that once flowed freely through himself. He enjoyed the island's vernacular, the rhythms of speech, the plain speaking of the islanders, and the constant exposure to the elemental power of the natural world.

I stepped in to look more closely at the plaque. As well as Roethke's name and dates there was a bronze figure, head and shoulders turned to look upwards, open-mouthed in amazement, at a flock of birds. The lines beside him came from Roethke's dream poem 'The Far Field':

> I suffered for birds, for
> Young rabbits, caught in the mower,
> My grief was not excessive.
> For to come upon warblers in early May
> Was to forget time and death.

Richard Murphy himself had first entered the powerful orbit of Inishbofin in 1952, a decade before Roethke's visit – and it was Day's Bar that pulled him in. He was one of a crew who'd been battling for nine hours to reach Clare Island. They were in a *púcán*, a boat that had been involved in the Cleggan Disaster twenty-five years earlier, when, in a single night, nine fishermen from the island had died, and another thirty-six from along the coast. The *púcán* had survived but the crew had not. In that 'haunted, leaking boat', Murphy and the others beat back and forth in heavy seas. When the boom broke, they gave up and ran down to Inishbofin. There followed a wild night in Day's Bar that ended at sunrise. 'I had been trying for more than a year to reach a mythical island in a poem,' he wrote. Now he'd reached one in a boat.

Looking back, Richard Murphy saw that journey as the 'rite of passage that changed my life'. The chance arrival on the island, the sanctuary it offered and the things he heard there that night combined to potent effect: 'That was how I started to love Inishbofin.' The poem that came out of that trip – 'Sailing to an Island' – kick-started his career.

Many of those he took out to Inishbofin on the *Ave Maria* were also 'transformed by the experience'. As well as Roethke, Murphy brought the actor Robert Shaw and his lover Mary Ure (still married to John Osborne, but already expecting Shaw's child). The trip began with Murphy running aground. But they were soon clear and it was a beautiful day with a fair wind. Mary lay stretched out on the foredeck, her bare legs hanging over the side. The following year, Sylvia Plath and Ted Hughes came and Plath enjoyed the *Ave Maria* in the same way. Ted Hughes sat in the cockpit with Murphy while Sylvia went forward, gazing down into the water, and at the bows of the boat slicing through it, 'inhaling the sea air ecstatically'.

Inishbofin's mystique rubs off on everyone who comes into contact with it – the floating island, suspended, unattached, where what is fixed can be freed, and the discrete territory can come to mean whatever you want it to. But at a price. The original story of Inishbofin ends badly. The first thing the fishermen saw when they landed on the floating island was an old woman beating a white cow. Cows being sacred, and white cows doubly so, one of the fishermen protested. He was instantly turned to stone. The woman and the white cow were also turned to stone. Hence the name of the island – *inish* – *bó* – *finne*: 'island of the white cow'. Pirate outpost, rebel stronghold, Cromwellian prison – the island traps as much as it attracts. While outsiders yearn to visit it, many residents dream only of leaving.

Sylvia Plath's trip to Inishbofin came in the last few months of her life. The island and Richard Murphy became things she reached for in her struggle to stay afloat. She'd met Murphy a couple of times; she was a judge on the panel that awarded him First Prize in the Guinness Poetry Awards. His stories of the west of Ireland had so enthralled her that in July 1962, she wrote to him saying she 'desperately needed a boat and the sea and no squalling babies'. Could she and Ted come and stay? Their marriage was already tenuous at best and it is clear that Plath loaded the trip with a good deal of expectation, an island cure for herself, perhaps a reconciliation with Hughes. She told Murphy: 'you would be a very lovely person for us to visit just now'.

They came for a week. The three of them drove down beyond Galway to see Yeats's Tower, and to Coole Park. They sailed to Inishbofin. Hughes lasted four days, before leaving suddenly one morning. Alone with Murphy, Sylvia made a play for him. He 'panicked', fearing the local community's disapproval, and she turned against him: 'Sylvia was enraged. All her warmth and enthusiasm, her gushing excitement . . . changed into strangulated hostility.' A fortnight later, she wrote to him from Devon saying she and Ted were getting a divorce, and could she come back with her babies and her work. In the letter is a hint of the frail state she was in: 'My health depends on me leaving England & going to Ireland, and the health of my children . . . Please have the kindness, the largeness, to say you will not wish me ill nor keep me from what I clearly and calmly see as the one fate open. I would like to think your understanding could vault the barrier it was stuck at when I left. Sincerely, Sylvia.'

Murphy prepared for her arrival. What was he expecting? He was a few years divorced. But then she changed her mind. He saw her once more in London. She said she was happy, living in the flat where Yeats had lived, and that it was best that she had not come to Ireland. Murphy remembers that 'her face looked feverish, and she seemed ecstatic'. Within a couple of weeks, she was dead.

For Roethke, the dream of Inishbofin also exposed his vulnerability. After a fortnight on the island, his behaviour became erratic. He drank too much in Day's Bar, he picked arguments. When Richard Murphy spoke highly of a Robert Lowell poem, Roethke hammered on the bar with his fists: 'Why are you always praising Lowell? I'm as mad as he is!' Half in jest, he put a knife to Margaret Day's throat.

In the end the doctor was called. Roethke was certified. A place was found in Ballinsloe County Mental Hospital. Murphy remembers him leaving the island 'in tears . . . stumbling down the slippery pebbled shore, past the Armada anchor dredged up in a trawl' to the wooden punt and the mailboat that would take him to the mainland and the hospital.

Two years later, he was found floating face-down in a swimming pool near Seattle. He'd had a heart attack.

It was late when I left Day's. The night was perfectly still. Walking down the slip to untie the Zodiac, I was surprised to hear the purr of a car engine on the quay. It came from the wreck of a Sierra. I went over and peered in. The interior was stripped of all but the driver's seat and a man was slumped half in it and half out. I had an instant thought that he was dead, but as I watched he gave a little splutter, and a hand came up to brush his nose. I left him to sleep.

The Zodiac skimmed over the black waters of the harbour; the half-moon's reflection skimmed beside it. Feeling restless and awake, I passed *Tsambika* and carried on to Port Island. I ran the bows up the sand and jumped ashore. Above the beach was soft grass and the outline of Cromwell's Barracks. The ruined walls were apparent not because they were visible but by the void their shape made in the night sky. I stepped into the roofless interior and shivered – had the temperature actually dropped?

I didn't stay inside for long, but walked out to the headland. I sat where the soil gave way to a low cliff and listened to the slop and gurgle of seas among the rocks. In the moonlight, I could make out the abandoned island of Inishark and the abandoned High Island to the south – and beyond it, nothing and no one but a silver infinity of water.

10

SOMEONE HAD TOLD ME ABOUT Omey, an island that was only an island when the tide was in. For a few hours each side of low water, it was attached to the mainland by a tether of sand. One man still lived on Omey Island. There was no safe anchorage, so I closed up the boat and went to the quay on Inishbofin to catch the ferry to Cleggan.

A small crowd was waiting there already. I greeted the party from Galway. They looked a little less cheery than they had in the bar last night. When the boat arrived, the deckhands dropped a walkway to the quay and a new batch of eager-faced visitors stepped ashore. After them came a trolleyful of food. There was a time when hotel food came from the island, but now a chef was here in cook's tunic and latex gloves to unload the trolley into his van: boxes of freeze-chilled French fries, shrink-wrapped steaks, beetroot, spring onions, plastic cartons of milk. When a bag of new potatoes fell and split open, they rolled and bounced across the quay. Two of the crewmen helped gather them up.

'Will you look at these things!'

'*Poreens*, we called them.'

'Cow food!'

'There'd be no price on them at all.'

The chef knew he was being teased. 'I wouldn't know about any of that. I'm from Dublin.'

'So you'd not be used to the real world, then?'

He flicked his arm at the island. Now there was anger in his voice. 'This place, you call this place *real*?'

The ferry pulled out of the harbour. We passed *Tsambika* and Port Island with Cromwell's Barracks, then turned to push out through the channel. With a deep growl, the engines opened up and I went on deck to look north, at what the coast had in store for me in the coming days. The usual: hostile water, surf-swept rocks, hidden breakers and cliff-edged islands. I made out Inishturk, and Clare Island and the mountains of Achill and Mayo beyond – all wonderful to behold, alarming to navigate.

I found Tommy Burke on board, out on the after-deck, and we stood together at the rail. He was going to the mainland to visit his mother. She had Alzheimer's. He liked to get out to see her once or twice a month, in her care home. 'Actually, I'm not that sure she really knows who I am.' In his huge hands he held a small bag of cakes.

I asked him about the Cleggan Disaster of 1927. I knew his family had been affected; everyone had been affected. He gestured out to sea. 'There were a lot of boats out that afternoon – just up there, on Inishlyon. It's a good place for herring. They noticed something different that evening. The wind was from the north-west but with it was a sort of drizzle. It was strange.' Tommy had a particular intonation. His whole delivery was quiet and gentle, but there'd be a moment when the tone would rise, like a key-change in a song, and it was so marked that it instantly conveyed whatever he meant it to – irony, paradox, or, in this case, peril.

'The storm came very quickly. On one of the boats, they just tucked under a tarpaulin until it went through. But it wasn't just a squall. It went on, and on. Those men were lost, and the boat washed up on the mainland. Another boat was close enough in and they quickly threw down a grapnel and it held. A boat near them did the same, but their anchor didn't bite at first. Then it did bite – and they swung round on it, and banged into the first boat. The force of the wind was so great that that boat was stoved in by the bows of the first boat – and it sank. There were two brothers – one on each of those boats and the one who could swim was in the water and the other couldn't save him. Another boat managed to run before the gale and get to Cleggan.

'My grandfather was on one of the other boats. It was swept out to sea, down towards High Island. He put out his nets as a sea anchor, put them out from the bows, and those nets held the boat into the wind and stopped it being swamped. All that night he stood there in the bows holding the nets, about nine hours. Sometimes he was pulling them in a bit, sometimes paying them out. The others were in the stern, baling, and they had their backs to the wind. When the wind died, they cut the nets and rowed round to Cleggan. My grandfather was blind for a while from the spray, and his hands were cut to pieces. But they all survived.'

Tommy said that the effect of the disaster was to 'take the spirit out of the fishermen'. People didn't want to go to sea. The boats stayed ashore, pulled up on the grass, their seams filling with weeds.

'There's a line in a poem by Richard Murphy about the crew of a boat away "in London drilling a motorway". And that's more than thirty years after the disaster.'

'What about you?' I asked. 'Do you ever go to sea?'

'I go out potting sometimes. But I'm not really a sea-person. I have sheep and cattle. I graze them on Bofin and some of the off islands. There was a short time that I worked on the ferry.'

'This route?'

He nodded. 'For about eight years.'

'More than a short time.'

'Well, it was, I suppose. I did about eleven thousand trips in all.'

On Bofin, where the shadow of 1927 still hangs over the island and its families, no one wants to claim to be a 'sea-person'.

From the quay at Cleggan, I walked west. The hedges were filled with flowers and the sky was filled with larksong. It was pleasant walking. I carried on over the back of the peninsula towards Omey. With the tide out, 500 yards of pale beach stretched across from the mainland to a rocky shore and the low hill of the island.

The sand was still wet. My boots splashed through shallow pools. I could feel the hard sand-ridges and see their mackerel-back patterning. Up on the island were a few closed-up holiday houses, and I followed the gentle up-and-down of the road until it reached the far south-west corner. There the road stopped. A cove lay to one side with a rim of machair. On the wind-stunted grass above, looking like something washed ashore in a storm, stood a mobile home. One large window was boarded up with a sheet of ply. It looked abandoned.

A collie appeared – doing that doggy thing of barking in alarm and fish-tailing in greeting. I bent to nuzzle its ear, then climbed the breeze-block step and knocked on the door.

Nothing.

I knocked again. The dog was sniffing at my leg. A faint creaking from inside.

'Come in . . .'

The boards of the threshold were spongy. In the main room was a camping table covered with ashtrays and old newspapers and a half bottle of Paddy Irish Whisky. On the banquette seat behind it sat Pascal Whelan.

'Sidown,' he croaked, and marked my arrival by inserting a fresh cigarette between his lips.

He was wearing baggy fawn trousers and an old white shirt, and braces whose red straps looped up over his shoulders. Silvery stubble grew from the grykes of his face, and his skin was pale. I lowered myself into a picnic chair and waited while he saw to the lighting of his cigarette. The sun fell through the side window. I could see rocks and reefs and in the distance the cliffs of High Island.

'Quite a place you have here.'

His face was hidden by smoke. 'Bloody beautiful.'

'The winters must be difficult.'

'Winters? Winters are bloody beautiful too.'

We talked for a while about storms: February gales with the 'sea gone crazy' and the wind 'hitting the caravan like a train'. He then paid close attention to the stubbing out of his cigarette and, very slowly, settled his head back down on his arms, and closed his eyes.

I looked around his room. Behind him, on a wire hanger, was a suit. On the other wall was taped a picture of a corncrake. Beneath that was a sheet with a woman's face on it. I stood to read what it said: HILARY – *Fortunes – Dreams – Tarot – Psychic Therapy.*

'She's good, she is.' Pascal had another cigarette in his mouth, his one good eye animated, as if nothing had happened. 'Put it this way – most of her business is repeat.' He chuckled, and the chuckle made a swift transition to a cough.

'My sister has it too – she has the sight. Me, I can do it only with the fish. I always know where there's lobsters. I watch others pulling up strings of eight or more pots, all empty. But I know where they are – just one pot, and I get them every time.'

'You have a boat?'

He scoffed. '*Had* a boat. Three boats. Lost them all in the gales couple of years back. One after another, taken away by those bloody hurricanes. Found my *currach* three fields in from the beach. The RIB all smashed to pieces. I'm building up me gear again, building it up slowly.'

Pascal had been born and brought up on Omey Island. In the early 1960s, just twenty years old, he left for Australia with his first wife and a tenner to his name. In Melbourne, he went into plastering. Someone taught him to wrestle and he began to do shows in boxing tents. He learnt how to take a punch, how to fall, discovered the rewards of entertaining small crowds, and signed up for drama school. He became a stuntman, expert in fist fights and sword fights, jumping off buildings and driving through fires. He worked on a James Bond movie, on *Butch Cassidy and the Sundance Kid*, and doubled for Paul Hogan. He then set up a live stunt team and toured with it.

'Used to lie on a bed of nails while they smashed concrete blocks on my stomach.' He once jumped from sixty-five feet in a gale. He was going to aim for the concrete, hoping the wind would blow him on to the mat. 'But I changed me mind.' The wind dropped, and he hit the mat.

Back in Ireland, he carried on with the stunt work, and set up a school for stunt workers. At one show in Waterford, an eighty-foot jump went wrong. One of his team fell badly. The man died in Pascal's arms. 'From that moment my heart was no longer in the business . . . and my career was over.'

With a couple of marriages behind him, he was alone. He lived in Dublin for a while, but there was nothing to keep him there. 'I'd never forgotten the island. Even when I was in Australia and everywhere, Omey was where I thought of.'

Drawn by a homing instinct, the pull of native places, he came back out west. All his family had left the island. Everyone had left the island. His childhood house was a ruin. But the idea of what it once was proved enough. He placed the caravan just fifty yards from the crumbling walls of his childhood home.

'Wouldn't want to be anywhere else in the whole world. But I miss how it was – all the old families and us kids running all over the island. Always up to something we were, usually trouble.'

He looked out of the window. A group of gulls was flying hard against the freshening breeze; High Island was under a shower. Pascal looked at me with an empty expression, then lowered his head again to the table. His cheek was squashed against the paper, stubble against newsprint, his eyelids grey. I sat listening to his rasping breaths. Between each was a pause which lent a certain tension to waiting for them. In those pained inhalations was the frail existence of all these islands. People have abandoned the periphery, sucked away by the centripetal forces of our age. Alone on the island, Pascal was already like a ghost.

Quietly I stood and left.

Outside I turned to face the weather. Above the horizon, low clouds were pressed together in thick grey folds, the sign of an approaching gale.

I heard the dog bark; a car was coming down the road. The caravan door swung open and Pascal stumbled out, pulling on his coat. 'It's him! He's here again. Me old stunt partner. Turned up yesterday, from Australia. Tracked me down after all those years! He's taking me to the pub.'

I made my way across the beach, up the dunes opposite, which rose to whitish sand-cliffs and a plateau of marram grass. On top, I looked back. The two men were standing by the car. Each had the same wide-legged stance, the same pugilist's build. They might have been twins.

I was back on *Tsambika* when the gale came through. It gathered pace overnight and reached its height early the following afternoon. I went out and stood on the foredeck. The mooring buoy was kicking back and forth. I'd put on an extra line, with a big shackle and a cable tie threaded through the pin to stop it working loose. It was this line now that was taking the buck and tug of the boat as the wind caught first one side of the bows, then the other.

A squall and the sky darkened. The wind brought a low mist, scooped up from the water by the rain and its downdraught. When it struck, the hull quivered with a movement I couldn't quite explain. After the squall, a blue line opened on the horizon, broadening swiftly. Soon all was sunlight, as if the curtains had been thrown open. But it wasn't long before the next squall was sweeping across the water. At four the darker clouds crossed the sky for the last time. I had cabin fever; I laced up my walking boots and went ashore.

Beyond the last of the houses was a soft grass track which cut into the side of the island. Across the sound lay Inishark and its lonely cluster of ruined buildings and roofless gables. There was a headstone just below the track:

In Memory of
Our Brothers
MARTIN LACEY aged 28
MICHAEL LACEY aged 22
and Cousin
PETER LACEY aged 38

It was Easter Sunday 1949 and the three men had been in church. They'd come by *currach* from Inishark, but the boat was swamped on the way home, and they were drowned. Eleven years later, the last six families left Inishark for Bofin. An eye-witness account of the evacuation survives, from a man who said it looked 'like a garrison surrendering after a lifetime's siege. The Atlantic beat them. It hammered them into submission.' One by one, he watched the islanders carry their effects along the pier to the waiting fishing boats: 'A huge, home-made wardrobe lashed to the shoulders of fifty-three-years-old Michael Cloonan. A dark brown cat in an old blackened cooking pot, with the lid half tied down . . . Eleven-months-old baby Anne Lacey in the arms of her mother . . . Anne Murray's geraniums, hens in baskets, geese in sacks, straw brooms and string-tied suitcases, iron bed-steads and baths . . . Thirteen cows, twelve dogs, ten donkeys, eight more cats, scores of hens, a hundred sheep, a stack of hay – and a tear in the eye of Thomas Lacey, the elder.'

Thomas was the father of the two men who had drowned.

I carried on, out to the far west. This side of the island was deserted – no houses, no fields, no trees, not much alive even to cover the bare rock. It felt like the otherworld, or that version of it that was the realm of the dead. I passed Royal Oak Cove, where a British troop ship was wrecked in 1779. Fifty-six men died. Squinting into the distance, I could see another crumble of rocks offshore, and another plaque and commemorative inscription: two students from Kansas who, in February 1976, 'lost their young lives by drowning here'.

I reached a place where the water had cut a narrow channel into the land. Cliffs rose on each side. A rock arch stood at the seaward end and I watched a young cormorant poised on the cliff-ledge. It was trying to fly. Its guano paled the lip of the narrow ledge. For a long time it crouched there, looking at the space below. When it did launch, its wings did little to break its flapping plunge into the water. It then bobbed about, reluctant to try again, while the faint traces of swell rose and fell beneath it.

On the way back to the boat, I dropped in on Day's Bar and fell into conversation with a retired marine scientist. He lived just inland, in a cabin clad in tiles made from recycled plastic bottles. Years earlier, he'd left the fisheries ministry in Dublin because of all the 'backbiting, bureaucracy, squabbling and ignorance'.

'I went to teach in the university and found it just the same. So I came out here to Bofin.'

He took another swig of his beer. Across the harbour, we watched a line of seven white geese walking a path through the rocks.

'Ravens,' he said.

'They're geese.'

'They're Bofin's ravens in the Tower.' When the geese leave the island, he explained, the belief was that the people too will desert, like the ravens leaving the Tower of London.

'But those birds,' he said, 'they've gone feral. They only ever walk now.'

11

THE DEPTH SOUNDER WAS FALLING: 2.2 *metres* . . . 2.1 . . . 2.0.

I'd checked the tides, the channels, the breakers, the course, the approach to the small island of Inishturk. Now I was heading out of Inishbofin harbour, and the water was disappearing. I'd checked everything but not right here. *Idiot*. I must have cut the corner. Now it was impossible to tell which direction to go to avoid the shallows. Over the side, I could see sand and darker patches of rock. At about 0.7 metres the keel would hit the bottom, and the tide was falling . . . 1.8 . . . 1.7 . . . 1.7 . . . Like a day trader, I willed the numbers to tick upwards. But they went on going down: 1.6 . . . 1.5 . . . 1.3 . . . 1.0 . . . They steadied at 0.9, dipped to 0.8 . . . 0.8 . . . and began to climb.

You're pushing your luck, I found myself saying.

Soon I was in the channel, heading out past Cromwell's Barracks, lining up the pepper-pot towers astern, leaving the protection of Inishbofin for the open sea, with fifteen, twenty metres of water below me. Clearing the end of Bofin, the swells started to mount. They were huge, each one a fluid ridge above scarp and slope and valley. Down inside them, the light dimmed a little and I looked up and could see only water and sky. They were running sideways to my course and, to avoid rolling, I waited for just the right moment to push down the helm and align the transom with the wave's force. I felt the surge as the hull pushed up beneath my feet. On top was a fleeting view of the wider seascape and the islands and the shape of the waves to come. The gale that formed them had long since died away. They were large but harmless, prize fighters in retirement, losing tone. *Tsambika* revelled in their bulk and dip, and I revelled in her motion. In the end it was a pity that Inishturk was not further away.

The harbour was no more than a short quay and a few moorings outside, sheltered from the westerly swells. I secured the boat and headed ashore. The lifeboat was in. Above the harbour was the chapel and a small crowd standing outside. I could see several of the lifeboatmen among them, in their thick yellow and blue oilskins, heavy with kit. It was the island's annual Blessing of the Boats, and the priest had come across in the lifeboat from Achill, an hour or so to the north.

Fifty-eight people live on Inishturk, and it looked like every one of them was there that afternoon, crammed into the chapel, spilling out onto the grass. Their entire existence depends on the sea – the weather it throws at them, the ferries it prevents or allows, the fish it provides or withholds, the boats it floats or destroys. Between them, the combined offices of Church and lifeboat had it all more or less covered – comprehensive insurance against the risks of island existence.

With Mass over, everyone followed the priest down to the quay. He stood high on the ferry's bridge-deck, white surplice and emerald-green stole inflated by the wind. He held a microphone and its lead ran back to a portable speaker which his acolyte clutched to his chest. The priest's lips were moving, but his words came from below.

'Bless this boat, and all its equipment. Bless all these boats and protect those who use them from the winds and the rain and help us, O Lord, to accept your shelter. Frail is our vessel, and the ocean is wide; but as in your mercy you have set our course, so steer the vessel of our life towards the everlasting shore of peace . . .'

It used to be said that Ireland's biggest export was clergy, but the pull of the priesthood was not what it was. The country now relied on imports. 'Father Krzysztof,' whispered the woman next to me. 'Polish.' His acolyte, she said, was from France.

Father Krzysztof took a plastic bottle of pre-blessed water and shook it over the decks of the ferry and the trawler alongside it. He shook the plastic bottle further, and the droplets glittered as they rained out over the smaller fishing boats beyond – their rigging hung with signal flags for the occasion – out to the black-tar *currachs* and a single kayak, which belonged to the husband of the island's nurse. Like a lone dissenter, *Tsambika* bobbed out of reach in the harbour.

In the community hall afterwards was a meal and speeches. Over the winter, the islanders had organized bring-and-buy sales and a 'Christmas Jumper Quiz'. Their efforts had raised 1,000 euros. The lifeboat branch secretary looked genuinely moved. 'From this small-est of islands, to have raised so much. I . . . I – there's nowhere on the coast quite like Inishturk.'

I'd been given the name of Paddy Colman O'Toole, and that evening I followed a green-centred track out west to see him. In the verges was sedge-grass and its blades flashed in the late sun. Paddy had a bungalow tucked in beneath a limestone cliff. He had always lived on the island and was something of a local historian and a folklorist. His family, children and grandchildren were stuffed into a curtained room to watch Ireland playing football on TV. We sat next door in the breakfast room, laid out for B & B guests. But there were no guests that day. I began by asking him about the island's name – and the pig.

'That's right, *Inis Toirc* – "Island of the Pig". But he's not an ordi-nary pig, the *torc*. He's a wild pig.'

Paddy had a natural enthusiasm, a storyteller's relish for chasing the tale, for leading his listeners away from the scent with elaborate deviations, while he himself always knew where the quarry was – in this case, the pig.

'Let me show you something.' We spread out a map. 'Here, there's the lake – a reservoir, for the island's water. When they were building it, they thought – better have a little look before it all disappears underwater. So they sent for some top people from Dublin, and they came and drilled down through the mud, and they struck gold.'

'Gold?'

'A lime tree.'

'Right.'

He smiled. 'If there were lime trees, there was forest, and if there was forest, there'd be pigs. It was all wooded, said those Dublin men. The whole island, probably. This would be about seven thousand years ago, seven and a half, perhaps.

'Tell me,' he asked, 'where you come from, do you know of the people called Tuatha Dé Danann?'

I said I'd read about them in the *Lebor Gabála Érenn*, the *Book of Invasions of Ireland*. They came to Ireland after roaming the lands of the north, acquiring the dark arts. They then defeated the Fir Bolg, the dominant race of Ireland at the time, and began their rule.

'It was those fellows – they used the pigs. They would send them into battle as a weapon, like we'd fire a missile or something. The Tuatha Dé Danann could do a load of things that we can't. I know some people say that they came from another planet. But, well – no one can be certain about that.'

The Tuatha Dé Danann occupied Ireland for a long time. Then came the Sons of Mil, last of the invasions of antiquity and forebears of the current population. The Tuatha Dé Danann were defeated by them. They were forced to live underground as *sídhe*, fairies or little people, in a world parallel to ours. The two realms come closest in certain hills and *sidhe* dwelling places, known also as *raths*.

'Then came the Christians – Columba's people – and they found the island full of spirits, so exorcism was the job of the day. They rounded up the *sidhe* and put them in the pigs, and all the pigs ran over the cliffs. The pig is a strange animal – very, very strange – one of the few that the spirit of man can enter. But he's intelligent – and normally he wouldn't go near the cliff – but all those pigs just ran out there and over the high cliffs.'

Despite the efforts of Columba and his ilk, some of the *sidhe* remained on the island, here and all over Ireland. 'They're the strangest clan that ever came to this country. You cross them at your peril. I've seen in my own time a man who didn't bother with them. Said they'd all gone. He was a builder, had a lovely piece of land, raised up. He said, that's where I'll build my house. People said to him, you can't build there, it's a *rath*. But he went ahead. And he lost his three sons – two had accidents, and the third drowned.'

Into that room, with its floral curtains and plastic cutlery trays, its electric toaster and the muffled sound from the flat-screen next door, blew an alien breeze. It was almost imperceptible, but as Paddy spoke of these things – not entirely believing, not entirely sceptical – I felt it brush past me, disturbing a hundred certainties.

'Just up from here –' he picked up a cork mat, and held it on its edge – 'there's a place of rock faces, like this. That's where the *sidhe* live, in little holes.'

I followed the track up from Paddy's house and into the island's hills. Where it was exposed in outcrops, the limestone glowed pale as bone in the dusk. Shortly before the lake, I cut in from the track and started to climb. The turf was broken by areas of flat stone; moisture oozed up out of the grass. Tracing the contour of the hill, I came out facing west. Below me was a large basin of open ground, scarred in places by bedrock and scree. A ridge rose on the other side, lower than where I stood, and beyond that – dim and pale in the almost-night – was the sea.

Paddy had said that up here was the *Teampall na Muice* – the 'temple of the pig'. It sounded faintly comic, but he billed it as a no-go area, a place people had always avoided. I scanned the place now with the boat's binoculars, not quite sure what I was looking for. A mound, a circle, a cluster of rocks? The whole site suggested a certain shape, a natural amphitheatre. There was a half-ring of raised ground on one side, with areas of rock face, and beneath that a gully, boggy and curling round through ninety degrees. On the inside of the curl rose a natural platform. At one end was a small assemblage of rocks. I looked at it for some time, trying to make sense of it. The rocks were definitely propped up, arranged. Once seen, they became the focal heart of the entire area. A Temple of the Pig – pig slaughter, pig worship, pig feasting? Maybe all three.

Paddy's pig-history of the island had been full of colour and images, but he hadn't actually answered my original question – Why the *torc*, the 'boar', in the name of Inishturk?

In the Iron Age, the pig was central to domestic life in northern Europe. Cattle were milk and traction, but the pig was meat. Hams and pig half-carcasses are common grave goods from the period, deposited with knives to enable the dead to feast on them. Pork was the preferred meat of the otherworld, and in the *Echtrae Cormaic*, Cormac visits an otherworld fort where a pig will only cook if truth is being said. Recent provenancing analysis of material from ritual gathering sites around Stonehenge has revealed an astonishing range of porcine origin. The pig is not an easy beast to herd and archaeologists have used the evidence to emphasize the high value attached to transporting it to such sacred sites.

Salted and cured and smoked, pig-flesh was a valuable export. The pig was also associated with plenty, and on Mull a bird named *Torc Sona*, or 'happy hog', helped ensure a ceaseless supply of grain. In general, though, pigs were not popular in Scotland. The devil was the *muc mhor dhubh*, the 'big black pig'. A taboo on eating pork long baffled observers. 'But the Scots never eat pork,' asserts a character in Walter Scott's *The Fortunes of Nigel*. 'Some folk think they are a sort of Jews.' Scottish fishermen would not utter the word 'pig', but spoke instead of the 'cauld-iron beastie'.

The name of the Celtic god Moccus is said to be linked both to the Roman god Mercury and the Irish *muc* ('domestic pig'). Ireland was itself known as *Inishmuice*, 'island of the pig'. The pig had the power of divination. When a pig was slaughtered at a feast, each part was awarded to the diners in a strictly hierarchical way.

Among the best of early Irish stories is *The Tale of Macc Da Thó's Pig*, the account of such a feast. The great warriors of Ulster and Connacht gather together at the hall of Macc Da Thó. Into the hall is brought the cooked body of a mighty pig. For seven years, the pig has been fattened on the milk of sixty cows. Forty oxen could be laid across its flank. Its snout is covered in seven inches of fat. But the men of Ulster and Connacht have been at war for three hundred years or more, and they cannot agree who should carve the pig and who should have the *curadmir*, the 'champion's portion'. A round of boasting follows. One by one the men recount their deeds, each more wonderful, more heroic than the last. Seasoned with surrealism (some believe the story is an early satire of such tales), the episode is held to represent something of ancient Ireland as a whole. The feast ends in a bloodbath: 'everyone hit someone . . . streams of gore reached the entrances. The hosts broke through the doors then, and a good drinking bout broke out in the courtyard, with everyone striking his neighbour. Fergus pulled up an oak by its roots.'

If the domestic pig – *an muc* – was all about food and fertility, its tusked cousin in the forest – *an torc* – represented brute savagery. In Denmark, on the side of the Gundestrup cauldron from the first century BC, a long-snouted boar squats on top of the warriors' helmets. The same belligerent stance can be seen in countless Iron Age figurines and statues of boar, found from Transylvania to Spain. Strabo noted that packs of wild boar made even wolves wary. Killing a boar was a rite of passage. Boar hunts were noted for their danger; often it was the hunters and not the boars who were killed. When faced with the ferocious nine-tusked 'Sow of Healing', one old Fenian hero announced: 'I shall deal with the sow and it is the same to me whether I live or die.'

What links Inishturk with *an torc*, the boar? Was it the shape, seen from the land? Was the beast introduced to its woods and the island set aside for ritual hunting? Were these the creatures, with all their associations of pre-Christian belief, that were killed with the coming of Columba? There's little now to work with, just disparate clues from place names, shreds of story, folk memory and excavations.

What is striking, though, is how many islands along this coast bear the names of animals. I'd come from Inishbofin, 'island of the white cow' – to Inishturk, 'island of the wild boar'. There is another Inishturk near Clifden harbour, and another Inishbofin off the Donegal coast. Down in Kerry, I'd sailed through an archipelago, the Magharee Islands, known in English as 'The Seven Hogs'; one of the islets was Mucklaghbeg, which means 'little place where pigs feed'. In Scotland, there is the island of Muck, and the name Orkney is said to come originally from the Old Irish 'arc', 'piglet'.

Like most place names, they probably have a fairly prosaic origin, each island labelled for its use, be it summer grazing or hunting. But on these western coasts, nothing is ever just itself. Mixed with the innate mystique of islands, the names themselves became suggestive, stirring memories of ancient heroics and mythical hunts. Temples and exorcism entered the frame here on Inishturk, mythical white cows and enchantment on Inishbofin. More than anywhere on the mainland, these places came to stand for the borderless spaces of the imagination. The shapes on the horizon became emblems, where the familiar moves towards the sacred, the literal towards the poetic, and the *sidhe* live side by side with the wild animals and giants of old.

There was to be a beacon-lighting – up at the island's highest point, the Napoleonic watchtower, at midnight.

I made my way up the hill. It wasn't quite dark; these nights were never fully dark. I came round a low bluff and could see, against pale drifting clouds, the stub of a ruined building. A dozen people were already there. I'd been on the island only about twelve hours, but I found I already knew most of them. Paddy had come with a group of his extended family, and there was Séan and Marie, whom I'd met at the chapel, and Maggie the nurse and her husband Stephen. A small pyre of ply sheets and beams stood beside the broken tower. Séan slopped some fuel on it, and we all watched as he took a box of matches from his boiler-suit pocket.

He threw on a match. Nothing.

He struck another, and it blew out. 'Right now, we're all in one of them health 'n safety videos. It all ends badly!'

He twisted a sheet of paper and lit that and threw it and – *whoosh*! Black smoke burst into the night sky, trailing away in the wind. The first flames were fickle and soon passed – but by then the wood had caught and a more solid fire began to build. Everyone stood around in their coats and hoodies and baseball caps.

'That's a decent fire.'

'Any sign on Clare?'

To the north, the shape of Clare Island rose some eight miles across the water. There were a few pinpoint lights, but they were electric.

'Beat 'em to it!'

The crackle of burning wood and all of us standing in its glow – the warmth on our faces as we gazed at the flames.

'Imagine the first guy who made a spark,' said someone.

'Must have been a hell of a surprise,' chipped in another.

'*B'Jesus, what's that?* his missus would go, and he'd be telling her, *I have no fuckin' idea, but it seems to be spreading.* And she'd say, *Well, you just keep it going, because it's keeping me warm!*'

When we looked north again, there was a flickering dot on Clare Island, and another beyond, on Achill – faint yellow blooms in the vastness of the night.

Was this an annual tradition? I asked. I was thinking signals, pig sacrifices.

'God, no! Someone on Clare said they'd be lighting a beacon and who else was up for it. Posted it on Facebook.'

It was well after one by the time we walked down the mountain. We were in high spirits. We passed the lake and continued down the harbour road. In twos and threes the people peeled off home. 'Good night! Good night!' – until I was walking alone to the quay, down the slip, wheeling the Zodiac stern-first into the water and motoring out to *Tsambika*. A warm breeze came flowing off the mainland. I sat out on deck for a while, leaning back against the mast, content in the moonlit arena of sea and shore.

A couple of hours later, I was awake. The pitch of the wind had changed. I left my berth and went up. The Mayo mountains were silhouettes against the coming dawn. The wind had strengthened, markedly. Steep waves were driving in on a fierce south-easterly. It was the one direction the harbour was exposed to. The bows were already involved in some exuberant see-sawing.

The warps were OK. I went back to bed.

When I woke again, an hour later, the wind had risen further. The boat's motion was wilder. I needed to grip the stanchions to reach the foredeck. The bows were dipping; with each sea now, the mooring buoy was going under. I watched the wild thrashing for a while, but there was nothing I could do. I went back below. This time I couldn't sleep but lay in the saloon, propped against the bulk-head. Through the companionway, the shore was just seventy yards off and it swung up and down, a violent vertical scanning – *water – rock – slope – sky . . . sky – slope – rock – water . . .* I was thinking, if anything broke, I'd have a couple of minutes only – then the rocks.

At seven o'clock, the wind was a gale, whining in the stays, the boat bucking like a steer. I went out again and stood on the foredeck. Every time the bow rose, the line yanked tight, throwing up a comb of spray. Eight tons of boat versus an inch or two of plaited mooring rope. Should I head off to Clare, or to Westport? I thought of my options; none looked better than sitting it out.

By nine, it was easing. There was still violence in the boat's pitch, but the wind was dropping. Later I went ashore and walked off my fatigue with a long circuit of the island. When I reached the harbour again, it was mid-afternoon. An elderly man named Pete nodded out towards *Tsambika*.

'That boat of yours,' he asked, 'timber, is she?'

He suggested bringing her in to the quay. He said it would be fine to lie alongside the ferry for a better night. We went back out in the

Zodiac. He didn't say very much but I could see him taking in every inch of the boat.

I nudged *Tsambika* in beside the ferry, against its tractor-tyre fenders. Pete was in no hurry to go. We sat in the cockpit.

'I used to have a wooden fishing boat.' His voice was quiet. Like all of the older generation, he appeared to carry a general sense of loss, the burden of all that these islands once were, or what they were imagined to be. 'I had to sell her.' He looked away, out over the water, with a mariner's stare – one that took in every minute change. 'There's more weather coming in again tomorrow.'

I told him I was planning to leave early for Clare Island. 'To try and get there before it.'

'They have a good harbour over there, a good harbour.'

He said it with weight, but no bitterness. It sounded like an inheritance that had somehow passed him by.

12

IN THE EMPTY INTERIOR OF St Brigid's Abbey on Clare Island, the walls dark with damp, the gale rising and falling in the eaves, was a pig. His tongue stuck out between two rows of teeth. Along the ridge of his back, hairs ran like a saw blade. He was carved in bas relief in the chancel, on a slab of dark limestone, and at each of the three corners above him and below were drawn-back bows ready with arrows. In the fourth was a ship. The buccaneering habits of the local O'Malley clan are well told in this, their armorial shield – arrows charged for vigilance and defence; ship for transport, commerce and battle; and, at the centre of it all, toothily grinning, shaped like a barrel, squat as a rock – *an torc*, the boar. Mess with us, it is saying, and it's him you'll face.

The O'Malley family still runs the ferries to Inishturk and Clare, but their dominance of the coast was once much more extensive. Though they trace their descent to the fourth-century high king of Connacht, their power never relied on high office. *Terra marique potens* is the family motto – 'powerful on land and sea'. Like the *sídhe*, they earned a certain respect from the possibility of sudden appearance, from the ease with which they passed from one element to the other, from land to sea. Their heartland is Clare Island here to the west, Achill to the north, the sacred mountain of Croagh Patrick to the south, and to the east the broad basin of Clew Bay. Masters of the clinker-built galleys, the O'Malleys were as familiar with the west coasts of Britain and France as with those of Ireland. They would think little of sailing to Spain. In the summer, to help with the task of persuasion, they would bring in ships full of gallowglass, well-armed mercenaries from Scotland.

In the late sixteenth century, this stretch of coast was the domain of Grace O'Malley, or Granuaile. Plunderer and protector, gambler and libertine, rebel and politician, she had the island of Clare as her base, but the sea as her home. Her eldest son, Owen, was born on board the ship she commanded; the very next day she fought off a bunch of Barbary pirates. The English governor of Connacht, Richard Bingham, identified her as 'the nurse to all the rebellions in the province'. He captured her and erected the gallows for her hanging, but at the last minute her son-in-law, who went by the name of the Devil's Hook, gained her a reprieve. Once free, they both rebelled. Bingham's soldiers murdered another of her sons on Omey Island.

By the time she reached her early sixties, Grace O'Malley's power was on the wane. Bingham's ships managed to hem her in, but then she outflanked him by sailing to England, to talk to his commander-in-chief, Elizabeth I.

A lot of froth has bubbled up out of this meeting – England's pirate queen meets Ireland's pirate queen. Documentation is scarce. But in the State Papers of Elizabeth I is enough evidence to confirm that it happened, and why. Grace O'Malley certainly sailed up the Thames, and she was recorded as being at court. In her written petition, she explained that she'd been reduced to 'utter decay and ruine' by Bingham. She duly implored the Queen: 'In tender consideracon wherof and in regard of her great age she most humbly besechethe your Majestie of your princely bounty and liberaltye to grant herr some reasonable maintenance for the little tyme she hath to lyve.'

Elizabeth granted her what she asked for, and Bingham was removed from the west. Nothing is known of Granuaile's final years, nor of her death. The stone tomb here in Clare's Cistercian abbey, with its tracery arch, is said to be her grave. But her spirit remains on this coast, her story told and retold, embellished and adapted, a presence as elusive and mythic as the islands themselves.

I dropped the abbey key back at the shop and sat outside to eat a roll. The gale hummed in the overhead cables. Low clouds hurried in from the west. I watched a hooded crow rise from the wall opposite and shoot away downwind, splayed out like a skydiver. I'd left *Tsambika* in Clare harbour, just below the ruin of Granuaile's tower, another cable tie pulled tight through the mooring line's shackle pin, another gale to sit out.

Someone had told me about a gannetry at the far end of the island. A track followed the line of the southern shore, the fertile shore. As I walked, the clouds broke and in a sudden moment of clarity, the sun picked out the old spade-ridges, green mounds that ran in corrugations down the slope. The island is haunted by emigrants. At the time of the Great Famine, Clare had ten times the population it does now.

I dropped in on a bungalow to check the way. Set a little above the road, the garden was filled with the frame of an old polytunnel. The shreds of its plastic skin clapped in the gale. An elderly man came to the front door.

'When you see the watchtower, follow the line of the cliffs. 'Tis a bit steep, mind.' He looked down at my feet, to check they'd be up to it. 'I'll tell you a funny thing about that place. Years ago, a man came into the pub. He said there were two white birds on that rock, nesting, like. And for a good few years after that there were a couple of pairs there. Then suddenly – summer or two past, there's been loads.'

We stood outside his door, looking past the polytunnel to the place offshore where the surf was breaking high around the rock of Mweelaun.

'Not a day to be out there,' I said.

He told me he used to have a *currach*. 'For the potting. Broke to pieces in a storm. I left it up on the grass and the water came up and smashed it. Wind broke the polytunnel too. Used to give lovely tomatoes. They were never that big – but there was a sweetness on them. Round little things like that.' He raised his hand, pressing his thumb and forefinger together to form an O. He then dropped his hand and let out a sigh at the inevitable passing of all things, particularly when wind and sea were involved.

The houses ended and then the track ended. I spotted the watchtower on the skyline and turned away from it a little, into open ground. I climbed a rocky shoulder of land and there, on the other side, was the sea, gale-shaken and scattered with breaking waves. I would be crossing that stretch of water within a day or two; and there too was the fear, a little diminished, but still firmly by my side.

The slope was as steep as a grassy slope can be without becoming a cliff. I couldn't see the rock beneath it, but knew it was there, just out of sight, because of the strip of white spume on the water and the gannets milling out from it, like wasps around a nest.

I side-stepped down towards it. I could hear the high chatter coming and going on the wind.

When the rock appeared, it looked less like a rock than a crown of white jewels. All around it was the glide of black-tipped wings, criss-crossing each other. There were fulmar too, whose burrows would be in the cliff just below me. Through binoculars, I looked down past the toe of my boots at their short-necked shape, so distinct from the weaponized gannets.

Then – *fhweeesh*! I didn't see it coming. A black-backed gull, dive-bombing, inches from my head. I turned and lost my balance, and had to twist, sharply, to make sure I fell in against the slope. After that, I sat down.

Clare's gannetry is the most northerly in Ireland. It's also the newest. It certainly didn't exist in the spring of 1909 when a tide of more than a hundred naturalists began to sweep over the island. For the next three years, they examined everything – the bird life, the botany, the butterflies and fungi, the liverworts and moulds, the reptiles and aphids and water bears, the coelenterates and echinoderms, the marine molluscs, the geology and antiquities. They made Clare, for a time, the most studied island in the world.

The project was led and organized by Robert Lloyd Praeger, who, though an amateur, is now regarded as the greatest of Ireland's field botanists. His day job was librarian at the National Library in Dublin, but his spare time was all wind and sun, bog and hill. Weekends began with a train ride deep into the midlands, or to the Munster mountains, then walking – 'fifty miles or so across country with a halt for the night in the middle, and a late train back to Dublin. That could be done on a toothbrush and a collar.'

He walked tirelessly and attentively. His mind was a precision instrument fine-tuned to putting things in their place – books into subject categories, plants into their taxonomy, people into efficient work. On Clare Island, the legacy of his note-taking, soil-prodding and sample-taking means that curious visitors are still known as 'praegers'.

A few years earlier, he'd conducted an exhaustive study of Lambay Island, off Ireland's east coast; in doing so, he revealed more than eighty species new to Ireland and five new to science.

Islands have always held a magical allure for field scientists.

Crucibles of endemism, where species go off in their own direction, diverging, developing traits of such originality that they can no longer breed with their mainland counterparts. For biologists to step on to the shores of such places is to enter a laboratory Eden, where the processes of speciation are amplified and accelerated. By the beginning of the twentieth century, island studies of places like the Faroes, Christmas Island and Krakatoa had revolutionized the world of natural science. It was the Galapagos that prompted Charles Darwin into his theory of evolution, the archipelago of Indonesia which did the same for Alfred Russel Wallace, while years sailing the southern ocean, observing both the diversity and commonality of island species, led Joseph Hooker to hypothesize about continental drift.

Clare Island held out the promise of such discovery. But it also represented the 'western island' of Irish mythology. Just as 'the western islanders . . . constituted a genealogical link with pre-conquest Ireland', the islands' flora and fauna might reveal something equally elemental.

For Praeger, Clare Island also held a powerful personal memory. 'My first experience of it began weirdly,' he wrote. He and his wife made the crossing in a mist that formed an arch over the island – 'solid enough seemingly to walk on'. The next day, they walked out to the cliffs and saw 'a blood-red sun, lighting dense inky clouds which brooded low over the black jagged teeth of Achill Head, rising from a black sea tinged with crimson. It was a scene fitted for Dante's *Inferno*, and if a flight of demons or of angels had passed across in that strange atmosphere, it would have seemed quite appropriate.'

Three years of study, more than seventy scientists, sixty-seven reports, countless data sets – the Clare Island Survey was organized by Praeger on an astonishing scale. No piece of comparable territory had ever been examined in such detail. Of the total flora and fauna identified – 8,500 species – nearly 2,000 had never been found in Ireland and 120 had never been found at all. The marine biologists defined eleven new genera of polycheate and oligochaete worm, including one, the *Grania maricola*, which they named after Grace O'Malley.

But in truth, Clare Island fell short of Praeger's expectations. It had no truly exotic species. It was too close to the mainland to have developed the menagerie of freaks that so ornamented the studies of more remote islands. Collating the reports occupied his 'leisure time' for six years and was completed in 1915. By that time, a great shadow had fallen over Europe. Many of those scientists who took part in the study were killed in the war. Praeger himself and his German wife only narrowly avoided internment.

Robert Lloyd Praeger's memoir, written in the 1930s, gives little space to the Clare Island Survey. It is filled instead with a nostalgia for the spirit of enquiry which first propelled him through Ireland's provinces, when byways and wood banks were packed with unknowns, and although the primary job was to catalogue the diversity of the natural world, there was plenty of time for contemplation and beauty. 'I recall the more leisurely, deliberate spacious days of Queen Victoria, the courteous quakerish naturalists who taught me truths that lie at the bottom of all true science.'

It was evening by the time I reached the harbour again. I sat at the top of the beach and took off my boots. A low surf folded its queries onto the sand. *Tsambika* lay just offshore, among the island's gale-bound craft, the *currachs* and potters and RIBs.

At the far end of the beach appeared a stock-dog. All the dogs on the island looked like they were descended from the same border collie, and this one was no different. It ran into the shallows and along the beach to the rocks. Then it turned and did the same going the other way, splashing for the sheer pleasure of it. Leaving my clothes on the beach, I took my cue from it, and stepped into the water. I swam out through clear water to *Tsambika*. Her gunwales towered over my head. I could see one or two dings in the paintwork, a small dent in the gunwale from the pontoon in Kilrush, another chip in the white gloss from Fenit. I rubbed the flat of my hand along the cove-line, washing off a faint green film of weed. What seas we'd crossed, what miles of water had already passed along these curves! But how much more we needed to navigate before the Summer Isles. From Kerry, I'd sailed no more than a third of the distance.

Later, in the community centre, there was music. A group of players from County Offaly was visiting the island and the dance floor was packed. Several girls stood in a close circle, step-dancing, their torsos held still, their feet following a frenetic routine below. All was noise and laughter, drink and sweat.

At the bar, a woman told me about her cousin, Patrick O'Toole, a traditional singer. 'Pat's won national competitions.'

'Is he on the island?'

'He is. You'll find him out towards the old lighthouse. Follow the lighthouse road and turn left on to the mountain road. You'll come to a house with a nice garden, lovely flowers and all bright shrubs and things. That's not Pat's. His is the one above.'

It was raining when I walked out next morning towards the lighthouse. I failed to find the nice garden, and knocked on a door at random. 'Can you tell me where Pat O'Toole's house is?'

'I can! That's me.'

I was struck immediately by his gentle manner, by his shy, toothy smile. In the main room, a chair was placed on either side of the stove, as if already set for hearty reminiscing. The peat glowed

146

soft-flamed behind the glass. Above it ran a row of children's swimming things, pegged on a string. The wind grumbled in the chimney.

Pat had spent a lifetime farming and fishing on Clare. From May onwards, he used to go out in his *currach* along the north shore where the cliffs are so steep it's only accessible from the water. He gave up the potting when he lost his *currach* and it meant going out in a 'boat'.

'A *currach* puts you close to the waves. It's not the same in them boats the boys have now.' He looked into the fire for a moment. 'For me it was never just about the fishing. It was just being out there. When it was high water along that northern shore, it was lovely.'

'What about low water?'

'Low water was lovely too.'

Most things were lovely to Pat, particularly when it came to places on the island. He'd never wanted to be anywhere else, and his love for Clare had bred an unrivalled knowledge of its names and stories, its *dinnseanchas*. When a 'fellow came map-making', it was Pat who talked him through every inch of the north coast.

I asked him about his music.

It had all begun one day when he was about twelve. He'd gone to a fair on the mainland, in Louisburgh. 'I was standing watching everything going on, when I heard a song. It made me stop quite still. I followed the sound behind some trailers and found a boy there. He was about my age, a tinker. Was that you singing? I ask. If you want the song, I'll give it you on a pennysheet. And another song too – but it'll cost you a shilling.'

'Grandad?' Paddy's six-year-old granddaughter had been watching us from the kitchen doorway. He waved her away.

'Grandad!'

'What is it?'

'Will you make me a smoothie?'

'Later, later . . . So that was the start of it all. Some songs I picked up over the years, some I swapped – a lot of them came from the islands round here, old ones, like. Composed a few meself. At one time I must have had one hundred and fifty or so.'

He looked down at the fire again. The purr of the flames filled the space between us, and there was the sound from the kitchen of his granddaughter tapping the table with her pen.

He started to sing, *Down Erin's Lovely Lee,* and the transition was so smooth it seemed less like a song than an extension of speech.

> 'On March the sixth in sixty-nine we sailed from
> Queenstown Quay
> With the Fenian boys from Erin's Isle bound for Americay
> While travelling with this happy band as you might plainly
> see
> I was forced to go from sweet Cloughroe down Erin's
> lovely Lee.'

For the exiles, the pain of emigration is redeemed a little when they meet some compatriots and recount the places back in Ireland where the heroes lay buried. The song was plain and unstrained and carried with ease an expanse of yearning that had nothing to do with any one singer or any one shared moment. Each melodic phrase was common inheritance.

The distinctiveness of Irish traditional singing is said to rest in ornamentation, the particular modulations given to each word. There are no dynamics, no change in volume and the sound itself comes from the far back of the mouth, with a faint drone to it. The effect is hypnotic.

'When I go home to sweet Cloughroe the boys will
welcome me
And they'll help to float a Fenian boat down Erin's lovely
Lee.'

When he'd finished he looked at me. His face was blank, as if
he hadn't performed the song but was simply the conduit through
which it had flowed. 'This is mine, this one:

'By the verge of the ocean
by the mouth of Clew Bay
there is a lovely island, covered in mist and spray . . .'

'I was up on the cliff here, one day. I was humming that air and
turning it over as I went and then I just started putting words on it.
It's a very ancient air.'

That use of 'air' was a reminder that all song is breath. But it's not
quite that simple. 'Air', meaning 'melody or tune', comes from the
Italian *aria*, a word which itself can be traced to the Middle French
air, meaning not just a 'mixture of gases' but 'manner, appearance',
and which itself stems from the common Greek root *aer*. It is tempting to amalgamate both senses in a single idea, invisible substance
and physical appearance – the Judeo-Christian God breathing on
clay to make life appear, our constant inhalation to maintain it, and
the capacity of music to conjure feeling from thin air.

Pat had turned to face the fire, thinking some happy thought. A
light smile crossed his face. I asked him what he knew of the waters
to the north of Clare, and about going round Achill Head.

'That's a nasty headland. Never been round it myself. But there's
not much to worry you before you get there. Just the one rock – the
Jane Black breaker.'

'Jane Black?'

'There's not a house on the island that doesn't have something off the *Jane Black*.'

Two years adrift. An unmanned hull at large in the Atlantic – until the westerly winds finally drove the *Jane Black* onto the rock to the north of Clare. It was January 1859. To most who read the reports, the explanation made sense – a storm that first crippled her rig, then forced her crew to abandon her. But there were many who knew better, who blamed her master, Captain Timothy Gorman, and the misfortune he took with him whenever he went to sea. On his first voyage in command of the *Jane Black* in 1842, he reached the Newfoundland coast before the ship was holed. The 417 passengers were left in the icy wilds for several days before being rescued.

But that was not the albatross around Captain Gorman's neck. A few years earlier, he was commanding another ship, also sailing back from Newfoundland. The *Francis Spaight* carried a cargo of timber and eighteen crew. In mid-Atlantic, in heavy seas, the ship broached, the masts were lost and the supplies spoilt. They managed to make the food they had last more than two weeks. But then it ran out. Captain Gorman gave his orders: one of the cabin boys must be killed and eaten. They drew lots and young Patrick O'Brien was selected. The cook refused to kill him. O'Brien tried to do it himself, slashing his own wrists. When that didn't work, Gorman told the cook if he did not kill the boy, they would kill him instead. O'Brien was despatched. By the time the wreck was spotted some days later, others had also been eaten. When Captain Gorman and the survivors were landed, they did nothing to conceal what they'd done. There was no question of prosecution or inquiry. It was accepted that out beyond the land, a different set of conventions applied. It was the 'custom of the sea'.

Gorman soon returned to Limerick and was given the command of the *Jane Black*.

It had stopped raining. Pat and I followed his granddaughter outside to the swing. She jumped on and pushed off – leaning forward, leaning back, gaining height. Pat pointed to the guy-rope which anchored the swing to the bank behind. It was fixed to a large lump of metal – a piece of superstructure from the *Jane Black*. The rope tugged each time the girl swung forward, straining at the piece of old ship. But it didn't budge.

'Look at me, grandad,' she called. 'Look!'

13

IN THE GREY MID-MORNING, I headed out around the end of Clare and straight into a large swell. *Tsambika* began the labour of pushing into it. The wind pressed her rail to the water and I found myself half-standing and half-sitting at the helm, raised up with the lean of the boat. From down below came a rattling and shifting; the rig creaked against its fixings. Everything found its place in this new strained and tilted world. Sailing uphill is one way of describing progress into the wind, and that's how it looked from here: Achill Head, some twenty miles away, at the far end of a steep slope.

It wasn't just Pat O'Toole who baulked at going round Achill Head. No one I'd spoken to on Clare and Inishturk and Bofin, among people who'd spent their life on these waters, had gone beyond it. It was an unspoken northerly limit, a barrier to one of the wildest stretches of coast in all Europe – Blacksod Bay, Belmullet and Donegal Bay. According to weather records, it is the stretch which receives the highest winds and largest seas of any of Ireland's coasts.

With me on board was Lance. He'd arrived on Clare by ferry that morning. He lived in Westport with his wife and sons, but was originally from South Africa. One evening, when I was on Inishbofin, he'd walked into Day's Bar, dripping and exhilarated after sailing from Rosmoney with a couple of others. I liked him at once. He was a professional pilot, but changing his flying licence to European standards was taking a while and, while he waited, he was up for a bit of sailing. He'd once sailed from Brazil to South Africa with a 'madcap' captain who'd made them all sit out a storm down below, with the hatches closed. 'Like being in a washing machine for three days.' With his sons, he was doing up a wooden boat in Westport, very slowly. The idea of *Tsambika* appealed to him; I was glad of his company and the extra hands.

It was a lonely day of it, zigzagging in and out of the black shore-line of Achill Island. The vast seas came mounting towards us. They heaved the boat upwards. They dropped it down. Some crested and bounced spray off the bows, or dropped lumps of water aboard, flash-flooding the side-deck and sluicing down the length of the boat to burst against the coaming. The wind didn't ease at all. The boat was never still. Lance became a little subdued, spending the time leaning over the side, growing somewhat familiar with the lee rail.

In the mid-afternoon, we put in a reef. I dropped the mainsail a metre or so and let it flap. Up at the mast, I tried to gather it in. I clung on, arranged the loose folds of sailcloth, then crawled back to winch the halyard back up. With each turn, the sail tightened – then, *pop-pop*! The fixings on the boom's steel track pinged up. I watched them drop in the water. I lashed the track down with a sail tie.

The headland edged a little closer with each tack. It was dark and jagged, a knife of schist half-wrapped in a broken sheath of cloud. Seas burst white against it, doing nothing to brighten its Stygian aspect. I gave it a few miles berth before freeing sheets and head-ing north. At once the boat's speed increased, the motion became firmer and Lance's spirits brightened.

'Jeez!' He was eating a sandwich now. 'Those seas were *horrible.*'

We passed a couple of miles inside Black Rock, a rogue fragment of land in the open sea. Its lighthouse, when manned, was known to be the one where Irish keepers were most often marooned. Whenever you looked, the rock had changed shape – from sleeping elephant, elongating, then rising to a pyramid. Abeam, it suddenly revealed a white streak of quartzite down its girth, like a ski-slope.

The Inishkea Islands grew more gently from the water ahead – flat and sandy after all the hard verticality of Achill. Coming round into the lee of the islands the seas steepened and surged, pressing the boat on, corralling us into shelter. Then the water was flat and the decks were level and we were in the broken circle of a bay. The sun seeped through thin cloud, covering everything in the same light, a strange lemon-yellow.

The islands have been deserted for more than eighty years. Ashore I could see abandoned houses. Further round, linked by a low-tide shoulder of ground, was Rusheen Island. Before the First World War, the Norwegians had come to the Inishkeas and set up a whaling station on Rusheen. They built a slip and an engine house to winch in dead whales and slice them up. They brought in vast tanks to boil the blubber and soften the bones. The artist Paul Henry, who visited the Inishkeas at the time, recalls the sight of islanders in blood-spattered aprons, with saws and 'murderous' flensing knives. He was warned not to approach the island's pigs, as they had become crazed by the glut of offal.

We dropped anchor, cooked and tidied and ate. We sat drinking beer, dazed from hours of hostile seas. Lance spoke of taking small planes in and out of Mozambique. He rolled up his trouser leg and showed me a wound from the Angolan war, and we discovered we'd been there at about the same time – him with the South African forces and me reporting briefly on UNITA's efforts against the Soviet-backed MPLA.

Last thing that evening, I went up on deck. I let out a little more anchor chain, then stood at the rail. The bay was filled with the same all-over yellow light, dimmer now. The sea and the sky were all one colour, and the beach and the machair was a stripe between them.

Beneath the boat, the water was so clear I could see the chain looping down and lying on the sand.

A few yards from the bows sat a small bird. A red-necked phalarope – a wader, but with little appendages on its feet for swimming. Most of its life is spent far out in the ocean but it comes ashore to breed. I'd just been reading about it in Robert Lloyd Praeger's autobiography. On the mainland near here, he and his wife had stumbled on the phalarope's only breeding location in Ireland. They were astonished by the bird's grace, by its lack of fear. Praeger describes it flying 'like a butterfly' and quotes the great Victorian ornithologist Henry Dresser, who compared its poise on the water to 'an eggshell'. Looking at it now, paddling towards me, it appeared weightless and carefree. I knelt down and leaned through the guard rails. For a long time we gazed at each other, each one of us on the far edge of our habitat, curious citizens of different countries, meeting at the border.

The night of 28 October 1927 marked the death of the community on the Inishkeas, as it did for the village of Rossadillisk near Cleggan. In all, forty-five lives were lost along the coast that night. From the Inishkeas more than twenty *currachs* were rowed out to the fishing grounds in the afternoon. The seas were calm, the weather quiet. A light rain was falling. The reports concurred with those from Inishbofin. When the gale came, it did so with such speed that the fishermen didn't even have time to haul in their nets. Ten died. It was enough to tip life on the island from the barely manageable to the unbearable. Within twelve years or so, all the inhabitants had moved to the mainland. Another island abandoned – another tiny extinction.

In the morning, I dropped Lance off for a run on the southern island and took the Zodiac up along the edge of Inishkea North.

Above the foreshore, the low skyline was broken by the profile of half-ruined houses. They were roofless, their bare gables like hands pressed together in prayer. I rounded a low headland and came in to the beach and the old *porteen*. Cutting the engine, I felt the stern lift on the surf and the boat surge forward, driving the bows into the beach. I heaved it up to the tide mark. In the soft sand behind me were two wheel-tracks and the deep scuff of my boots. I felt shame at the signs of my own intrusion in this ghostly place.

Eight decades deserted, and the sand had filled the gap left by the islanders. It covered the interiors of the houses to the window ledges. It lay in drifts against the outside walls. It smoothed every surface, was bared in patches in the machair, showing as pale scalp between the marram grasses and thistles. It was a fine white sand, light and endlessly mobile. I felt if I stood still here too long, it would rise up my body and bury me.

The Inishkeas are sinking. In the Middle Ages, records suggest that the two islands were one. The sea split them apart in the coming centuries and in the early 1900s another breach appeared in the north island. Winter storms regularly push water far inland, and toss large rocks up over the machair. Everything about the Inishkeas is transient (even the name, 'Island of Geese' suggests a temporary roost on a migration). They are a variation on the mythical island, the island raised into existence by hope. These worn blocks of schist, 200 million years old, are as solid as anything on earth. But that doesn't make them permanent. Like everything else, they're on the move, subject to the law by which, grain by grain, all that is above the water will one day be submerged.

In April 1937, with the island almost deserted, a Frenchwoman stepped out of a *currach* and on to the Inishkea sand. Françoise Henry was then in her mid-thirties. She had studied prehistory and the early Christian period at the Sorbonne, but during a brief visit to a friend in Tipperary, she'd fallen for Ireland and all its medieval stone and story. It was a love that lasted her whole life. She studied Irish on the Aran Islands. She joined the French department of University College Dublin, and later became its director of studies in archaeology and art history. She was one of the great advocates of the genius of early Irish art, and a notable figure in Dublin's colourful world of letters. Frank O'Connor proposed to her, but the marriage ban for female public servants was still in place. She was forced to choose between him and her job. She chose her job.

The Inishkeas became central to her life and her interests, not just for the archaeology but for the purity and presence of the islands' past. Her journal of the first visit has little about her work and much about the simple glee she feels on arriving in such a place, the sense it gives of imminent revelation. She sets out from the Mullet Peninsula in a *currach* with a crew who are all called Pádraig. They row 'like devils . . . the foamless sea swells and sinks and the three row, row and announce that they are headed for America'. One of them suggests Françoise might like to settle down and live with him on the island. At one point she sees a girl in one of the houses and is struck by her beauty: 'her face is made stunning by her huge blue eyes surrounded by black lashes'. Late in the day, she returns to the mainland and looks back: 'To the west a curtain seems to be rising slowly over undefined spaces of brightness. The two islands are only thin lines embossed on the surface of the waves.'

A year after her first visit, she gained permission from the Office of Public Works for a six-week dig. In August 1946, she was back again. By now, the island was completely deserted and her journal more melancholy. 'This dying island,' she wrote. 'The sea gnaws at it, breaking the granite slabs, throwing them back on top of the cliffs, devouring the sand wherever it can reach it. The wind wears it away, little by little removing the dunes. The rabbits undermine it.'

Françoise Henry's most striking discovery on the Inishkeas was a factory. Just to the north of the mega-dune of Baily Mór, she uncovered a workshop building from the early Christian period, several slab-lined pits, a large hearth and a number of 'pot-boilers' – stones pulled from a fire and dropped into water to heat it. What identified the site, though, was the vast quantity of dog-whelk shells, *purpura lapillus*. It was a factory for making purple dye.

The making of purple dye was always more than just manufacture and process. It was alchemy. Originally production was in the hands of Phoenicians and their colonies throughout the Mediterranean; their range can be mapped by middens of whelks. The discovery of the shells' secret is told in a Phoenician story about the sea nymph Tyros and her lover, the god Melqart. One day the two of them are walking on the beach when they see that their dog's mouth is covered in a vibrant purple: it had been biting on a mollusc. The name of the Phoenicians' native region, Canaan, lends itself to the word for 'purple' in several Semitic languages. The Greeks named the people 'Phoenicians' using, it was thought, their own word *phoinix*, 'purple'. (In fact, it was probably the other way round – the Phoenician name for themselves gave the Greeks their word for the colour.)

Pliny has left a description of the dyeing process. Twelve thousand whelk shells were needed to dye the trim of a single robe. It took nine days of boiling. The dye came from the mucus of a gland used by the gastropod as a sedative for its prey. Mystique attaches to everything about the dye. When it is first secreted, the liquid is clear – its tones emerge only when exposed to sunlight; then, rather than dim with age, they deepen. Bede writes of Britain's vast numbers of dye-producing molluscs. They produce a colour, he explains, 'which the intensity of the sun nor exposure to the rain can ever succeed in fading, but the older it is the more beautiful'. In the Roman Empire, it was as valuable as silver, and only certain noble families – *purpurarii*

– could wear it. In ancient Greece, red was worn by storytellers and poets when they recited the *Iliad*, while for declaiming its sister-text, the island-hopping *Odyssey* – the one more deeply tinted by the imagination – performers donned purple.

The word in Old Irish for purple is *corcur*, thought to derive from Latin *purpura*. Production in Britain and Ireland was abandoned in the eleventh or twelfth century, so completely that the role of the whelk was thought to have been forgotten. But in the late 1600s, the Englishman William Cole heard that far out in the west of Ireland, there was someone dyeing linen handkerchiefs 'from some liquid substance taken out of a shellfish'.

The purple-dye factory on Inishkea is one of the most complete known examples in northern Europe. Françoise Henry dates it to the late sixth and early seventh centuries, when monks were living on the island in beehive dwellings. The dye, she argues, was extracted not for cloth but for something more devotional – for manuscripts and the mystery of the written word.

There's not much to see now. Just a few bumps in the sandy soil. I wandered around its base, struck less by the past than by the plastic tangles of monofilament and bottles and canisters. Elsewhere were flowers – squat yellow cinquefoil, tiny blooms of lesser stitchwort and, on salt-shortened stalks, the gaze of miniature eyebright. I picked a little wild thyme, put it to my nose, and climbed to the peak of Baily Mór.

It's only about sixty feet high. But, surrounded by flat ground and the water, the hill asserts a strange authority over the area. I had noticed it as we approached the island last night. Now I could see *Tsambika*, obedient at anchor, and Rusheen Island beyond, far-off Slievemore to the south, and the Mullet Peninsula across the silvery sound. Siting the factory below such a hill looks deliberate. How much of *here* did the dye carry with it? I thought of it travelling off in tiny cloth-bound vials to scriptoria on Iona or Lindisfarne. I pictured a brush poised over the page and an initial letter half-hidden in a thicket of interlacing or fretwork, and the purple-tipped bristles stroking the vellum. For both scribe and reader, the colour's appeal lay not only in its natural vibrancy and the painstaking process of extraction, but in the knowledge of its origin, a monastic island far out to the west, poised on the threshold of the otherworld.

Françoise Henry concludes her greatest work, *Irish Art in the Early Christian Period to 800 AD*, with talk of patterns, the defining characteristic of early Irish visual art. She points to the intricate designs of the manuscripts – the *Book of Kells* or the *Book of Durrow* – or those on the Ardagh Chalice, and identifies them as part of 'one of the most fastidious and subtle systems of decoration the world has ever seen'. Whorls and spirals and interlacing, trumpet scrolls and pelta shapes, triquetras and interlocking compass-drawn curves – the effect is dazzling.

The Monogram Page of the *Book of Kells* is the 'epitome of Irish art', wrote the art historian Margaret Stokes. James Joyce also saw the manuscript as 'the most purely Irish thing we have'. He had a copy of Edward Sullivan's illustrated study and became obsessed by the pages' endlessly twisting paths. He sensed in the visual effects something of the meanderings of his own prose. He wrote to his friend Arthur Power about Sullivan's book: 'In all the places I have been to, Rome, Zurich, Trieste, I have taken it about with me, and have pored over its workmanship for hours ... Some of the big initial letters which swing right across the page have the essential quality of a chapter of Ulysses. Indeed, you can compare much of my work to the intricate illuminations.'

It is not purely abstract – in amongst the geometry are figures or parts of figures, angels, rats and cats, an otter with a fish in its mouth, grotesque beasts. On examination, many of the patterns are derived from foliage or animal forms. Some of the letters themselves are legible at once, others deliberately obscured. To spend time with the pages is to slip into a trance-like state where everything is in flux, to slip under the spell of an expressive instinct that is wild and borderless. The whirligig patterns that spin across the manuscripts, mixing picture and letter, image and meaning, predate the written word. They are found on shields and mirrors, harness ornaments and brooches from the first millennium BC. They are found on carvings from two thousand years before that, on the megalithic carvings of Newgrange above the River Boyne in County Meath.

All is transformation, one thing becoming another. It is the ambiguous country of the *Song of Amergin* and the otherworld, the voyages of St Brendan and Bran and Máel Dúin and all the enigmatic islands that drew them on. 'This multiform and changing world where nothing is what it appears to be,' wrote Françoise Henry, 'is but the plastic equivalent of that country of all wonders which haunts the mind of the Irish poets.'

The cloud was thinning. I walked back through the village. On the cottage walls, sunlight sparkled on crystals of mica. One building had a roof. It was set a little apart from the others and as I was looking at it, thinking how recent the roof looked and wondering when it had gone on and why, a woman appeared in the doorway. She was barefoot, and a terrier ran out from behind her, barking.

'Quiet – *quiet*! I'm sorry.'

'That's OK,' I said, wanting to ask a dozen questions all at once.

'He's all right. Will you come *here*!' The terrier trotted back.

She was from Dublin. She'd arrived yesterday, dropped off by fishing boat. She and her family had come to visit her father – and her father had been alone on the island for months, since before the winter. It was the first time they'd seen him.

'He's in there now, meditating.'

I followed her inside. The roof tiles showed above the purlins; the floor was painted concrete. A table stood in the window, with a lived-in spread of food packets and books and plates. There were rugs over old chairs, a dresser scattered with spice jars and torches and candle-stubs, and more books on bareboard shelves (Blake, Yeats, the *I Ching*, Françoise Henry, James Roy's *Islands of Storms*). At one end of the building was the storeroom – sacks of rice and grains and pulses. At the other end hung a red-and-black Kirghiz felt hanging. She gestured at it. 'Behind there.'

When the islanders left in the 1930s, she said it was her grand-father who helped them settle on the mainland. In return, they had given him the old schoolhouse. It had lain empty for years. What use was a single house on an abandoned island that you couldn't even reach? But last year, when her father wanted to go on retreat, it came into its own.

The Kirghiz hanging lifted and Brion entered. At once his presence filled the room. He had a handsome face, blue eyes and swept-back white hair, and he moved and smiled with an easy charm. 'I saw you come in last night.' He gave the impression he'd been expecting me.

Nine months alone on the island had left Brion glowing. Perhaps he glowed anyway, back in Dublin, where he practised as a psychi-atrist. But standing in his renovated house, among the ruins, he looked like a man whose feet were set firmly on the earth.

'The first months,' he explained, 'they were the hardest. The gales, the long hours of darkness, the wind. My god, the wind!' With spring had come light and clarity of mind. His overall focus had been his years of work with Mahayana Buddhism.

'Something changed after a few months. The words of my teachers began to fade and I could think only of the most insignificant gesture – how they pulled a chair up to the table, or the particular way in which they held a cup of tea. That's when I learned to appreciate being here – here on this island.'

'Dublin must seem like another planet.'

He smiled. 'Everyone leads such crazy lives now. We're all in too much of a hurry. You remember the note Christopher Robin pinned to the door – the one that baffled his friends in the wood? *Gon out – Backson – Bisy – Backson.*'

I asked him if he felt any connection to the islands' early monks. He didn't answer immediately, but a little later he stood up and said: 'Let me show you something.'

He pulled on a sun-faded coat with DALLAS COWBOYS stencilled on the back. We stepped out and crossed a series of old fields behind the house, with their salt-stubbed grass and ankle-high remnants of wall. Among them was a small roofless building: St Columba's chapel, said Brion – built in the sixth century. We stood inside its cramped interior, silent for a moment.

Brion raised his head towards the sky. 'What always surprises me is – why in here? All this openness, and they came in here to worship.'

I said that Osip Mandelstam had had the same thought in a tiny church in Soviet Armenia. '"Whose idea was it to imprison space inside this wretched cellar, this low dungeon."'

Brion pointed at the east wall, at a niche in the stonework. 'Look – in here. Even when it was in ruins, the islanders continued to use it. They were said to have kept an idol in there. The priests were furious!'

Insular remoteness, vulnerability, or perhaps just the maverick mentality generated by the far west. Whatever it is, the Inishkeas have always encouraged the more unorthodox expressions of belief. The islands drew the most committed of the monks, set them working at bubbling vats to produce drops of sacred dye, had them pray through the extremes of the seasons. The islanders themselves were said to have erected a temple they called *Caisleán Phleimeann*, 'Fleming's Castle', where they propitiated those gods responsible for weather at sea.

The Inishkeas' 'idol', or sacred stone, is better known, if equally prone to rumour. It was what was housed here in the chapel niche. It was many things – pagan, Christian, a statuette of Jesus brought from Italy. It was the *Naomhóg*, the 'little holy thing', like the *currachs* of Kerry. It was wooden; it was terracotta; it was stone. It came from the slopes of Baily Mór. The islanders dressed it in a suit of red flannel. They passed it from house to house. They warmed it by the fire, wrapped it up in its own bed.

In the mid-nineteenth century, a local Anglican vicar heard about the stone. He was appalled: the 'gross superstition in . . . Inishkea where a stone idol was invoked for the protection of the inhabitants'. Reports began to accumulate of the islanders' idolatry, how in times of distress they carried the stone to the water and held hands around it. A priest was sent out from the mainland. He had the stone taken from the chapel and buried. When he tried to leave the island, though, a great storm forced him back. Another priest came. He ordered the stone to be thrown into the sea, and that priest died soon afterwards. The stone was recovered and another priest came and burnt the robe of the *Naomhóg* in the house of the island's king, and that priest died too. The *Naomhóg* was smashed to pieces by a pirate, but the islanders gathered the pieces together and wrapped them in a new suit of clothes. Then the people of the South Island came and stole it.

During the Second World War, the writer T. H. White was

living as a conscientious objector on Achill, near the Inishkeas. He became obsessed by the *Naomhóg*, or the 'godstone' as he called it. The islands had only recently been deserted and he was immediately drawn to their tantalizing profile on the western horizon, and the stories of them told by the exiles.

'I was off at full tilt. Why could it not be Tir-na-nÓg, the Island of Youth, where the mythological hero Oisín – the Ossian of the eighteenth century – was taken by the golden-haired, immortal beauty whose name was Niamh? And the "óg" in Tir-na-nÓg! Niamh-óighe! Was it possible, could it be possible, let it be possible, that Inniskea was the veritable Land of Youth'.

He asked to be rowed out in a *currach*. It was mid-winter and he camped alone in an abandoned house. He was somewhat spooked by the place, by the spirits of those who'd lived there before, and by the 'heathen god' he'd been told about.

'If I had had paper,' he said of that night, 'and could have written, it would have been a fountain of feeling about eternal things.' He did have an envelope, though, and with the fire crackling in the old grate scrawled a ten-stanza poem.

White's short stay on the island left him with a deep attraction to the holy stone. 'I chased that *Naomhóg* for five months . . . my mind bejingled with ideas about paganism and phallic pillars and the claptrap of a half-baked archaeologist.' He devised a questionnaire for surviving islanders about the stone, and recorded their answers in detail. He sought out every reference of every traveller to Achill who mentioned it. He travelled to Dublin, where he'd been told it was kept. It wasn't.

When Françoise Henry published her work on the Inishkeas, she did not mention the *Naomhóg*. But she did talk about finding a couple of 'ascetics' pillows' in the island's early dwellings. T. H. White took that as the most appealing explanation of the stone's origins and the 'wild goose chase' that had occupied him for so long. Back on Achill, he let the islands and his fruitless quest settle into memory: 'Bathing on summer days in the lace-work of the Atlantic rollers, frothy like milk just spurted in the pail, or stretched among the snail-shells on the sand dunes of Drumreagh, I often thought kindly of [the saint] with his solitude and his old head-rest. His islands of repose stood lonely in the distance, their hazy silhouette topped by the sea-mark of the south one – a finger pointing to the heaven he had longed for. I never went to the islands again.'

The *Naomhóg* of the Inishkeas hasn't been seen for almost a century.

I took the Zodiac back to pick up Lance and we returned to the schoolhouse. It was late afternoon, and Brion's grandchildren and son-in-law had come back from walking in the north of the island. We all sat around drinking tea and chatting. We pulled down books from the shelf, the children made patterns with the shells they'd found, and the dog lay curled up by the door. Brion sat at the table. The children revolved around him, lodging briefly on his knee, then wriggling off again to run around the room. The smile on his face was something wonderful – the reward of a long vigil.

'Why not stay?' he suggested as we rose to leave.

'I'd like to.'

But we needed to catch the tide. We needed to reach Frenchport if we were to cross Donegal Bay tomorrow, and we needed to cross tomorrow to use the good weather, and I needed to keep going if I was ever to reach the Summer Isles while it was still summer.

'Busy,' I said to him. 'Back soon.'

14

It was evening by the time Lance heaved the anchor up out of the Inishkea sand, and I pushed down the helm to point the bows north. We took the inshore route, and Lance read out loud the pilotage as we weaved between the hazards. It sounded like some sort of allegory. Beware the Pluddany Rocks and the perils of the Usborne Shoal. Do not be tempted by Carrickmoneagh and Carrickmoylenacurhoga. Ensure a virtuous depth of water beneath you by keeping the Ears of Achill in line astern – first with the rock of Turduvillaun, then with Shiraghy. Look out for the guardian presence of Carricknaronty – which was there, where it should be, Cerberus-like on the approach to the strait between Inishkeeragh and Corraun Point. We were close enough in to see weed-patches on the point and hear the loud *shhhh* of waves on the reef, and then on the rocky shore of the island of Inishglora.

Inishglora! Tiny Inishglora, where the Children of Lir lie buried in thin soil. How did they end up here? Their father was Manannán Mac Lir, God of the Sea. For him, the ocean presented no impediment. It was Mag Mell, the 'plain of delights', where all the horrors of the deep were neatly dealt with by becoming something else, something terrestrial: the fish were leaping lambs and the waves just bushes blowing in the breeze. When his wife died, Manannán remarried and his new wife could not bear the affection he showed his children, his four beautiful children. So she turned them into swans. Nine hundred years they spent trapped in swan bodies, travelling through Ireland, from region to region, from lake to lake until, on Inishglora, St Brendan freed them from the curse. For an instant, they were children again, fair-haired and butter-faced – then the centuries caught up with them and they dropped to the ground, dead. That is what happens to those who return from the otherworld. They re-encounter the linear laws of earthly time. 'In the Otherworld,' wrote John Carey, 'all of time exists simultaneously in an eternal present.'

The magical, age-warping qualities of Inishglora are mentioned in the *Konungs skuggsjá*, a thirteenth-century text in Old Norse: 'Though men die there, they are not buried in the earth, but they are raised up round about the church in the churchyard, and stand upright like living men with all their limbs all dried, and all their hair and nails unscathed, and they never decay, and birds never perch on them.'

The ruins of St Brendan's oratory showed as broken teeth on the island's ridge. Rounding the eastern tip, I steered between Inishglora and the rock of Leacarrack. The low sun crept over the back of the island. Corrugations of waves lined up to break over a shallow reef. The surfer in me felt drawn to their symmetry, their clean slopes; the sailor wanted them to go away. I felt a lot happier when the digits of the depth sounder began to rise.

We spent a short night in Frenchport and weighed anchor at sunrise, hoisting the mainsail and running free from the inlet. Nothing can beat the pleasure of leaving harbour at such an hour, with the freedom of open water ahead. I stood at the helm while Lance made coffee below. He was good to have aboard, with his pilot's practicality and his bonhomie – but most of all because he liked it.

I turned to look at the dawn. It was a fair-weather dawn with a few ribbons of gilded cloud. The land below it was still black, the skyline sharp as a blade. A ruined house stood in silhouette and as I passed it, the sun flashed through its empty windows. The forecast was for a steady south-easterly. Seventy miles across Donegal Bay to the island of Inishkeel – fourteen hours, at five knots.

Pushing down the helm with my thigh, I watched the bows come round to line up on Eagle Island. I leaned over, loosed off the genoa, slotted in the winch handle and wound it in. I cut the engine. Water hissed past the hull. The boat leaned and settled in the waves. Off to seaward was a line of six gannets in flight – the gaps between them so regular, their pace so uniform, that they seemed connected by an unseen rod.

For weeks, I'd been thinking of Donegal Bay. In idle moments in the saloon, I found myself reaching for the charts, the pilot book, scrolling through the Navionics app. To go into Sligo? Or Killybegs? I'd trawled the internet for every hint of shelter, safe haven, for pontoons and moorings. In the end, I took the Gordian knot approach – I'd cross it in one. 'Donegal Bay,' mused a seasoned sailor I met on Inishbofin, 'that's the loneliest bloody expanse of water I ever saw.'

Eagle Island lay a mile or two ahead, Donegal Bay beyond it. The acolyte of Cross Rock stood to the east, and between that and the mainland cliffs, a gap was opening up, slit-wide to start with, but broadening until it looked possible to navigate. Beyond it, the flat horizon grew longer. If we continued on our course, the next thing we'd hit would be the ice of the Arctic.

Now I could lay the crossing, 065°M, out into the bay. We set up the autohelm – first the Raytheon, which runs on battery, then the Windpilot, which uses only the air and the water and is capricious but like a dancer when you get it right. It took a while to tune. The compasses wouldn't agree, the breeze came and went. But suddenly everything was OK. The wind steadied at eighteen knots abeam, the compasses settled their differences, the sails were just right and the boat was spanking along at seven and a half knots. Lance and I lounged in the cockpit, talking about South Africa and Ireland and which was best (Ireland), and his wife, who ran a care home in Westport, and his pride at how she'd turned it round. He told some colourful stories about camping in the Transvaal, about flying into Mozambique, and the terror of finding himself in no-go areas in Cape Town.

I checked the Windpilot, then went forward. I sat with my back to the mast, manoeuvring a little to avoid the cleats and fittings. Across the bay, the land was an undulating line that swept round, bulking up with the peaks, for sixty miles or more. Again I had the sense that this was not Ireland, not even Europe – but somewhere altogether larger. With the wind coming from the south-east, the seas were steep and narrow. I watched the blue-green translucence where the sun shone through their crests. I dipped into the travel-worn copy of Yeats's *Collected Poems*. A thing about Yeats, I've found, is that he makes more sense in extremis – perilous bus rides, dawns in the wild, or at sea: some of the allusiveness and layered symbolism falls away to clarity so sharp it has the sheen of revelation, even lines like: 'The gyres! The gyres! Old Rocky Face, look forth—'

Bang! One of the seas peaked hard against the side, rose up and dropped on the foredeck – on me, on the book.

In his *Reveries over Childhood and Youth*, Yeats spoke of doing exactly this. He was out sailing in Donegal Bay with some of his seafaring family, sitting with his back to the mast. He didn't recall exactly how old he was, nine or ten perhaps. What he did remember was that it was the day he first drank alcohol. When a wave broke green over the bow, soaking him, he was given whisky and taken home in an open cart, standing up and shouting to everyone how drunk he was.

It is not the Yeats we think of – the long-fingered, floppy-tied *flâneur*, the aesthete who was so concerned about his appearance that he painted his heels to hide the holes in his socks. But much of Yeats's early imagination was shaped by the sea. As a boy, a large part of his adventuring had to do with boats – sailing several hours into Donegal Bay, while he 'mocked' his English friend, doubled up on the bottom boards, for feeling hungry. He collected wood in the yard to build a ship and seek heroic death in a sea battle. 'All my dreams were of ships,' he wrote of his childhood. They were assembled from the stories he heard on the Sligo wharves, from deckhands and cabin boys. They were coloured by his sea-captain grandfather, who lived nearby – 'You most of all, silent and fierce old man / . . . the daily spectacle / That stirred my fancy' – and who owned only one book apart from the Bible: *The Shipwreck* by William Falconer.

It was the sea, and Donegal Bay in particular, that first convinced Yeats that 'the world was full of monsters and marvels'. The quays and inlets of Sligo were his playground, the Liverpool steamer the means of returning there from school in hated England. In London, he boasted of the crossing to his classmates. He adopted a feet-wide-apart gait, as if walking on a rolling deck. He remembered asking his grandmother once if God was as strong as a sailor. The sea and seamanship helped form the dreaming part of him: 'I have walked on Sinbad's yellow shore and never shall another hit my fancy.' Crossing water, the sea voyage, passage to the otherworld – all these became abiding images in his later work.

In 1900, his brother Jack recalled their childhood here in a painting called *Memory Harbour*: an elevated view of the port at Sligo, the rigging and bustle and the river mouth beyond. It is a haunting picture, full of the suck of the open sea, beyond the Metal Man, beyond Rosses Point, out into the wilds of Donegal bay. When W. B. was looking at the image in his late forties, it thrilled him to be reminded of the figures and places of his childhood. But it struck him too with the bitter-sweet logic of nostalgia: of loss and unfulfilled hopes. 'I feel melancholy,' he reflected on the picture, 'because I have not made more and better verses.'

We reached the Donegal coast with the glow of evening bright on its stony slopes. Past Malin More Head, the high cliffs were all gleam and shadow. Empty moorland rose to a host of rounded peaks. We'd passed no boat since Clare Island, but now a single ketch appeared half a mile out to sea, working hard to windward. On land, there was not a tree in sight – nor any sign of road or dwelling.

'Reminds me of the bush,' mused Lance – then suddenly: 'Oh, I miss South Africa! I miss the space, the sky, *this*.'

We found an anchorage in Church Pool, and in the morning headed ashore. Lance was due back with his family. There was a mile-long beach with surf breaking on it. We surged in on white water and Lance rolled up his trousers. Briefly we embraced, then he shouldered his bag to wade through the shallows. I turned the Zodiac back into the breakers. The bow rose high, and slapped hard down behind it. I twisted the throttle and rose more gently over the next, passing out of the surf line.

Looking back, I could see Lance standing on the empty beach, trousers still rolled up, the bag at his feet, waving.

I took the Zodiac across the bay, past *Tsambika*, to the deserted island of Inishkeel. Above the beach was a fringe of pasture and above that the deep unbroken blue of the sky. The sight of a single cloud in that sky, on that morning, would have been absurd. Up on the low cliff, one by one, appeared three rust-coloured cows, looking as heroic as any domesticated animal can ever look.

Those hours on Inishkeel were filled with a strange joy, drawn from some secret fund of hours reserved for certain moments and certain places in our lives. I climbed up over the rocks. I stumbled at first on the hoof-pitted turf, then found my feet. The sky, the sea, the green – the depth of colour was extraordinary. In a single patch of grass shone the bright yellow of ragwort, tormentil and cinquefoil, the purple of knapweed, self-heal, clover and sow thistle, blue of the cornflowers – and each one amplified to an otherworldly degree. I wandered round the semi-restored church, roofless, its old blocks numbered and reassembled. I sat in a hollow out of the wind, and looked north. The seas were running from the island, their white-tops winking like stars, and the entire surface gave the impression of something galactic and ceaseless. A single herring gull dropped to the water and, in a perfect arc, soared up again; not once did it move a wing.

Inishkeel is Donegal's holiest site. Historically, it owes its sanctity to Conall, who came here in AD 500 as penance for murdering his father. St Conall settled on the island and over time became known for his profound devotion. His example drew others, other 'holy wanderers', and for the 1,500 years since, pilgrims have been coming to the island to commemorate St Conall and his brethren.

But it is tempting to believe that Inishkeel was always holy, a place of pilgrimage long before Conall arrived. No more than half a mile across, it is a piece of the earth where barriers to the sacred seem lower, where worldly concerns dissolve. The very form of such islands suggests the shape of the human soul, at least how it looks in deep contemplation – somewhere discrete and earthbound but immersed in eternity, a tiny fixed presence in a restless universe.

In this life though the soul is attached to the body and Inishkeel is not entirely an island, or rather it's not always an island. At low-water springs, when the tide recedes, the waves pull back and it's possible to reach it on foot. In practical terms, that makes pilgrimage a lot easier – no need to commission a boat, to risk a short but exposed passage. The isthmus acts as the topography of hope – wait for just the right time, the right place, and transcendence will be a quick stroll across a finger of sand. Just don't expect to stay too long.

One of the mysteries of the early Irish Church is how a set of monastic practices that had developed in the Egyptian desert, pioneered by hermits like St Antony, should so rapidly and widely have sprung up here, thousands of miles away. An díseart, 'the desert', was the generic name given by early Irish monks to the places chosen for the contemplative life. Links to Egypt through France, through St Martin of Tours, or through sea routes to the eastern Mediterranean, explain lines of possible influence. But they do not explain the zeal with which the eremitic life was pursued in Ireland.

A report from the first century AD suggests the sanctity of such islands in the pre-Christian period. Demetrius of Tarsus said that 'many of the islands off Britain were uninhabited and widely scattered, some of them being named after deities and demi-gods.' He himself managed to explore a number of the islands and found that on one of them were a few inhabitants who were holy men.

Offshore islands have always drawn pioneers of the spirit. For some of the Christian peregrini, though, they were not enough; they were no more than stepping stones to other imagined islands over the horizon. These men opted for 'white martyrdom'. If land is body and sea is spirit, then a voyage into the ocean is a renouncing of the physical, the corporeal – and death out there is the purest death of all.

Over the years, I have come across a few people, perhaps half-a-dozen at most, who appear to have perfected the secluded life.

There was a Coptic monk in Egypt's western desert, an Armenian Vartabed I knew in Jerusalem, a couple of Ethiopian nuns and monks in cliff-top cells. And one man here in Ireland, down in County Kerry, earlier in the summer. The mission of Monsignor Pádraig Ó Fiannachta was not one of eremitic isolation but of scholarship and pastoral care. He acquired the empty convent of the Sisters of the Presentation, right in the middle of the town of Dingle, with its fifty-two pubs. There he established a 'Centre of Irish Spirituality and Culture'. But the name he gave it in Irish revealed the roots of his own belief. He called it simply An Díseart.

The monsignor spent his career in study, writing and publishing works on early Irish literature. He translated the Bible into Irish, then donated his collection of 6,000 books to Dingle library. Having spent a few days with them, I went to see him. He was in his office, a tiny cell of a room off one of An Díseart's echoing halls. Large patches of damp bubbled from the paintwork. A plaster-of-Paris figure of Christ was the only adornment. Otherwise it was all papers and typescripts and books, and the monsignor himself huddled amongst them, bent and weak and radiant.

He had been born some eighty years earlier just to the west of Dingle. 'At my birth, the midwife told my mother: "He has a very big head – he will probably be a priest."'

His childhood was hard. The local landowner, Lord Ventry, pushed his family out of their cottage when he needed more land for his horses. Two of Pádraig's brothers drowned out fishing, another at birth. The midwife was right – in due course he went off to seminary. There he developed a love for playing Gaelic football, and one day he received a kick in the head. 'It made me a little violent, that kick. When the doctor came to examine me, we had an argument about the Old Testament – and I hit him.'

It was hard to imagine this gentle man hitting anyone. The

seminary had little sympathy. They sent him off to a 'mental hospital', where he was given ECT, without sedation.

'They didn't even consult my mother. Very tough, it was,' he said with an apologetic smile, as if it was wrong to mention his own suffering. The bishop refused to have him back. So he went to Wales. There he spent six years studying Welsh and the early Christian centuries, a period that became the grounding for his life's work.

I asked him about the connection between the early Irish monasteries and the Eastern Church.

He steepled his fingers to his lips before answering. 'No one knows for sure . . . Let me answer it like this. Many years ago, I went on a visit to the Soviet Union. In Moscow, they asked me where I wanted to go and I said: Armenia. The oldest Christian country. I travelled down there and visited the monasteries in the mountains. I looked at the cells and thought of the monks and I was struck by the strong feeling – more than a feeling, it was as if I was in two places at once – that I was back here in the west of Ireland. There was one site with seven churches, just like on Inis Mór.'

'That sounds like Geghard. The churches in the cave?'

We both recalled what we remembered of it, and of the other monasteries, and he said, 'I don't know of any historical link – maybe it is only in spirit. But I felt it.'

He then told another story from the same trip. He was invited to visit the Madenataran – the great national library of Armenia. 'They said – now, we would like to show you something special. They brought out the *Gospel of Echmiadzin*. This, they said, is the most beautiful book in the world. It was certainly beautiful! But I told them that it's not the most beautiful book in the world, because we have that one in Ireland – it's the *Book of Kells*. Of course, that started a bit of an argument. "Do you show your book?" they asked. I told them that every day there are queues and queues of people to see it in Dublin. "Well, that proves it," said the Armenians. "We do not show ours at all."'

He smiled and his eyes glittered at the memory. Such a smile in so frail a body! Living proof of the triumph of spirit over the physical.

A few weeks later, I turned the pages of the *Irish Times* and there again was the smiling face of Monsignor Pádraig Ó Fiannachta. It was his obituary.

I walked back over the top of Inishkeel. I could see the Zodiac lying high up the beach. Beyond it, the waves were breaking across the sandbar, sliding in from each side, meeting in the middle. The tide was still falling.

On the beach was a small waiting crowd and when the water dropped further, the first of them broke away. Soon a line of people was leading out towards the island, through the shallows. There was something biblical about those distant silhouettes – lone figures in single file, clutching their shoes, small family groups, a couple hand-in-hand, and, striding out in front of them all, a man with a child hoisted high on his shoulders.

15

I WAS LYING DOWN BELOW, WAITING for the tide. I had pulled
down Thomas Merton's *The Seven Storey Mountain* to look for a
passage I half remembered – about how he became a Trappist monk
in 1941. He'd received his draft papers to join the US army, but failed
his medical for not having enough teeth. Reading up about monasticism in the *Catholic Encyclopedia*, he found the idea immediately
resonant: 'What wonderful happiness there was, then, in the world!
There were still men on this miserable, noisy, cruel earth who tasted
the marvellous joy of silence and solitude, who dwelt in forgotten
cells, in secluded monasteries.'

It was Bridget who'd introduced me to his work; she who had
given me his book. I read it for some time, then laid it down on
my chest, daydreaming – about Merton and Pádraig Ó Fiannachta,
about Bridget and her Carmelite nuns, and about Sutherland, the
mountains of Assynt, and the Summer Isles.

I'd done what I needed to do. I'd heaved the outboard up on deck
and fixed it to the after guardrail. I'd taken the spinnaker halyard
down into the Zodiac, clipped it on, then winched the whole thing
up, swung it aboard, deflated and stowed it on the coachroof. I'd
checked the bearing up to Aran Sound, spotting the breaker dead
on my course (along this coastline, there's always a breaker on your
course). I'd tidied, stowed, fiddled, then come down to read – and
wait for the tide.

Sunlight was beaming into the saloon. I watched it glint on the font of the hurricane lamp and on the brass shade above it, then shift across the ceiling as the boat swung, an oblong of brightness on white paint, crumpling as it crossed the varnished beams. There was something anticipatory in its sliding. Will it reach the suspended half-coconut shell, souvenir from *Tsambika*'s two years in the Caribbean, which now held three ripe bananas? The line became my own progress up the coast. Would I reach the Summer Isles? I watched the light approach the bananas. I saw it catch their ends, yellowing the yellow. It spread up along their shafts – then it stalled, hovering for a moment, and began to retreat. The hull was swinging the other way against the chain. The sunlight shrank back, returning over the timbers, to flash on the lamp and move across the ceiling on the opposite side.

On the chart, the next stretch of coast was chaotic. It looked like someone had taken a hammer to a slab of toffee. It wasn't clear at first which of the pieces were land and which water, and which were intertidal rock. To reach the harbour of Burtonport, you had to weave up into Aran Sound, first through the South Sound and then the South Sound of Aran. (Confusing place names were just one of the cautionary boxes which littered the relevant pages of the ICC pilot book. Another was the 'rocks too numerous to mention', and the unreliability of chart data.) There was no channel as such, just an arcane shuffle between reefs: 'Leaving Turk Rocks beacon not less than 1 cable to starboard, bring Carrickbealatroha Upper beacon in line with Ballagh Rocks beacon 354 to leave Clutch buoy to port,' etc., etc. I'd read and re-read the passage, checked the charts. Now I was watching sun-shapes, waiting for the tide . . .

I heard the main halyard flicking hard against the mast. The wind was getting up. Action! I shoved Merton back on the shelves and hurried up on deck.

Clearing the end of Inishkeel, I found a long swell driving in from the west. Small wind-blown waves were travelling in the opposite direction, scooting up and over the mounds of rolling water like ocean-bound vessels themselves. I watched the Donegal coast unpeel ahead, with its sea caves and cliffs, its treeless slopes scattered with small white houses, its ridge line of bulbous granite.

In the South Sound of Aran, I went forward to prepare for landing. It was the last piece of clear water before the approach to Burtonport. I secured the bowline. I tied fenders to the guardrail. I could see beyond them down into the water. It wasn't the graded blue-green of deep water. It was pale, and amidst the pale were dark patches of weed. Too early! The tide was barely covering the flats.

What is it about not going backwards? A stubborn refusal to retrace my steps drove me on, into the shallows, that mess of surf-ringed islets and reefs. I dropped the sails and crept forward under engine. The depth was hovering at around two metres. Wyon Point and Illancrone and Turk Rocks were already behind me. I'd learned the names and repeated them out loud, as if reaching for some sort of liturgical providence: the Clutch, Aileen Reef, Carrickbealatroha Upper and Lower, Lackmorris, Dirty Rock. Opposite Arranmore, I picked up the transit on Inishcoo, and the channel into Burtonport. I pushed down the helm and steered back towards the gap that separated the granite shores of several small islands. Its gateway was two rocks a few boat lengths' apart. On one was a green concrete tower, and opposite it a red. The red one marked the edge of Rutland Island, and all I could think of, as I chugged down that narrow, granite-flanked corridor of water was how English it all sounded – Burtonport, Rutland Island – on this most Irish of coasts.

*

William Burton was one of eighteenth-century Ireland's great improvers. Before improving here, in the north-west, he'd already done some impressive improving at his home at Slane Castle on the Boyne, experimenting with the cultivation of rice and the importing of vigorous Spanish rams. He'd built a mill so large it had no equal in Ireland or Britain, a beautifully adorned building which became hugely profitable. The glories of the distant past attracted Burton no less than the prospect of a productive future. He pioneered the study of Ireland's antiquities and helped set up the Royal Irish Academy. When his uncle, the first Earl Conyngham, died childless, William and his brother were beneficiaries. William added Conyngham to his name and received large pieces of the country in return, including 100,000 acres of Donegal.

The west coast and its islands encouraged William Burton Conyngham, as with more romantic souls a century later, to let his imagination run free – not with the fire of solitary worship, nor with mythic ideals of Irishness, but with dreams of progress and plenty. The herring fishery of north-west Donegal had been yielding vast returns. The shoals were so thick that in places people were complaining it had become hard to row anywhere. As many as 3,500 fishermen were going out after them each winter. If all the fish were caught, they said, they could fill the holds of every boat in England. What the fishery lacked was shore-based facilities, and access to markets.

William Burton Conyngham identified the island of Inis Mhic na Doirn as the site for an entirely new fishing station. Loyally, he renamed it after Ireland's lord lieutenant, the Duke of Rutland. He set about building a port on the mainland (named after himself) and a road to it across the boggy wastes of Donegal. On Rutland Island, bedrock was blasted and the natural harbour enlarged. Quays were built. Net lofts and fish cellars followed. There were facilities for gutting, coopering, rope-making and producing salt; an inn, a schoolhouse and the region's main post office – all built from scratch.

A map survives of the original plan for the settlement. The ideal of a Georgian city, with its neat grid of perfectly parallel streets and its bold right angles, has been transposed onto this rough-edged raft of broken granite. Burton Conyngham was an active member of Dublin's Wide Streets Commission and knew the value of generous boulevards and orderly design, and he brought those principles out to the island. But the grid doesn't quite fit. A bit of Duke Street runs across the strand. Church and Duchess Streets run into an area of 'Sand Hills'. No account is taken of slope.

With sufficient will and budget, anything can be done. Such was the credo of William Burton Conyngham. Building progressed. Three-storey warehouses went up; the keel for a sixty-ton vessel was laid, the hull was built over it and the ship launched in the harbour. To man the station, Burton Conyngham advertised for 'intelligent' settlers from England, and even America, to try and galvanize local agriculture and 'my ignorant and indolent tenants'.

In its first years, the station was a success. Tens of thousands of fish were landed, processed and sent out to markets in the east of Ireland and England. But fish being fish, they proved fickle. Some people said it was the sound of building on Rutland Island that drove them away, others that it was 'sharks with heads like Dutchmen'. It was probably over-fishing. By the mid-1790s, the herring had all but disappeared. Burton Conyngham died in 1796. The buildings on Rutland Island were already being abandoned. Out on the western shore, the Sand Hills began to break up. Gales sent clouds of fine sand spilling down the streets. It began to rise against the walls of the buildings, to drift against the doors, burying the dead settlement.

I could see the ruins as I passed. A few of the smaller buildings had been restored as holiday houses. Others stood as they had been left, roofless, their bare gables the emblem of these western islands, the topography of man's brief occupation, of hubris.

The channel ended and I took a sharp left, following the line of buoys into Burtonport. Swinging round to come in alongside the quay, I turned in too tight. The wind caught the boat's side and there was a crunching of gunwales, a scraping of hulls. No damage to their steel, but a few painful bruises in *Tsambika's* teak toe-rail, and some judgemental stares from the quay above.

I tied up alongside a fifty-foot trawler. The *Kesteven* was not going to sea anytime soon. Patches of green weed bloomed in her scuppers. I stepped across her deck and climbed the ladder up on to the quay. It was six islands ago since I'd last set foot on the mainland.

Burtonport had rundown fishing harbour written all over it. Along the shoreline stood a number of derelict shipping containers and an old Thermo King refrigerated unit. Beside them were empty cable drums and oil canisters, broken pallets, boat trailers with missing wheels, perished RIBs, coils of rotting cordage. Discarded nets had sat long enough to accumulate soil, to become habitat, to host cock's foot and mugwort. A couple of rusting hulks lay on the hard. *Tom Doyle of Cork* read one transom.

'You should have seen it in the old days. Then it was something!'

He had pulled up on the quay and opened the driver's window to talk to me. A plump and jolly man who exactly fitted the driving seat of his little Fiat. He certainly wasn't going to move from it, nodding at the view around him.

'Five deep in the old days, boats moored here against the pier and coming and going at all hours. The lights were on all night and forklifts going back and forth. Now they've all gone down Killy-begs. There's huge money being made down there, so there is. Huge money.'

He was a priest. He had a parish in the south of Donegal, not far from the busy fishing port of Killybegs. But this is where he'd been brought up, where he came back each year on holiday, alone.

'My mother used to bring me out here. She'd show me all the things they were doing. She had uncles with boats, trawlers and things, and they'd be gone for days at a time. Think she wanted me to be a fisherman but –' he tapped his collar – 'I became a fisher of men!'

I laughed with him. It was clearly a joke he'd made before.

'I remember the sight of all those boats – and the men in those days. I saw them at Christmas when they came to call. They were wild men – to me they were storybook heroes.' He directed his gaze out over the harbour to Conyngham's ruins on Rutland Island.

'Ah, but it's all a long time ago now, a long time.' The driver's window had already started to slide up. 'God bless.'

I had the number of a retired academic who lived a few miles inland. Cormac Gillespie said he'd be down later, but now he was off to have his dog clipped. When the two of them arrived in the early evening, sitting side by side in the car, they looked equally well trimmed.

'Thought I might as well do the same!'

With a grin, Cormac patted his white hair. He had a natural spar-kle, a fizzy blend of enthusiasm and humour which filled the car as we drove back to his home in the Rosses and he talked – of every-thing. His dog sat behind me, licking my ear.

'*Stad de sin a Bharley!*' Will you stop that, Barley!

Barley was a wheaten terrier from Wexford, and Cormac

addressed him only in Irish. The two of them lived in a bungalow down a sleepy, grass-centred lane. In the sitting room were house plants and books and graduation pictures of his daughters on the piano. The girls had left home, left Donegal for good jobs in the south-east. His wife had recently had a stroke. She was now in a care home. She had lost movement in her right side and also the power of speech. 'But not song. Play her anything by Bob Dylan and she'll sing along. She's his number one fan!'

Cormac pulled down a dictionary of maritime terms in Ulster Irish. It was his own work, and weaved together several strands of loss – the shrinking use of Irish, and of the skills of sail and paddle. A third strand was the use of interviews with 'the last representatives of the now deserted island communities of Gabhla, Inis Meáin, Inis Oirthear, and Inis Bó Finne'. A further strand was that the dictionary existed only in typescript. It had taken him years, interviewing dozens of people – elderly mariners, in the main – but he'd been unable to find anyone interested in publishing it.

Flicking through it, I found myself pulled into its particular world – a local variant on my own onboard life.

'You'll see that newer fishing gear and techniques tend to have English names.'

There were a few older terms too that were similar to the English: *taic* – 'tack'; *landail* – 'to land'. Many more were distinct. Each entry was accompanied by a citation from his interviewees, a glimpse of deep experience, the demands made on vocabulary by centuries of separate seafaring and fishing out here in the far north-west: *aice* – 'lobster- or crab-hole'; *rith* – 'sailing with a following wind'; *lubog* – 'cringle'.

The entry for *bolg* started one of those associative chases through meaning that are as intoxicating as they are uncontrolled. *Bolg* is the word for 'bilge'. I remembered from my own sketchy study of Irish that *bolg* (with a glottal stop between the *l* and the *g*, so '*bol-ug*') also meant 'stomach', and that Ireland's early inhabitants, the Fir Bolg, and Belgium traced the origins of their name to it.

'It is not that the Belgians are "people of the stomach",' explained Cormac, 'but rather that the Romans named them after a small pouch they were accustomed to wearing around their waist, next to their stomach.'

The route to the nautical term 'bilge' in modern English may also be linked. It is said to have come through the Old North French *boulge*, which in turn came from Late Latin *bulga*, which may well have come, originally, from the Gaulish *bulga*. So the belly of a ship, its sump, where the floating part tapers downwards and inwards, may owe its name in Latin and English to a Celtic or Gaulish root, with the suggestion that the Celts and their displacement hulls had an early dominance in the water.

Or is that all just bilge? ('*Bilge* – nonsense, 1921', *OED*, from the foul water in the bottom of a ship). When you throw in the Gaulish pouch – which may be derived either from its own bulging properties or from its proximity to the stomach, and also the hypothetical Indo-European root *bholga*, then you have a lexical soup which has simmered for so long its ingredients can no longer be separately identified. But we had a lot of fun that evening sipping away at it and speculating.

We spoke of the bardic tradition, and the old bardic schools, where the training once lasted for years, and the Contention of the Bards in the early seventeenth century, when a regional conflict was fought by rival poets firing verses at each other. Cormac then recited an anonymous ninth-century poem, twice – the second time to point out the 'astonishing' internal rhythms and rhymes.

'The "Ungenerous Payment" – it's about a stingy patron.'

> 'Ro-cúala'
> *ní tabair eochu ar dúana:*
> *do-beir a n-í as dúthaig dó:*
> *bó.'*
> I know him:
> He'll give no horse for a poem:
> He'll give what his kind allows:
> A cow.

He grinned. 'What a barb! It's like haiku.'

'But I thought cows were highly valued?'

'Ah! But if you were a poet, you had no land. A cow was useless. What you wanted was a horse to speed you around the country.'

Much of Cormac's work as an academic had concerned the Norse and Icelandic Eddas and sagas. He was an expert in both the Irish traditions and the Icelandic. He remembered as a student, years ago in Dublin, a delegation coming from Reykjavik and their soft-spoken cool. Was it them, I asked, that made you study the sagas?

'Yes! No – not entirely. It was before that.' He paused, recalling the exact moment – and the place – that changed the direction of his life, that swivelled it northwards. 'There's a cove along the coast called Port An Doruis. It's a very magical place, with high cliffs all around – you can only get to it through a cave. I was there with my dog – not this one, it was years ago. There was a full gale blowing and the white clouds were booming across the sky. The massive waves took me by surprise – my four-legged friend skedaddled and bolted for home. I think the spray must have burnt my eyes, because it was then that I first dreamed of Iceland, the great north somewhere beyond that cove.'

He was about to spend his twenty-first winter in Iceland.

When we reached the quay, we were still talking, so we sat in the car. I said I'd been reading Seamus Heaney's rendering of *Buile Suibhne* – *Sweeney Astray* – the wonderfully weird medieval story of Sweeney's odyssey around Ireland, as an owl. 'Much of the time reading it, you don't even notice he's an owl.'

'Those Irish stories!' Cormac put his hands to his head in mock exasperation. 'Honestly, sometimes they're too much.'

'Are the Icelandic ones any different?'

'Much more pragmatic, more real. The Irish ones are just mad. So much imagination! I think it must have been bad bread. Messed with their minds.'

The met charts had looked OK. For a week ahead they'd been covered in shades of sailable blue and green. But in the last thirty-six hours, I'd watched the isobars increase and the lows slide in from the Atlantic to reveal red and orange centres, like some dangerous confectionery. The gales had been relentless. For weeks now, I'd been running along the coast like a fugitive. Down in Mayo, I'd met one of the O'Malley clan and he'd said: 'Summers are not the same any more. The only decent weather we get is in May and June. With the turn of the year, it all goes downhill.' By 'turn of the year' he meant midsummer. That was many weeks ago now.

From Burtonport, my plan was to sail up to Tory Island. Doing last-minute checks – fuel, oil, course and tides – I flashed a torch in behind the engine and saw that the bolts for the prop-shaft bracket were loose again. How long had they been like that? I pictured days waiting around for an engineer – to do what? Hours taking things to bits, ordering parts, waiting for them to arrive. I wriggled down into the bilges, plugged the deadwood holes with matchsticks and managed to get enough purchase to tighten the bolts. But I didn't want to risk Tory Sound, in this weather, with such a bodge.

Cormac had a cousin along the coast. I'd met him a day or two earlier. In the small harbour of Bunbeg, Conan kept a wooden boat, which he'd restored from a wreck; I figured he'd have all the right stuff for a less basic fix. On the phone, he said: 'Sure, come round. But don't try and come into the harbour yourself. You'll never find the channel. I'll come out and meet you.'

Clearing the narrow corridor from Burtonport, I sailed out into open water and hardened sheets round the top of Owey Island. The cliffs on the north side were high and jagged, as though someone had snapped off a piece to take home as a souvenir. I was close enough in to hear the swells echoing beneath them, and see the water sluicing back green from the slabs.

It always felt good to be out at sea again, on the move, with the sails full. Now the bows were pointing for the first time towards Bloody Foreland, the headland that ends the west coast of Ireland. But something was changing – there was a new urgency, to get the miles behind me.

In the distance, fifteen miles or so north, Tory Island sat on the horizon, its eastern end rising to cliffs that, even from here, looked precipitous. Closer at hand were the Stag Rocks, a cluster of three sea-stacks – the petrified remains of three brothers. When St Columba landed on Tory Island, bearing his civilizing Christian message, these three wanted none of it. They leapt in the sea to escape. They only got this far. I watched them as I passed, their forms moving against each other like trees seen from a slow train. They were story-makers, those rocks, filling that empty stretch of water with a presence that far outstripped their size.

A warm wind was pushing out of the south. The undersides of the clouds looked like crumpled bedding, a sure sign of bad weather.

The mountains of Donegal were as grey as the sky – except for the perfect shape of Errigal, whose quartzite slopes made it glow like a giant tooth. The wind was freshening. When I turned in to pick out the end of Gabhla Island and the entrance to Bunbeg harbour, it turned out to be more or less on the nose. I put in a few tacks, but as the clear water narrowed, I had to switch on the engine. I couldn't help thinking of the matchsticks beneath my feet, the bolts shaking loose, and then the bracket breaking free, spinning round with the prop and gouging out a hole in the hull.

I called Conan. He said it would be another hour or two before the tide reached his uncle's boat and he could set off.

So I gilled about, up and down the strait to the east of Gabhla. Dusk settled over the deserted waters and the deserted islands. The earth stilled. The wind dropped a little and I toyed with the idea of anchoring for the night off Gabhla, but the forecast was for a force nine. The waters looked oily in the thickening darkness – the unfriendly tone which the sea gives off pre-storm.

Suddenly a breech – grey body rubber-piping up out of the water, blowhole and meaty fin, and cigar-shaped snout. Bottle-nose dolphin. Then another off to port. The two surged ahead and crossed off the bows. I flicked on the autohelm and went forward to watch them from the foredeck. There were four now. They were slower than common dolphins, and bulkier – but still skittish. They rode the bow-wave in pairs, diving with a flick of the tail that sent spray up over the deck and into my face. I found myself grinning. A fisherman friend had once told me that whistling attracts dolphins. So I whistled, and they stayed – veering off, sounding, and then reappearing with their fins in unison, weaving around the bows.

I called Conan again. No answer. Was he on his way? The wind had come in once more, and had built quickly. It was now more than thirty knots. At my reduced speed, it kept blowing the bow off its course. I'd wanted to avoid doing so, but I now upped the throttle. There was a moment when a metallic rattling sent me reaching to cut the engine. But it was just the kettle, jiggling on its gimballed hob.

Night was settling in. I could see the flashing green and red navigation lights in the channel. But no sign of Conan, no text or call. I had the fanciful notion that the dolphins were there to guide me in. They were still at the bows, and would lead me in, surely. I pushed into the channel entrance, and there it was – a red and green pathway to shelter. Why not give it a go?

A noise overhead – and I could see the underside of a plane coming in to Donegal airport among the dunes, wobbling a little in the wind (the next day, I heard it had been blown off the runway as it landed). When I looked down again, I made out a small boat, unlit, invisible until it was almost upon me. Its hull was dancing a different tune to mine in those wind-whipped seas. I could make out Conan, standing in the bow in a black beanie. His uncle was bringing the boat in close in the almost-dark and our decks were way out of sync, but when Conan stepped across, it was with the ease of someone passing from one room into another, stretching out his hand, with a calm: 'How are yer?'

'Glad to see you!'

After that it was a blind slalom up the channel, Conan standing amidships, calling back his pilotage to me at the helm. 'Ignore those lights. Come in close to that port-hand buoy . . . that buoy's in completely the wrong place . . . the sand's shifted there, come round to starboard. There's a low cliff there and you must pass it close . . . Now head in.'

In the morning, we had a look at the prop bracket. We repacked my matchstick repair. Conan said there was a good yard on Lough

Foyle, a famous yard specializing in wooden boats; they could take a proper look at it before I headed to Scotland.

The weather came in fiercely that morning but there was a gap the next day. I took the chance and caught the last ferry to Tory Island.

16

OUT ON THE NORTH-WEST CORNER of Tory, off the north-west corner of Ireland, itself off Britain and the north-west corner of Europe and the great land mass of Eurasia, stands a hut. The cliffs drop sheer behind it and the sea stretches out beyond them, filled that day with a host of whitecaps. The wind was in a hurry to get ashore, dashing across the water, scouring the surface, soaring up the rock face – to fiddle with the granules of quartz at my feet. Of all the peripheral places I'd been to in the past months, this hut, on this island, was the most peripheral. It hardly felt like land at all.

My boots crunched up the last few feet of path. The door stuck for a moment in the jamb but, with a shove, peeled open to a musty smell of warmed plywood and age. Cobwebs softened the room's high corners. Flies buzzed in the casements. A table and chair stood beneath a large window and, through its single clouded pane, facing away from the wind, I could see the west end of Tory flatten to the shore, the gale-tossed sound and the distant mountains of Donegal. I spent a happy few hours in that hut, sitting before the window, reading and writing and gazing, and not thinking at all about boat things.

To my right – an old corner cupboard; behind its glass doors, the basic requirements of life in a hut, circa 1971: LUX soap flakes and a tin of pork luncheon meat, a teapot and kettle, a quiver of candles in a jug, a jar of Melba sauce, a half bottle of Hennessy brandy (not entirely empty), TCP, Floret insecticide, blue ink and pastel fixative.

For several decades, from the late 1950s, the hut was used as a summer studio by Derek Hill, the English artist. Hill first heard about Tory Island on a train from Dublin, when he fell into conversation with the island's lighthouse keeper. At the time, Hill lived in a leafy spot of mainland Donegal, in a rectory decorated with William Morris wallpaper, framed photos by Cecil Beaton and painted plates by Picasso. In the wardrobe were Dior jackets and snakeskin slippers. He also spent a good deal of time in England – a convivial bachelor's round of painting and visits to patrician friends, and painting the portraits of his patrician friends. But in the following years, he discovered solace here in this hut, which he took on a long lease, spending months each summer sleeping on a fold-up bed, bringing from the lighthouse buckets of water and cold cuts from a leg of lamb he kept in the keepers' fridge.

'The happiest times of my entire life,' he recalled, 'were spent on Tory Island, up in my hut.'

Hill grew to love Tory's people (the hundred and fifty or so who still live there) and its landscape. He painted each with the same dedication. He found here something profound and rare, an island quality that distilled everything to its essence. He never gave up his rounds of visits in England, but over the years came to see days spent anywhere else as days not spent on Tory.

As a realist painter in the abstract expressionist 1950s and 1960s, Derek Hill occupied a somewhat marginal position in the art world. Initially he had the support of John Berger, Britain's most influential critic. Berger came to visit Hill on Tory. He was struck by its isolation, likening the islanders to 'survivors huddled in the stern of an open boat'. He wrote a laudatory note for an exhibition of Hill's in Dublin. In 1961, when the Whitechapel Gallery proposed a Derek

Hill retrospective, Berger agreed to write a longer essay. Then he changed his mind. His position as champion of abstract art would be undermined by enthusiasm for such a painter. To Hill, it was a betrayal, and he was devastated.

On the hut's walls were pinned a handful of sun-faded prints of Hill's Tory Island paintings – the Tau cross above the harbour, the lighthouse, panoramas of the island and its rocky shores. Even in reproduction, I could see their rough, earthy quality – heavy skies, hard cliffs, a sense of the moment, and the sort of light that changes in an instant. They project an unspecified longing: I looked at them each for some time, filled with the same longing. Hill's biographer, Bruce Arnold, wrote of Hill's 'haunting and evocative creative spirituality'.

Hill's work also has the mark of all true landscape painting – an instinctive sense of line, the simple shape that a cliff makes against the sea, or a ridge against the sky. It's always puzzled me why one painter's line looks right and another's wrong. Topography, after all, is the result of random forces, haphazard accretions and weatherings and erosions played out over geological time. The resulting shape should be random too – but it's not. In its irregularity, landscape conceals an integrity, an innate harmony which is apparent only when you see it rendered carelessly. Like music, the line of the land speaks to our recognition of a deep patterning principle, one that operates far beyond the capacity to explain it.

Tory Island was central to Hill, a lodestar in his sociable and lonely existence. He is remembered with affection by the islanders. 'He pierced his heart for the love of Tory,' said one. 'He always carried a powerful smile that would reach you walking towards him even if you were hundreds of yards away.' With his encouragement, a group of islanders became artists; their work has been exhibited in Dublin, Paris and New York. James Dixon already painted, and the story goes that one day he saw Hill at work, leaned over his shoulder and said: 'I could do better 'n that.' Derek Hill gave him materials. Dixon was used to bits of old cardboard and wood, so was glad of the paint and paper, but he told Hill he preferred his own brushes, which he made from the tail of his donkey.

When he died in 2000, some of Hill's ashes were scattered on Tory – on the ground outside his hut. The cliffs, the ocean, the shoreline and its people had come to represent for him all that could not quite be touched on this earth. Asked once how he imagined death to be, what that otherworld might look like, Derek Hill said: 'Probably it will be like going on a trip to Tory Island.'

Tory Island – out on the fringe of the great western ocean, a stepping stone to the otherworld, potent with myth, and most of it malign. Seen from the mainland, or from the waters around it, the dramatic profile of Tory has always been the shape of danger, of piracy and ill deeds.

In prehistory, the island was the stronghold of the Fomorians, goat-headed giants with one hand, one foot and one eye, who inhabited Ireland long before the Irish. The principal enemy of Ireland's early settlers were the Fomorians. They fought dirty, had terrifying powers, and for a while ruled all Ireland from Tory. They were tyrants, demanding not only vast amounts of tribute but a proportion of all the children born each year.

The Fomorians crop up in the *Lebor Gabála Érenn* (the *Book of Invasions of Ireland*), that concoction of early texts and oral traditions that were gathered together in the eleventh century to establish a suitable genealogy for the Irish nation. The book begins with the Creation, runs through the stories of Adam and Eve, Noah and Japheth, involves a lot of sea-roving, fighting, and journeying to and from Scythia, Egypt and Iberia, follows wave upon wave of invaders to the Irish shore, and ends with the Sons of Mil arriving in south-west Ireland.

Among the first to study the text in detail was the French philologist H. d'Arbois de Jubainville. Despite its propagandist purpose, he discovered in it traces of earlier beliefs, of the pre-Christian gods and heroes, and, beyond them, evidence of an animism that predated the Irish pantheon: 'the earth and the sea and the forces of nature seem for a moment in the *Book of Invasions* more powerful than the gods'. He found too that alterations had been made in translation. Many of the heroic settlers were said to have reached Ireland from Spain – 'Hispania' in the Latin. But the Irish original does not have Spain but 'Mag Mór', the 'Great Plain' – and the Great Plain was not in Spain. It was the western ocean.

So behind the pseudo-history of the *Lebor Gabála*, with its emphasis on the Mediterranean as provenance, as source for Ireland's various settlers, are hints of an alternative myth of origin. The limitless expanse of water, out beyond the shoreline, where the sun dropped to the horizon, was the great cosmological arena of early Irish belief, the place where the physical world fused with the imaginary. It was the destination of the soul after death. But it was also the place of eternal youth, the Tír na nÓg, 'land of the young'; Tír na mBeo, 'land of the living'; and Tír n-Aill, the 'other world'.

The ocean was not just a place of the afterlife, but the before-life. Death proceeds from life but precedes it too – less of an end than a return to source. If the figures of the heroic age came from there, they brought with them something of the magic of the otherworld and the islands of the west. Tory Island had its place in that system – a real shape on the threshold of Mag Mór, a gatehouse or guardpost, an island of giants and gigantic imaginings.

*

I rented a room above the shop in West Town. It turned out to be several rooms, and I wandered from one to the other, unsure quite what to do in them. The sitting room alone was bigger than the boat. In the bedroom was a bed and in the bathroom was a bath, and I looked at each for some time before using them. I shoved a bundle of clothes into the washing machine and went to stand at the floor-to-ceiling window in the sitting room. It framed the tumult of the harbour and flexed in the gale, so that not just the water but the road beneath and the sky above all quivered. There was a knock on the door and two men came in with a length of 2×2. They jammed one end against the hearth and the other against the window. 'That'll stop the glass blowing in.' I used it to hang out my washing.

A large island off the coast of Tory. That was how a school-child here once responded when asked to describe Ireland. Self-contained, isolated, Tory's people have always lived in their own way, surrounded by hostile waters, by suspicious mainlanders, by story and traditions. It is the last Irish island to have its own king, a role that drew on that of the Brehons, the lawgivers of prehistory. The king of Tory stood in when there was no priest, dispensed the island's sacred clay and decided who should receive any wreckage that washed up on the island's shores.

I asked to see the current king and was directed up the hill to a bungalow which glowed mustard-yellow in the evening sun. Set into the ironwork of the gate was a sign: *Teach an Rí*, 'House of the King', and beside it, hand-painted:

Patsy Dan Rodgers
King of Tory
Celebrating 45 years as a
primitive artist

Patsy Dan appeared at the door, compact and smiling in a dark blue Breton cap. We walked over to the social club for a drink, and before we'd gone the fifty yards, we'd covered the island's early history and how the post of king was established by St Columba. 'It was he who appointed the first king – to keep the island's pirates at bay.'

At the bar sat the island nurse and her partner. No one else. The barman was polishing glasses, holding each one up to the light before putting them away. The barman was married to the king's daughter and they chatted for a while about family, and then we all chatted about the island and its people – but we seemed too few, too small a group in a hall built for crowds of dancers and singers and revellings.

King Patsy Dan said: 'There's some weather we have.'

I wasn't going to argue. 'What a summer!'

'That's one thing you can say about St Columba,' said Patsy Dan. 'He knew his way round the weather.'

I remembered Adomnán's *Life of Columba* being full of weather predictions. 'It seemed to give him power over his followers – his forecasting.'

'Well, prophecy was his business. He talked of horses that wouldn't need barley, that will stand by the door until you needed to use them. And now look – we have tractors!' Patsy Dan climbed off his stool. 'One moment!'

I heard the outside door bang closed behind him.

When he came back, he had six paintings, three under each arm. He laid them out on a banquette seat. There was a puffin and a boat, a half-decker with foremast and mizzen, and studies of the light-house by moonlight and at sunset.

'I do them very quickly,' he said.

One struck me in particular – a boat moving up the picture

diagonally, giving a palpable sense of sea-motion. I'd seen something similar in a picture by his fellow islander, James Dixon, his *Gypsy Moth Rounding Cape Horn*, and also, down in Kerry, in An File's picture *The Blasket King and the Frenchman*. In St Ives, Alfred Wallis had tinkered with boats and the plane of vision in the same way. And each of them men who knew from the business end the true nature of seafaring.

When I asked Patsy Dan about Balor's Fort, the great natural complex of cliffs and plateaux at the eastern end of the island, he shook his head. 'Not me, I'm not the man for that. You must speak to Anton Meehan.'

Quiet-spoken, solidly handsome, with eyes of a striking blue, Anton met me at the island's gallery, a couple of rooms in an old building near the harbour. As well as pictures on the damp walls, there was a ragtag collection of shore bounty – a deckchair from the *California*, famous for ignoring the flares of the *Titanic* and which – divine retribution? – later foundered on Tory's rocks. There was a bell from the *Wasp*, which went down in the sound with the loss of more than fifty lives. The boat held English bailiffs collecting arrears, so its wrecking was no surprise to anyone on Tory.

We left the gallery and walked east. Heavy rain was gusting in over the cliffs. Our coats were soon shiny, our hair lank and wild with wind. We followed the broad track between treeless bog. Where the turf was broken, it revealed a low scarp of black peat and Anton bent to crumble it between his fingers.

'A lot of people think the soil of Tory is holy, like holy water. Boats would come here specially to place some in their bows. If they saw a whale or something, they'd throw the soil and drive it away.' He cupped it in his hand. 'Last week someone called and asked for some. I collected it in a jar, and sent it across on the ferry.'

Anton's early life had followed the course of most islanders. He left school at fourteen and went to sea, fishing and potting the waters around the shore. But Derek Hill used to come to their house. 'I was quite shy then. I didn't speak much English. I must have been attracted by painting because, one day, I asked him about it. He said the painting life was really a very difficult life. I don't think that worried me at the time.'

Hill helped Anton get a scholarship to art school in Letterkenny. 'The teachers found it hard to teach me. I could read a little but could hardly write or spell.' He left after only eighteen months, and returned to Tory.

It was at about that time that Anton came across a book on the lives of the great painters. 'I read a few of those – Van Gogh and Turner and others. The thing about all of them was that none seemed very happy. They didn't have families. I chose to have a wife and children.'

'But you still paint?'

'Every day!' His work has been exhibited in New York and Paris.

The east of Tory rises to a series of spectacular heights. When I'd first seen Tory, sailing round the top of Owey Island, it was that end that drew my gaze. From close up, it's a dizzying complex of high towers and gullies and unreachable plateaux. Somewhere in there are the traces of an Iron Age fort – but Balor's fort is a mythical construction, built from suggestive topography and buttressed by imagination.

We passed the old harbour of Port-a-Doon, no more than a narrow inlet between steep rocks. Storm seas broke green into it and drove up over the shingle. There was breaking water on the other shore too, which at this point was just yards away. A narrow strip of land was all that came between Balor's crags and the bulk of the island.

Up the first sheep-cropped slope were the ramparts of the Iron Age fort. Above that, the land grew thin, the wind grew fierce and a series of edges brought violent updrafts. The grass gave way to a stony surface and bedrock. As we climbed, so the ground narrowed, until we found ourselves on a projecting finger of land, sheer cliff on each side. We walked slowly, then crouched, then crawled out to where the point pushed out into space. On our stomachs, we inched on until there was nothing before us but void and a flat-topped pinnacle.

Far below us, to the west, the sea was a deep blue-green, sheltered from the gale by land that rose high above it. Invisible gusts were diving down from the tops, zephyrs which dented the water below and fanned out as shifting patches of white. Stands of spray rose thirty or forty feet and scooted off in a zigzagging dance.

Anton stretched out his arm. He was pointing in the other direction, at a cliff which pushed hundreds of yards out into the sea. It appeared to exist only in two dimensions, a rocky wafer rising edge-up from the sea. The more you looked at it, the more improbable it became.

Anton leaned in towards me. I could see his mouth opening, but the wind swallowed his words: 'Prison . . . daughter . . . Balor . . . Balor . . .'

I pieced the story together later.

Balor of the Evil Eye, Balor of the Mighty Blows, leader of the Fomorians, bogeyman of the Donegal coast, terror of Ulster, scourge of all Ireland!

Anyone who fell under the gaze of Balor's single eye was killed instantly. Among his own people, he kept it closed, wrapped in seven veils. In battle, it was a weapon. Using a specially polished ring, four men hoisted the eyelid's veils, one by one. At the first, ferns started to wither, at the second, grass glowed red, with the third, trees became affected and their boughs and branches began to smoulder, and so on until the land was a continuous blaze.

Balor himself lived in the shadow of an evil fate. A prophecy had revealed that he would be killed by his own grandson. So he kept his only daughter, Eithne, where no man could reach her – here on Tory, among the pinnacles that stretched out from these cliffs. One day Balor came from Tory and stole a cow from the mainland. (What trouble might have been avoided in old Ireland if people had not coveted others' cattle!) The cow's rescuer reached Tory disguised as a woman, and as a woman he managed to slip into Balor's Fort. Once there, he seduced the imprisoned Eithne. She had three sons. Two were killed by Balor, but the third managed to escape with the help of Manannán, God of the Sea. Lugh was the name of the boy, and he was trained up to be skilled in many crafts.

In time Lugh rallied the men of Ireland behind him to attack Balor, his own grandfather. Balor ordered his eye to be opened. But Lugh hurled a thunderbolt at him and it pierced his eye and came out of the back of his head, spattering his men with the poisoned eye-stuff.

Balor said to Lugh: Behead me now, but what I ask of you is this: place my head on your own so my power might continue through you. But when Lugh sliced off Balor's head, he did not do as he was asked, but placed it on a pillar, where it still leaked its evil, so he jammed it in the fork of a hazel tree.

Mythologists have examined the story of Balor and discovered in it the universal story of vegetative regeneration. The American folklorist Alexander Krappe linked it to old Breton cycles. Alan Ward took it further, finding parallels in Vedic stories and Indo-European narratives, equating Balor with the drought god who stifles natural growth, imprisoning it, while Lugh, the storm god, destroys the drought and restores the land to plenty. Such interpretations owe much to James Frazer and *The Golden Bough*, and the idea that myths are universal, essentially the same everywhere, like the human body. Others have linked Balor with the classical Cyclops, the race of primitive giants. Lugh's victory – like that of Odysseus – is the triumph, through cunning, of light and progress.

But the Balor myth has endured also because of here, because of the cliffs of eastern Tory. They have acted as a visual aid to the imaginative flights of all those who have lived and worked in the coastal regions of Donegal, who have potted and fished, and those untold generations who shuttled between the west coast of Ireland and the west coast of Scotland. For those others too, refugees from famine and oppression, who set off from Belfast to America, Tory Island was the last glimpse of the old world, and the view of Balor's impossible stronghold was what they took with them to the new world across the Atlantic.

17

BACK IN BUNBEG, I HAD a call from Conan, who'd piloted me in the other night. He said he had a few days off and could join me for the passage along the north coast. I said I'd be glad. Then his cousin Cormac Gillespie rang and asked if his son – also Cormac – could come along too. He'd been working in computers for years, but had signed up to work on a yacht in the Gulf of Mexico, and wanted experience.

So the next afternoon there was quite a send-off on Bunbeg quay: Conan's wife and their boy, and young Cormac's father and a couple of others from his family, all standing on the harbour wall and waving.

That evening we dropped anchor near the deserted island of Inishsirrer. We rowed ashore and fanned out to look around. The roofs of old buildings cut angles from the evening sky. No more than a dozen households had lived here. But by the end of the 1970s, there were none. The promise that had once attracted them, of an island existence made possible by a little farming, a little fishing, a little endeavour had died on them. It wasn't sustainable. These squat ruins are all that remain.

A broken door stood ajar. Inside the space was crossed by half-collapsed roof beams. Pennywort had sprung from the plaster; stands of hogweed had burst through gaps in the floorboards. In another house was a twelve-foot paddle and an upholstered chair and a collapsed box bed; in another, a herring cask stood with its hoops fallen like skirts to the floor. The interiors had a musty, fungal smell – the smell of abandonment, of material being reprocessed by armies of microbes. Season by season, these island houses were reverting to garden, the stuff of domestic life becoming compost.

I walked with Conan up along the western shore. His competence at sea gave him an easy, unflustered manner. Over the past few years, he'd been living aboard his boat with his young family while doing various marine jobs from Brittany to the Hebrides. Now he was back home studying for his master's ticket for ships of over 200 tons. In the failing light, we looked across a narrow strait to Gabhla – his own island of broken promises. When he'd come back here in his late twenties, after years at sea, he'd bought a piece of land on Gabhla. Others were beginning to spend summers there again, doing up the old houses. Conan saw an opportunity and set up a ferry service from Bunbeg. 'But there were those who didn't take kindly to a new ferry, if it wasn't them running it.' He was forced to quit.

I went up on deck early next morning to check the anchor. Dawn was a bright glow to the south of Bloody Foreland. Old storm swells were sweeping in around Inishsirrer, as they had been all night, rolling the boat as we slept. Now I could hear them ashore, probing the spaces between the boulders with their glugging.

The day unfolded in a spectacular display of crystalline light, all the brighter for the gales preceding it. A breeze picked up from the south and we sailed between two islands, into Keelasmore Sound and up along the eastern shore of Inishdooey. Sheer cliffs rose high above the mast. There were indentations, zawns and caves, and they all dropped far down into the water, so that, even close to, the depth sounder read eleven, twelve, fourteen metres. We couldn't anchor on such ground, and there looked nowhere to land. But at the top of the island was a scatter of rocks spread out beneath the cliffs in imitation of a beach.

I asked Conan if he'd take *Tsambika* while I went ashore. Young Cormac rowed me in. I jumped into calf-high water and swung him round so that he could get back out through the surf. I waved him off, and he nodded in response, his hands working hard at the paddles. He had the screen-paled complexion of a software expert, but he was also a Gillespie from Donegal, with generations of Lough Foyle pilots behind him. He knew how to handle a small boat. Soon he was alongside *Tsambika* and climbing aboard.

The swells surged up over the pebbles, chinking them together like billiard balls. They were not native stones but schists and sandstones and porphyrites driven from elsewhere, wet and polished smooth as agate. I climbed up from the beach, via a low cliff and out on to its thrift-pillowed top. Dusting down my knees, I set off across the soft ground. Stepping ashore on these islands always brought its own thrill of anticipation, like meeting someone new, or reading the first pages of a book. What would they be like? Would you grow to love them? Last night on Inishsirrer was all gloom and desertion. Inishdooey at once felt different.

There was no recent community to mourn, for one thing. No summer stock grazed its pasture. In its pathless expanse, the season was turning. Tall grasses stood dry and blond and in among them were the diaphanous capsules of yellow rattle, long emptied of seed. I put up six greylag geese from a pond and watched them fly south, shielding my eyes as they shrank to dots and swung round in a great circle. I heard water ahead – and was suddenly looking down into a shadowy trench of shingle and kelp. The sound of waves breaking funnelled along the gully.

Long ago, when magic was still on tap for the righteous, Saint Dubhthach and Saint Columba had a competition. They both wanted the challenge of ministering to Tory Island, so they stood beside each other on the mainland, and each saint swung his crozier with huge force. Columba's landed on Tory, some five miles off. Dubhthach could only manage a couple of miles and his reached here, on Inishdooey.

The walls of Dubhthach's monastery were still discernible. I stepped inside, with an immediate awareness of hallowed ground. Lumps of quartzite dotted the stonework. Above the east window, the stones of the lintel fanned out like a sunrise. The opening itself was little wider than a slit, designed to celebrate the daily wonder of light returning, by capturing so little of it.

Back home in the UK, a service was being held that morning for a friend who had died too soon and too quickly. I thought of everyone gathering in the Devon graveyard, filing into church, gathering in the pews. I remained in the old chapel for what I imagined its duration, grass and nettles up to my knee, roof open to the sky. Then I headed up over the ridge again.

Out on the high cliff, I lay face down to look down over the rim. A pool was spread out far below, enclosed in an almost complete circle of sheer rock. The circle was perforated at sea level by several low arches, and the sun shone through these arches, filling the sea inside with a brilliant green translucence. Rays of light penetrated the top layer of water, flickering beneath it like fish backs. It was a minor miracle, an everyday occurrence that went on happening even though there was no one to see it; the sort of prospect that once prompted those solitaries living in such places to write:

> Delightful I think it to be in the bosom of an isle
> On the crest of a rock
> That I may look there on the manifold
> face of the sea.

From across all the golden centuries of Irish letters, few lines now have the raw impact of the verses known as the early 'nature poems'. What survives of them – a fraction, probably – suggests a tradition that began in its written form in about the eighth century. They were unlike anything else in medieval literature. What their authors drew on was what was normally sublimated to the collective or the divine, something that out here on the rocky fringes of the world was often in full flight: the individual sensibility. Their subject was the natural world – so familiar, so quotidian, it was rarely considered worth writing about. But the verses' ease and confidence suggest that it had been expressed for a long time.

'Comparing these poems with the medieval European lyric,' wrote the scholar K. H. Jackson, who anthologized them, 'is like comparing the emotions of an imaginative adolescent who has just grown to realize the beauty of nature with those of an old man who has been familiar with it for a lifetime.' Seamus Heaney sensed in them the 'tang and clarity of a pristine world full of woods and water and birdsong'. He marvelled at the 'little jabs of delight in the elemental' noting that, in their distinctiveness, they make 'a spring-water music out of certain feelings in a way unmatched in any other European language'.

The poems were the work of Irish monks, part-Christian in spirit and part-pagan, who pursued their devotions in the remotest of places, like here on Inishdooey. Some of the works were formal, or merged into longer cycles of story – in *Buile Suibhne* or *Immram Brain*. Others were more direct – simple observations, for instance, of the sounds heard outside a hermit's hut:

The voice of the wind against the branchy wood
Grey with cloud;
Cascades of the river,
The swan's song, lovely music.

Or of summer:

The smooth sea flows,
Season when the ocean falls asleep;
Flowers cover the world.

Or of a cherished island:

Gleaning of purple lichen on its rocks,
Grass without blemish on its slopes,
A sheltering cloak over its crags;
Gambolling of fawns, trout leaping.

From the late nineteenth century onwards, the nature poems were rediscovered, translated and celebrated by Celticists, along with every other surviving word of early Irish. In 1911, Kuno Meyer defined them by their modest intent: 'To seek out and watch and love Nature, in its tiniest phenomena as in its grandest.' And he was not shy in declaring their significance: 'these poems occupy a unique position in the history of the world'.

Like Japanese *haiku* and *tanka*, the Irish poems achieve their effect through immediacy. The act of recording what makes up a particular moment – birdsong, trees, sun and clouds – is more than just an assembling of scenic elements. It's a way of saying something timeless and urgent: do away with the not-here, this is what there is, the simple intensity of being alive:

> The woodland thicket overtops me,
> the blackbird sings me a lay, praise I will not conceal:
> above my lined little book
> the trilling of birds sings to me.

Plain statement gives the verse the crisp purity of snow. 'Its makers,' thought another of its scholarly advocates, Gerard Murphy, 'possessed a secret of keeping the reader's mind alert and happy, which they seem to have learnt from the story-tellers of the Old Irish period. It consisted in never saying more than was necessary, in passing rapidly over the abstract and discursive.'

Similar nature poems, of the same period, are found in Welsh. But one thing that distinguishes the Irish ones is their treatment of the sea – 'a genuine delight mingled with terror'. It is the view of people for whom the sea was a part of everyday life, a coastal or island view of what brought pilgrims and supplies, storms and raiding Norsemen, and which offered the physical backdrop to prayer and contemplation. 'The ocean is full, the sea is in flood / Lovely is the home of ships.'

The same focused attention can be found in marginalia of the period. While the monks dutifully transcribed Latin text from one manuscript to another, they often jotted down their thoughts, in Irish, on the edge of the page. In themselves they are hardly revelations, but in the context of their time, their confessional tone is remarkable. On one manuscript from the early ninth century – Cassiodorus's commentary on the *Psalms* – is a series of scribblings that offer an almost filmic glimpse of an Irish scribe, a sentient individual. He complains about the vellum. One folio is too 'hairy', another too 'bald'. He is feeling slow: 'My brain is heavy today. I don't know what the matter is with me.' The scriptorium he works in is chilly and gloomy: 'It's cold today. It's only natural. It's winter.'

'Welcome to us is the season coming next. We won't hide what it is – it is summer.'

The changing seasons produced some of the most powerful of the Irish nature poems. To celebrate the hinge-points of the year were the two great annual festivals – Bealtaine and Samhain. At the beginning of November, Samhain marked the moment when the harvest was all done, the fruits gathered and the meat ready for salting. But the Irish winter poems go far beyond the practical. In their unadorned details, they manage to suggest not only deep threat but also the sensation of the coming season, in all its wild beauty. It's hard to read such lines without shivering:

> My tidings for you: the stag bellows,
> Winter snows, summer has gone.
>
> Wind high and cold, low the sun,
> Short his course, sea running high.
>
> Deep-red the bracken, its shape all gone –
> The wild goose has raised his wonted cry.
>
> Cold has caught the wings of birds,
> Season of ice – these are my tidings.

I looked north, across the water, towards Scotland. The evenings were growing longer, the early mornings chillier. There was still a long way to go before the Summer Isles, and autumn was now waiting at the days' edges.

*

Back on board, we raised the sails. The wind had freshened; we made good progress. In the early afternoon Horn Head slid astern, a dark hulk of rock above a glittering sea. We entered Lough Swilly and found anchorage behind Lenan Head, where there was a small quay and little else. I rowed ashore and found a cove and swam out beyond the rocks. A crab boat was unloading at the jetty and a thirty-two-ton artic was backing up to load the catch. The *ping-ping-ping* of its reversing alarm sounded out across the water like some giant shore-feeding bird. Behind it on the harbour wall was daubed: FREE GAZA.

There was one more headland – Malin Head, the most northerly point of Ireland. We would reach it in the morning, then head down to Lough Foyle. I had calculated the tides. Back on board, I checked them. I'd made a mistake. We would need to weigh anchor much earlier than I'd thought.

'How much earlier?' asked Conan.

'Four a.m.?'

'Fine by me.'

That evening we lounged about in the cockpit. The late sun retained a little of the day's warmth. Cormac had cooked and he was telling us about his upcoming voyage in the Gulf of Mexico. 'I set up the whole thing online. I have no idea who these people even are.'

'If you can cook like that,' I said, finishing the last of his vegetable stew, 'you'll have no trouble making friends.'

Just a few hours later, leaving Cormac to sleep, Conan and I raised the anchor and slipped out to sea. The darkness was total. Black cloud above, black sea below. Coming out of the bay, the blaze of Fanad light filled the night: *Five flashes – pause – five flashes – pause* . . . I steered on it to clear the land, then came round to pick up a compass course for Dunaff Head. Within an hour or so, we began to make out shapes – the land a deeper shade of black in the blackness. The forecast had been for little wind – now there was plenty of it, twenty knots and more.

The chop coming up to Malin Head was unpleasant. The tide had stirred the seas into a nasty jumble of lumps and angles. I couldn't soften the impact by steering off their tops, because I couldn't see them – so the boat was being thrown around, and so was I. Conan was not. He stood in the companionway, the consummate mariner in a black beanie, staring ahead with one hand lightly placed on the coachroof. Occasionally he would turn to see me stumbling, or trying to steady the helm. We said little.

Day seeped into the sky, replacing the black with a gloom that wasn't so much light as a film of greyness smeared over the water and the clouds. In that grey, we rounded the apex of Ireland. Now we could loosen sheets. The motion changed. The boat settled to a steady heel and picked up speed and the seas came abeam, then off the quarter, reforming themselves into something regular and rhythmic. Cormac appeared, came up on deck to share the sailing.

The tide began to work in our favour, adding another knot over the ground. We took the inside passage through the Garvans – surf-surrounded rocks that looked grim in the heavy light. Now we raced along the shore. The slopes rose straight from the water, with steep facades of treeless green, and tops lost in the mist. There was something fjord-like in their scale, something vast and melancholy and Nordic. Silvery cords of run-off hung down their sides. Damp dripped from the hoods of our oilskins. The morning began as soggy endurance but as the hours passed, it transformed itself into something familiar – the wet and stoical pleasure of being at sea.

We spotted a ship on the horizon. It looked like it was carrying a clutch of whirligig toys ready for assembly – they were the towers and blades for giant wind turbines. Conan explained how he'd worked for some time on windfarm maintenance vessels. When he received his master's ticket, he might go back to it – but what he really wanted to do was to work in the sail cargo sector.

'There's not a whole lot going on right now, not yet – but when you think of the damage shipping does, using sail for freight begins to look like the future.' He trotted out some statistics. 'If the world's shipping sector was a country, it would be number six emitter of greenhouse gases. It produces two hundred times the amount of sulphur dioxide than all the world's cars put together. You'd think that sail might begin to find its place in the mix – if we still want to trade as we do. The wind's not going to run out.'

'Not if this summer's anything to go by.'

Towards midday we rounded Inishowen Head and entered Lough Foyle. Soon we were easing into the port of Greencastle, tying up alongside a ten-deep raft of potters and dayboats. Conan and Cormac gathered their kit and I walked with them up on to the quay. I wished Cormac luck in the Caribbean, thanked Conan for all his help. 'I couldn't have done it without you.'

'Ah, you'd have been fine.'

'Not coming into Bunbeg. I wouldn't have stood a chance.'

'That's true,' he chuckled.

Back on board, as I tidied up, I was aware of how cold and empty the boat felt. I missed them already.

I needed repairs. The prop-shaft bracket had held, somehow, but before crossing to Scotland it required proper attention. A stern cleat was loose; there were several other niggles.

Just above the harbour slipway stood a large shed and a sign which read in Gothic script: MCDONALD BOATS. Conan had mentioned the yard some days ago. I'd been hearing about the McDonalds all along the Donegal coast, and seeing their signature boats, the wooden clinker-built Drondheims.

The high double doors were open and a Cygnus 40 stood up on chocks; an old wooden Folkboat appeared further into the shadows. Otherwise there was the usual paraphernalia of boatyards – benches and engine-parts and hull-sections – but no one tending to them. The back office was covered in the same film of wood dust, the same scatter of boat bits as the workshop, with the addition of papers, and a desk, and the figure of Brian McDonald himself.

I moved an unopened parcel from the chair, and sat down opposite him. We chatted for a while, before I asked him about the work.

'Aye, that'll be no problem.' Brian accepted each item on my jobs list in the same quiet-spoken way. 'We'll take a look at that for you. That'll be OK.'

I watched him as he jotted it all down. I was struck by his fingers. They were both stout and delicate. They gripped the biro as if it was a chisel. Brian had been building boats here since the 1960s, when he joined his father and uncle as an apprentice. They had begun in the same way, taken on by their father, and his father the same, all the way back into the nineteenth century. In fact, McDonalds had been building boats in Greencastle since 1750. They had developed the Drondheim from Nordic inshore craft that first came in on the decks of cargo ships from Trondheim – hence the name.

Brian himself had never spent any time at sea, but his dedication to boatbuilding was absolute. 'I do take Sundays off, but I never had a holiday – at least not until a couple of years ago. I went to Rome. It was my first time out of the country.'

He'd been to Glasgow a few times, but that was to meet boatbuilders, and anyway, for those in Donegal, Glasgow hardly counted as 'out of the country'.

The sky cleared later. It was a lovely afternoon. Greencastle harbour was busier than any port I'd been in since Kerry. With a resonant hammering, new net-drums were being fixed to the beam trawler *Keriolet*. A half-decked crabber was pulled up on the slip; laid out along the wall beside it were rollers and brushes for antifouling, and a large bar of Galaxy and packets of Tayto Onion Rings for the antifoulers. A Belfast man was prepping the aluminium wheelhouse of his 1957 naval support-vessel; down below, in the stripped-out chaos, he showed me with some pride its two Rolls Royce engines, each one the size of a single bed. Astern of him lay a colourless hulk, slumped and beat, emitting from its side a parabola of water which slapped on the mud below.

I walked up along the lough. On the opposite shore lay the United Kingdom. After partition in 1921, the two sides could not agree who should control this piece of water. The Brits said it was theirs, the Irish said it wasn't, and the treaty failed to resolve it. And so it has remained – a legal non-place, where only the laws of the tide hold sway. I could see the ebb of it now, sliding out to sea, its force visible in fast-moving eddies and up-swellings, a great exhalation of water from deep inland. To the south, where the lough narrowed to estuary, the water was dropping along below Derry, beneath the Peace Bridge, exposing the banks of the River Foyle and its centuries of sediment. All around the vast lough – its forty miles of shoreline – shingle beaches were widening, wrack was settling on bare rock, cockles snapping closed and lugworm wriggling deeper into the mud – while just visible now to the south-east breeched the first whale-backs of sand.

Lough Foyle is still known in modern Irish as Loch Feabhail, and before that it was Loch Febuil. But long ago, before the *tomaidm*, or 'bursting forth' – the cataclysm that saw its pastures flooded – the area was Mag Febuil, the 'plain of Febuil'. An account of Mag Febuil survives. It comes in a brief and enigmatic text called the *Lough Foyle Colloquy*, dating to the high-point of early Irish literature, around the eighth century AD. The conversation is between Saint Columba and a young man he meets on the shores of Lough Foyle. Columba quizzes the youth about the lore of the site. One thing that Christian scripture had lacked, as it gathered in the souls of Europe, was the context of the local. The places of the Bible were far-off dusty towns, semi-desert; its struggles were those of pastoralists and wanderers labouring beneath a hot sun. Like St Patrick in the *Acallam na Senórach*, St Columba was gathering the area's *dinnseanchas*.

The tension of the encounter in the *Lough Foyle Colloquy* is the contrast between Columba's Christianity and the fantastic traditions of old Ireland. The man that Columba met is believed to have been Mongan, a figure who combined history and myth in one body. He was a real seventh-century king, but also a demi-god – his father was the great sea-deity, Manannán Mac Lir.

'Whence do you come, youth?' asks Columba.
'I come from lands of strange things, from lands of familiar things, so that I may learn from you the spot on which died, and the spot on which were born, knowledge and ignorance.'

At once Mongan is tilting the scene, reversing the roles of questioner and questioned. He knows Columba and his followers bring a new way of thinking.

Columba continues:

'A question. Whose was it formerly, this lough which we see?'
'I know that. It was yellow, it was flowery, it was green, it was

222

hilly; it was rich in mead, and strewn rushes, and silver, and chariots. I have grazed it when I was a stag; I have swum it when I was a salmon, when I was a seal; I have run upon it when I was a wolf; I have gone around it when I was a human.'

Therein lies all the mad poetry of the past – with its wonders, its fluidity and its identity-shifting. The sense emerges that Mongan is taunting Columba with the extravagance of his pagan life and of his imagination.

'And these islands to the west of us,' asks Columba, 'what is under them?'

'Not hard to answer: there are long-haired men with broad territories; there are fearsome greatly pregnant cows, whose lowing is musical; there are bovine oxen; there are equine horses; there are two-headed ones; there are three-headed ones – in Europe, in Asia, in lands of strange things, in a green land . . .'

'That is enough!' Columba commands. He then takes the youth aside. All night they talk 'about the heavenly and earthly mysteries'. When Columba returns to his followers in the morning, they gather round to hear what he's been told. But Columba holds up his hand. He is unwilling to relate a single word of what he has heard from the youth. It was just too potent, too subversive in its cosmic scope: 'It is better for mortals not to be informed of it.'

There is another story about Lough Foyle, from the same period or earlier – just as exhilarating in its strangeness. It begins in the antediluvian age, when the seabed was the great prairie of Mag Febuil and the land was ruled by King Febul. It is the opening section of the earliest of the otherworld voyage tales, the *Voyage of Bran*.

King Febul has a son called Bran. One day Bran is out walking when he catches the strains of music so beautiful that they send him into a deep sleep. When he opens his eyes, he sees a branch of silver hung with white blossom. He takes it to the house of his father, the king. A great gathering of nobles is underway and they are all in the great hall. A woman appears and sits on the floor. It was she who brought the branch with its silver twigs and its white blossom, and she who brought the music. She addresses Bran in fifty quatrains:

> A branch of the apple-tree from Emain
> I bring, like those one knows;
> Twigs of white silver are on it,
> Crystal brows with blossoms.
> There is a distant isle,
> Around which sea-horses glisten:
> A fair course against the white-swelling surge,
> Four feet uphold it.

For stanza after stanza, she describes the splendours of the island – the colours, the bucolic moods of its plains. On that island is no suffering and no deceit, sickness is unknown and there is no death. Golden horses and sheep of a heavenly blue graze its pastures. Nor, by any means, is it the only such island of wonders:

> There are thrice fifty distant isles
> In the ocean to the west of us;
> Larger than Erin twice
> Is each of them, or thrice.

In the *Voyage of Bran* are all the elements of the other *immrama* – the islands with their otherworldly features, the journey to a land of perfection or horror, the Christian gloss given the stories by those monks who first wrote them down. There is the same overall sense of a parallel world across the sea which is a distorted version of our own, and in which – it hints – is contained the answer to all mysteries, the quenching of all desires. It is not a place beyond death but one accessible to the living. And she gives the same exhortation as that given to St Brendan, the same plea to keep moving, the same reminder of the moral imperative to seek out the wonders of creation:

> Do not fall on a bed of sloth,
> Let not thy intoxication overcome thee,
> Begin a voyage across the clear sea . . .

The repairs took longer than expected. It was some time before Brian said the boat was ready. I settled up with him, bought victuals and planned the passage to Islay. At ten on a hazy morning, I climbed up the ladder of the harbour wall, untied my lines from the rings and climbed down again. I walked them out over the decks of the fishing boats. I spotted a figure crossing the green above with a familiar lopsided gait. It was Brian.

'You off, then?' he called down.

'Just leaving now!'

I could see him looking the boat over. His soft voice hardly carried: 'Well, good luck now! Good luck to you.'

I leaned down to push the engine into gear. The bow swung away to point out beyond the harbour. When I looked back, Brian was still there, watching my stern pull away from the quays. It was what McDonalds had been doing for generations – shaping boats, assembling them, fixing them, preparing them – then, like parents, watching them leave for the open water beyond.

18

AHEAD – PALE GREY SKY, pale grey sea. Astern, the slopes of Inishowen still sharp, shelving upwards. Yesterday there'd been a gorse fire up there. It had reduced the sun to a hazy orb, an orange half-floating in a brown soup of smoke; all afternoon it had covered Greencastle harbour with a sickly light. Now from the headland there rose a thin transparent spire, a pale trace of the fire.

I picked up a heading of 050° and peered into the gloom, looking for Scotland. The self-steering was dead; I'd clipped the arm on the tiller, pressed *auto* on the instruments and – *zilch*. The Windpilot too had developed a bias that I'd been unable to fix. So I was stuck, standing with the helm against my thigh, staring ahead.

The waters around me were a sunless slop, the sky a damp ceiling of cloud. The engine putt-putted beneath my feet and the mainsail hung idle overhead. Ireland shrank behind me, its dark profile fading behind the mist. I entered no man's land, and time itself seemed to enter a state of limbo.

There was movement at the edge of my sight. A fulmar swung in round the stern to come up alongside, slowing to my pace – *three wingbeats, glide . . . three beats, glide . . .* It managed to remain in the same place above the cockpit, at the same angle to my shoulder, as though we were engaged in a mid-air refuelling. *Three beats, glide . . .* I looked across at its squat body and thick neck and the black marking around its eye, and for an instant we locked gaze and I imagined

I shared something with it, something of its confidence and entitlement out here on the water. Then it skipped the glide and was off, banking round my bows and away again, shrinking over ashen seas.

I was a couple of hours out of Foyle when I spotted the distant outline. Islay! The four-hundred foot cliffs of the Oa. For a long time the cliffs sat on the horizon, growing no clearer. *Tsambika*'s bows split the surface of a flat sea, which was thick and lubricious, not like water at all. In places, sketchy lines separated ruffled areas from smooth. Although the lines were slender, they suggested movement below the hull, an immense agitation, one stirred not by the usual agency of wind but by the great body of water emptying out of the Irish Sea and the North Channel and the Sound of Jura, a suitably vast drain between two countries, between Ireland and Scotland.

But they're not two countries. The north and west of Ireland and the west of Scotland share similar history, language, ethnicity. A genetic marker – M222 – is found in males from Ireland and from south-west Scotland, and is believed to go back to one man who lived on the Inishowen peninsula about fifteen hundred years ago. The traditional view is that the Scotti were an Irish tribe who, in the post-Roman centuries, moved north into Scotland to establish the kingdom of Dal Riada. Adomnán mentions the early movement of settlers from Antrim into Argyll. Now the suggestion – in the contrarian way of scholarship – is that the migration might have gone in the opposite direction, that Gaelic-speaking groups moved south to Ireland. Archaeologists compare the brooches, the ring forts, the *raths* and the *cashels*. Toponymists pick apart the place names, arguing over their Goidelic and Brythonic roots. None of them has much to go on.

Comparable too is the geology. The 'Dalradian Supergroup' is not a Glaswegian rock band but a band of rock, 'a metasedimentary and igneous rock succession that was deposited on the eastern margin of Laurentia between the late Neoproterozoic and Early Cambrian'. Right. It makes up a large part of the defining features of both Ireland and western Scotland, the same mountains, the same high sea-cliffs, the same curiosities (Giant's Causeway in Antrim, Fingal's Cave off Mull), the same peaks and open moor, the same islets and reefs, the same sense of a primal clash between rock and ocean. And it is that backdrop – the gritty topography, the fractured shoreline, that has helped sustain the coastline's metaphysics, helped generate the wilder projections of outsiders and inhabitants alike, phantom islands from beyond its headlands, otherworlds from beneath its turf.

In Ireland, they are *sídhe*, in Scotland, *sìth* – each is pronounced the same: '*shee*'. The fairy populations share a folk DNA, as the human ones do. The definition of the Scottish folklorist John Gregorson Campbell covers them both: 'The Fairies, according to the Scoto-Celtic belief, are a race of beings, the counterparts of mankind in person, occupations and pleasures, but unsubstantial and unreal, ordinarily invisible, noiseless in their motions, and having their dwellings underground, in hills and green mounds of rock or earth.'

In a piece published in the *Scots Observer* in 1899, W. B. Yeats noted how prevalent the 'fairy belief' remained in both countries. Over the years, though, the *sídhe* and the *sìth* had diverged. The Irish ones, he claimed, were much better, or at least rather nicer: 'For their gay and graceful doings you must go to Ireland, for their deeds of terror to Scotland.' He cited the Scottish tale of a child cutting turf. The child is struggling, until a hand is pushed up out of the bog with a sharp knife. The child's brothers respond by slicing off the hand with the knife. Yeats claimed that would never happen in Ireland, where 'there is something of timid affection between men and spirits'. In Scotland, he claimed, an innate mistrust existed of that unseen world: 'You have made the Darkness your enemy . . . you have discovered the fairies to be pagan and wicked. You would like to have them all before the magistrate.'

As for islands, the western coast of Scotland frays into many more actual islands than that of Ireland, but fewer imaginary ones. One tale that is found, though, in several versions in the Hebrides begins with a man in a boat, lost in fog. He comes across an unknown island, and landing on it, he meets a woman. He stays with her, they have children. After many years on the island, he goes back to his former life. One day when he is old and blind, the man is brought a fish that no one can identify. Fingering it, he recognizes its shape. He asks to be taken out to the waters where it was caught, and there is the island. He is put ashore, and he and the island disappear.

It is a simple and beautiful story, and one that challenges Yeats's partisan point. Many aspects of fairy belief do not stand up to any kind of literal scrutiny: little people living in holes in the ground, stealing the substance of people, or changing into animals. But behind them lies a more persistent thought – common not just to the closely related fairies of Ireland and Scotland but to belief worldwide: that other versions of our own lives exist. They could be in the past, in the future, or in the never-never. They might be over the horizon, or on an imaginary island. But at one time or another, we will go looking for them. Perhaps we're always looking.

At midday, a breeze began to fill in from the north-west. It appeared at first as furred patches on the surface of the water. Within half an hour, the patches had joined up. There were short little waves. I had the main up and the genoa pulled out and they were already full when a sudden gust shoved the mast over. The boat came alive. The tiller tugged at my arm. I freed off the mainsheet and propped one boot on the leeward seat. It was a half-standing, half-sitting position that kept me more or less upright while the hull tilted beneath me. With the autopilot down, I kept that position for the next three and a half hours.

The sky darkened. The water below it became tussocky. Looking over my shoulder, I felt the weight of the breeze on my face and saw the wave-crests flash in the gloom. I always think that 'white horses' is a description first coined from the land; at sea, they look vulpine, a pack of pale predators cantering across the open plain. There was a suddenness in the wind's strength that was alarming. At what point would it stop increasing? Twelve miles stood now between me and Islay. *Tsambika* began climbing each of the seas, then lurching down them. The wind grew stronger. Water began to break over the bow. Beyond the guardrail, away from the weather, I watched the waves roll through, following their foam-streaked backs, and as I watched there came a moment when I suddenly felt an immense calm, when the boat and the weather and the water fused into one.

Up ahead, the cliffs of the Oa were now more distinct. High on their summit was the stubby monument to the 160 US servicemen who drowned in these waters in February 1918. Their troop carrier *Tuscania* was torpedoed. Just eight months later, another US troop carrier went down nearby; 400 died. Coming up to the headland, the seas became wilder, and then I was in the lee of the cliffs and they settled. The wind remained fierce and I raced along the shores of the Oa. All was rock and heather and short moor grass, and it was hard, looking at it, to think of that many people even alive.

The approach to Port Ellen was straightforward enough. A reef or two to avoid. The wind blew hard off the land. I wound in the genoa and bundled the main. I slid into a pontoon berth and secured the lines. Stepping on to the pontoon, I felt like a newborn foal, legs jellying about on the firm ground. I stumbled into Port Ellen, and made for the hotel bar.

In the *immrama* of Bran and Brendan, they go to an island of sheep, an island of strong men and ripe fruit, an island of women and easy love, an island of laughter and joy. They do not go to a whisky island. Islay is a whisky island. I stood at the bar and looked at the backlit mirror behind it and its sea of orange bottles. Like the waters I'd just left, they were moving. Beneath them the glass shelves rippled and shifted while the labels flicked like flags in the wind. My body wasn't ready to abandon the motion of the passage. But which to choose? Lagavulin, Laphraoig, Kilchoman, Eight-year-old, Ten-year-old, Twelve-year-old, Single malt, Cask, Reserve, Heavily Peated, Smokehead, The Classic Laddie . . .

The couple next to me were already experienced navigators of these peaty waters. They were from Virginia. They had come to the Scottish islands because of the whisky, and to Islay because it was the whiskiest island of all.

'Try the Kilchoman – that's a beauty. We done three distilleries today, got another three tomorrow. This island's something, I tell you. Practically *rains* whisky.'

Perhaps it was arriving in a new country, or an awareness of the miles still ahead, but the next morning I was taken over by a strong urge to clean and fix things. I scrubbed the decks, oiled the chrome, polished the cooker and all the brass. I ordered a new deck-plug for the self-steering. I tackled a problem with the pump. I drew the last of the fresh water, poured some vinegar down the intake to sterilize it, and filled it again. I got it into my head that fresh water might also have found its way into the fuel tank – a classic cause of engine failure at sea. For some time, I fought with the sump valve, lying on the cockpit sole to lean in upside down to try and loosen it. It didn't loosen. I drained the filter instead.

I am not naturally practical. It's always a surprise to me to feel the weight of a tool in my hand, still more so when it is put to any effective use. In Robert Pirsig's *Zen and the Art of Motorcycle Maintenance*, I was the 'romantic' Sutherland on the road trip, not the 'classical' narrator, who disapproved of Sutherland's ineptitude and considered the regular adjusting of his bike's valves a moral duty. My whole journey so far had been an exercise in Pirsig's dualism. Instinctively, I was drawn to the books on the saloon shelf, to loafing about with them on my bunk or in the cockpit, reading or jotting down stuff, looking and thinking. I resented the need to pull out the tool box and apply its contents. But there was always something. Now I saw it all differently. Running repairs were an essential part of the process. The route to those shimmering islands offshore was closed off if the engine was dodgy, if the anchor didn't run out smoothly, if the self-furler was jammed. I could do nothing about the weather or the shape of the coast, but it was only through things not breaking, and being fixed if they did, that I had a chance of getting anywhere.

Another gale was forecast. Through the course of that tinkering day, several boats arrived for shelter. A tubby old motor launch pulled in next to me on the pontoon. I took the lines from a woman at the rail and a well-clipped head leaned out of the wheelhouse. 'Thank you!' he called. I saw him later, coming out on deck in a boiler-suit, wiping his spanners down with oil.

'Diaphragm stuck on the bilge pump,' he said.

'There's always something,' I said, suddenly all *au-fait* with such things.

He used to be in the navy. 'You'd be surprised how much those naval ships needed fixing. We'd be happy if we put to sea with eighty per cent of stuff working.'

Somehow that made me feel a lot better.

That evening, thinking of the task still ahead, I pulled out my old copy of Frank Fraser Darling's *Island Farm*. There on the cover was the familiar image: the view looking north-east from Tigh an Quay along the cobblestone pier, then the narrow straits and the mainland around Achiltibuie, treeless and smooth, and broken only by the peak of Cùl Mòr. The same view was reproduced in the book's frontispiece, in an etching by G. C. Leslie, and again on a plate inserted into the text painted by the artist William Daniell in 1815. Frank and his wife Bobbie had one of those Daniell prints when they lived on the Summer Isles. They hung it to face the view itself, 'providing us with a working drawing for our restoration'. I had found the quay idly reproduced in several sketches in my own research notebooks, sketches I'd forgotten even making. I remember Bridget looking at the front cover – the quay, the mountain, the water between – and saying it looked like something from a dream.

What was striking about those pictures, and had become more so as I worked north towards the Summer Isles, was how placid they looked. Frank's photograph was taken on one of those Highland days – rare and unforgettable – when the cloud is high, the air is still and the water is glassy. When William Daniell left London for Scotland in May of 1815, he was aware of how difficult the west coast would be to travel to and paint. But the summer of 1815 turned out to be exceptional – week after week of settled conditions. He covered the whole of the west coast, went round the top, worked down to Dundee, and produced from it 139 prints.

And my summer? Mixed, in a word. Since May the storms had been queuing up in the wings, an endless troupe of gales waiting to come on stage and perform their little routine. The jet stream had been strong, the North Atlantic Oscillation in positive territory, and the surface air in a state of almost constant agitation. It left a sense of unease. Wind always suggests change, and big winds suggest big change. Constant exposure to them out here in the west had fed into that planetary anxiety, the anxiety of our age – that the whole system was now more charged, poised on the edge of uncontrolled violence.

What William Daniell didn't know as he sketched the Summer Isles in those sunny weeks of 1815 was what was brewing in the upper atmosphere. That April, in Indonesia, Mount Tambora had erupted. It had filled the air with dust and the dust was already spreading westwards, cutting out the sun as it went and throwing the Eurasian land mass into a chilly gloom; 1816 became known as 'the year without a summer'. Europe shivered beneath thick grey cloud, crops failed to ripen, the harvest was wrecked and hundreds of thousands of people died.

Now it was excess heat that was swilling around in the atmosphere, speeding through the conduits of global energy, moving from the tropics to the poles and spun into ever deeper vortices by the Coriolis effect, and driven eastwards. Surface winds were projected to increase even further along these northern shores.

And it made the Summer Isles, that version of them in the fair-weather photo, look ever more distant.

I was woken that night by pea gravel flung on the deck. *Hail.* I lay for a while listening to it, to the gusts behind it and the squeak of fenders and the slop of water. I must have dozed a little, because a sudden huge gust woke me. I pulled on oilskins and boots and went up. My warps were tight, *Tsambika*'s bows just inches from the end of the pontoon. I heaved on the spring to set her back. I tweaked the others. When I looked up, I saw a strange thing. All the other boats were being tended in the same way. The same change in sound had brought crews from their berths and we were all there in the dawn light, in the same foul-weather gear. And there were smiles from beneath the hoods, and thumbs ups. I ran out another stern line. I had one last look, then went below, peeled off my wet waterproofs and crawled back into my sleeping bag.

By afternoon, the gale had gone through. I left the other boats in the pontoon, and headed on.

A mile or two out of Port Ellen, a squall hit me with such ferocity that I lost my nerve. I had intended heading north-west, squeezing through the Sound of Islay, anchoring for the night in Loch Tarbert, on the west coast of Jura, before pushing on up towards Oban. It was exposed and remote; plan B was a much easier route up the eastern shore of Jura. So, plan B.

The squall had come up astern – a curtain of rain with a hem of spray, sweeping across the water. In the moment before it reached the boat, a *hisss* . . . Then – frantic flapping, a fifty-degree wind shift, downdraughts, and a gybe which might have been catastrophic had I not had the mainsheet in tight. I had been watching the shoreline of Islay and the island of Texa and the distillery: LAGAVULIN writ large on the side of the maltings. Now that all vanished – first behind bars of rain, then inside a featureless maelstrom of wet cloud. The boat was racing blind. I was heading too far north but could do little about it. I didn't want to gybe again until it had gone through. Rain was pouring down my face. I couldn't wipe my eyes as I had the genoa sheet in one hand, with a couple of turns round the winch, and the mainsheet in the other, and the helm between my legs. I felt I was playing some crazed colt on a lunging rein.

For five minutes, the squall continued. Then it eased. The rain was running off the boom and the noise was falling away. I cleated the genoa and the main and was checking for damage when it came again – a blast of wind. The boat stumbled, dipping the lee rail. I had to free the sails fast to avoid us being knocked down.

But that was all. It was over. The wind dropped, the sun came out, the water sparkled and I pointed the bows back towards McArthur's Head and the Sound of Islay. I forgot about plan B. Such are the fickle extremes of single-handed sailing.

McArthur's Head rose like a gatehouse at the sound's entrance. High above it, the bare hills shone luminous green. Areas of brown fern broke up the green and above them both, in the regions between drifting clouds, a patch of wet scree flashed in the sunlight. I felt able – with *Tsambika* beneath my feet – to do anything.

The land narrowed. The twin shores of Islay and Jura were funnelling me between them. I sailed over the submarine gorge that divides the islands. The wind was dying. I was aware that my progress through the water was slow compared to the way the lighthouse was rushing past. The tide was running in my favour – and running fast. The water on each side of the hull was swirling, a mass of mini Vesuviuses erupting from the depths. The bows were being pushed this way and that. I put on the engine to gain some steerage and, with the land hurrying astern, with the rocks and the beaches, the willow scrub, the treed grandeur of Dunlossit, the ferry slip and lifeboat, I rode that tidal gush for its full eleven miles.

After the narrows, I was spewed out into open waters. The twin tops of Colonsay lay ahead, the lower slopes pale with mist. Further north, some thirty miles off, ran the grey suggestion of the Ross of Mull. With the Paps of Jura at my shoulder and the island's northern peaks appearing, there was a new sense of enclosure, but on a wholly different scale. Here was the real start of the Hebrides. It was like emerging from a high-sided alley in a medieval town to find yourself in a famous square, blinking at it all.

I motor-sailed up the shore of Jura and into Loch Tarbert. It was early evening, but the light was still strong. I picked an anchorage on the north of the loch, sheltered by a row of skerries to seaward. I could see the rocks, and between them the rounded backs of swells and surf as they broke. But here inside, the water was barely troubled.

On the skyline above the beach appeared a lone form. I picked it out in the binoculars. Head and horns, four legs, shaggy pelt – a wild goat. Three more followed it over the ridge. Jura is twenty-seven miles long but has no more than 200 human residents. Its feral goats outnumber them by more than two to one (and red deer outnumber the goats by ten to one). They dropped down towards the beach, crossing the stripes of shingle in single file. There was something military in their progress, as if they were on an important mission.

I let the anchor go in four metres of water and waited for the boat to fall back towards the beach. I paid out fifteen, twenty metres of chain, then added three more before making it off. Going aft, I stood in the cockpit and picked up a couple of landmarks – a foreshore rock below a skyline peak, a V on the ridge with a large patch of weed on the beach. I waited for the boat to settle against the marks, then gave the engine a kick of reverse to dig in the anchor. I checked the marks again – no movement, no dragging.

Bending to pull the engine stop, I was suddenly struck by silence. It was a silence that stretched out across the miles of moorland and water. I felt as if the whole scene was a vast bubble of perfect trans-parency. Here inside it, every little sound was amplified, magnified, intensified. I was acutely aware of the tickle of water on the hull, the fibrous creak of the mainsheet as the boom swung, a halyard rubbing the mast, and, from the skerries, the distant brush of surf.

Then suddenly – *screech*. A herring gull dived on a flying heron. It came in again and again, ducking and weaving around the larger bird. Its cries echoed off the cliffs. The heron was unbothered, continuing its slow-motion wingbeat. Then at last it gave a squawk, but more from pique than aggression.

I cooked rice and vegetables and ate out in the cockpit. I watched the sun drop from its bank of cloud. The boat filled with honey-coloured light. Ashore the beach and the low cliffs all shone. The story of the land's formation, told in million-year chapters, could be read in the evening's spotlight clarity – the glacial scourings, the tilted bedding planes. A mile or two to the south, across the water, was a scooped-out glen, and along the upper half of its slopes ran a line of the same yellowy sun. One of the Paps rose at the head of the glen. Its upper slopes looked pure rock, almost entirely free of vege-tation. Its peak was beautifully rounded. Pap means 'breast', and I thought of the story of the Irish Saint Colman, who found he was able to suckle two children:

> Two paps has Colman Ela,
> A pap of milk, a pap of honey;
> His right pap for fair Baithin,
> And his other pap for Ultan.

Something made me turn. A head in the water, just a few yards from the boat's quarter – two big eyes, whiskers, pale blotches on the neck. A grey seal. We looked at each other. It was hard not to read in its gaze a sense of surprise, an anthropomorphized reaction to this intrusive form in its bay: Who are you? *What* are you?

Seals were always *selkies* here, along the Atlantic coast. They led semi-human lives. They lived in their own world beneath the waves, one that mirrored that of people's above. They were capable of human speech and human emotions, and they had underwater houses with doors and windows, the same as us. Once a year, they gathered at a place off the Donegal coast and elected from their number a leader a *selkie* king. Sometimes they could be heard singing of the seal city underwater, its coral gardens and its mother-of-pearl facades. To those who heard the song, it had a hypnotic effect: a delicate air, and words which spoke of a place ten thousand times more beautiful than the sky. The *selkie* world was a version of the otherworld.

Selkies could make near-seamless appearances on land. Female *selkies* would slip out of their sealskins and take on the form of women and sleep with men. Male *selkies* would also take on human form and father children. They might take those children back to the sea, or they might leave them on land. You could never be sure which were the *selkie* children; they might be very good at swimming, or very small, or 'very sharp indeed at the learning . . . particularly at the Hebrew'. Then one day they'd just disappear. There were whole families in Ireland and Scotland who were known to have the seal blood in them, and the Scottish folklorist John Gregorson Campbell speaks of the *Clann 'ic Codrum nan ron* of North Uist, 'the MacCodrums of the seals', so named for their seal ancestry.

In the 1950s, David Thomson travelled in the west of Ireland and Scotland gathering *selkie* stories. In the tender account of his journeys, *The People of the Sea*, he tells of meeting a man of the road down in Kerry who was descended from seals. 'The seals are a class of a fairy,' explained the man. 'They come out of the north of Ireland, from some place by the County Donegal.' He then told Thomson about a boy who, collecting kelp one day, stabbed a seal. The boy watched as it turned into a red-headed man and ran away. Years later, when the boy was a man, he was fishing near Tory Island. When he went ashore, he saw that red-headed man, and the man said 'thank you' to the boy for what he'd done years earlier. He'd been freed from his seal-state by the stabbing.

Thomson not only recorded the habits of *selkies* and their place in the world, but also the relish with which their antics were told. The *selkies* could be malicious or a threat, but they were also characters, recalled like any old-time village eccentric. He remembered one man in north Mayo telling a *selkie* story: 'Do you remember the seal we met outside chapel? You remember how it was walking like any dog.' He said that someone hitched it up to a cart and put it in a hay shed and it spoilt the hay – no cow would touch it. It was Finoola Finney who drove the seal, he recalled, and she was a girl who was up for 'any mad thing' – and the man laughed so much that for some time he was unable to finish his piece.

Thomson heard another account of a man travelling to the annual fair in Belmullet. He was late and all the *currachs* had already left to cross the estuary. So he sat on a rock, feeling sad. A seal came up and addressed him by name. The seal said he was also going to the fair. So the man jumped on his back and they swam out to cross the tide. They were joined by other seals, all going to the fair. When they reached Belmullet quay, the man jumped off and waded ashore, then turned to thank the seal. But he was gone. Instead he saw 'a fine gentleman'. 'I am the seal,' said the gentleman. The man took him to the pub and they drank rum together. Rum was the 'seaman's drink'.

The *selkie* stories were sustained on these coasts by the constant presence of seals. Some strange congress takes place when you look at a seal, some hint of recognition, reinforced by the sense that it appears to be mutual. In many places, seals were believed to be fallen angels, the ones who, expelled from heaven, fell into the sea. But it was less their angelic nature than their human habits that were recalled again and again. Seamus Heaney said of the seal belief that it represents 'the old trope of human beings as creatures dwelling in a middle state between the worlds of the angels and the animals.'

Yet shape-shifting is less about affirming man's separation from the beasts than the possibility that we remain a part of them. It implies a world in which the boundaries between things do not – or should not – exist. It is the same parallel country of fairies and angels, the spirit world, into which we might occasionally glimpse or even travel. We might be locked within our frames, within our own mortality, but a bit of us remains mobile. 'Of bodies changed to other forms I tell,' Ovid declares in the opening line of *Metamorphoses*, and goes on to make the case that our souls are essentially fluid, and 'adopt / in their migrations ever-varying forms'. Introducing his own version of *Metamorphoses*, Ted Hughes reflects on the moment of transition, repeated in each of the poems: 'Ovid locates and captures the peculiar frisson of that event, where the all-too-human victim stumbles into the mythic arena and is transformed.' The tales might be salutary, cautionary or retributive, but they hold out the promise of transformation – and transformation answers to that perennial itch at the core of our condition: the dissatisfaction of being, and the promise of becoming.

The endurance of the *selkie* myth can also be explained as an example of the poetic faculty, where everything can be revealed by finding its parallel. It comes from that strange region of cognitive territory where the chaos around us is briefly ordered by analogy, and the analogy grows into story and the story evolves and mutates into myth, a species in itself, both true and untrue. *Selkie* belief is a measure of the abiding need for such ambiguity. We might think that belief means certainty, but it doesn't – it works better as the accommodation of paradox. Seals can be people and people can be seals. That's it.

In the *Ordinalia*, a series of medieval mystery plays written in the Cornish language, there is a discussion about the question that lies at the heart of Christianity, the same question that has vexed and divided Christians for 2,000 years: how can Christ be both mortal and divine? The Cornish play has an answer:

Look at the mermaid
half fish and half man.
God and man clearly
To that we give belief.

I woke in the night and lay listening. Every ten seconds came the sound of a wave being dumped on the beach. I went up on deck. The boat had drifted round to face north-west. Not a breath of wind. My masthead light was glittering on the water. Over the Paps a large moon was half-hidden in shreds of cloud, and I listened to the anchor chain below, mumbling as it dragged its links over the sand.

I became aware of another sound. It was coming from the skerries. I realized that it had been there on the edge of my sleep for some time. I focused the binoculars: in the moonlight, a jagged silhouette of rock, a black void, and, above the water, three softer shapes. The moonlight on their backs gave them a roundness, the sort of shape that only animate things can hold. Seals. The noise they were making was part foghorn and part wolf-howl – and for the briefest of moments, I thought I understood what it meant.

19

A FEW HOURS LATER, THE STERN swung again. It came round to face the dawn, and sunlight burst into the boat, down the companionway, through the saloon and into the forecabin. I woke at once. I couldn't stay in bed. I went up on deck for a full appreciation of the morning. A brisk force five was forecast for later, sou'-sou'-westerly, good visibility. Out beyond the skerries the wave-backs were already running. I was eager to be among them.

I put down the swimming ladder, climbed up on the coachroof and dived in. There was the momentary shock of cold, the rush of water. Surfacing, I kicked for the shore and stood on the shingle. I thought of trying to find the King's Cave in the cliffs, where royal bodies were kept on their way for burial on Iona. But it was chilly out, so I swam back. I dressed and checked the boat – fuel, batteries, halyards, self-steering – then heaved in the anchor and headed out of the loch.

For an hour or two I bowled north along the coast of Jura with the genoa full and white crests flaring on every side. The boat's motion was easy, a gentle lunge and surge as the waves passed through. I put on the autopilot and read. A lot of the time I wasn't reading – I was looking over the top of the book at the bright blue of the water and the burnt brown slopes of Mull beyond. Towards the top of Jura, the mountains grew smaller. Then there was the dark bulk of Scarba and, between the two islands, the Gulf of Corryvreckan.

The chart marked the waters this side of Corryvreckan with wave symbols and the words 'The Great Race (dangerous tidal streams)'. It was spring tides, and I was steering clear of it. I knew the stories. Martin Martin's description in 1703: the water forming into 'Whirlpools' and 'Pyramids' which 'spout up as high as the Mast of a little Vessel'. George Orwell, while writing 1984 on Jura, getting caught in it, his dinghy overturning, his rescue by a lobster boat. Then in the 1970s, the folklorist Horace Beck being told of a ship of 450 tons taking cattle to market in Oban. They thought they were well clear, but the whirlpool started to suck them in. The engine made no headway against it. They started to slip back, listing heavily, taking on water. Their position only improved when they pushed the cattle overboard.

So, I was keeping away. Off to the east, I could make out the place where the sea was dark and agitated; to one side lay the shadow of Scarba's slopes and above them was a line of thick, low cloud. In a patch between was an area where the sun was out and the air shone with a greenish brilliance. Through binoculars I watched a crowd of seabirds, feeding and diving into the water. There were hundreds. They looked like insects buzzing around a corpse. They were gulls mainly, but there were fulmars, shearwaters, terns and gannets, and they swirled and crossed in the bottle-coloured light, stirred by the sand eels, who themselves were stirred by the churned-up zooplankton and phytoplankton. I watched them intently, aware of a feeling deep in my stomach, a thrill at the frenzy and the sheer number of them. But I didn't want to be there.

Then they were ahead. I put down the binoculars. I had been pulled into a patch of waveless water, an acre or so as smooth as a dolphin's flank. The seabirds were working a patch just beyond. I could hear them now, shrill and half-crazed by the feeding. When I came to them – or rather when they came to me – the boat dropped off the side of a low wall of water. *Out here? This far out?* I pushed down the helm and gripped the guardrail. The sea ahead was just turbulence – white caps and back-waves like a river's rapids, with a noise like rapids. Briefly I thought, *What a thing to witness!* Then I hauled in the sheets and hurried west. It was hard to tell what way I was making. The log was giving five and a half knots, but the water was moving the hull as much as the hull was moving through it.

For a moment, I thought I'd lost control. I fixed some landmarks, to work out which direction I was going in. I put on the engine and pushed the throttle up. It bellowed, rattling a dozen loose fittings. The book fell off the seat. I watched a peak on Scarba against the pale of the mainland beyond. For some time, it stayed still. Then, very slowly, it began to move astern. The sea started to settle. The cries of the seabirds grew fainter. I looked back and saw the agitated water stretching away into the distance. The spinning centre was in there somewhere. I had only passed through the suburbs.

Panic turned to relief, and deep gratitude to the boat. It was me that had led us into this – but *Tsambika* who had got us out.

I sailed on up to Oban and spent the night off the island of Kerrera. A couple of days later, I reached Tobermory at the western end of the Sound of Mull, happy at the progress made, and waiting for decent weather to round Ardnamurchan, the mainland's most westerly point.

Ardnamurchan has always been something of a threshold for mariners. It used to be said that anyone who sailed beyond it was entitled to come back with a piece of heather tied to their bowsprit – but those were the days of bowsprits and poor engines and derring-do. It was still a formidable headland, well known for nasty seas, and beyond it, facilities were somewhat thinner.

Tobermory did not lack for facilities. I refuelled and topped up the water tank. I filled the food locker. I found a chandler's in town, or rather a chandlery part of a larger store. I stood looking at all the blocks and cordage and galvanized chain, the spikes and keys and blades, the charts and plotters and thought: *I'll take the lot.* I left with a snap shackle, a roll of duct tape and some brass screws in a brown paper bag. The weather was rubbish, a low-pressure carousel of gales and rain and more gales. In the harbour office each morning, I joined the other stubble-chinned yachtsmen hunched over iPads, hoping for a few decent days left at the end of the season, tutting and head-shaking as they scrolled through the forecasts. One evening in the pub, I found myself gazing at a knot in the oak table, mistaking its concentric circles for the contours of a deep Atlantic low.

It was impatience more than an improvement in conditions that led me to head out of Tobermory and sail for the end of Ardnamurchan Point. Rain was falling when I left, but the wind was light. The rain thickened. It crackled on my hood; it leopard-skinned the water's surface around the boat. I gazed ahead. Ardnamurchan's profile stretched westward, ten miles of glowering barrier, its top muzzled in cloud. It was the geography of impediment, its entire scale a warning, its slopes beneath the white mist built of hostility. As the morning spun out, and more of the headland slid astern, it took on a certain majesty. I could see the end of it now, half-hidden by mist. The rain pressed down the swells, gave them a furtive, slippery look. Everything was damp and grey. I settled into a damp and grey mood.

An email pinged into my phone as I rounded the head. I read it a couple of times before taking it in. When I looked up again the scene was the same, but altered utterly. The email was from Maria Simonds-Gooding, down in Kerry where it all began, and it concerned the very first visitor I had had on board.

. . . I am sorry to bring the very sad news of Danny Sheehy's death . . .

   After their naomhóg capsized off the Iberian coast, all four crew
stayed with the upturned boat, which then swept them upon a beach.
The stern was severely damaged. Danny became ill just before reaching the shore and it is believed he had a heart attack and could not be
revived when the rescue people arrived. Of course the whole peninsula is in mourning and we are waiting for more news as it comes in.

I tried to remember his face – the stubbly white beard, the smiling blue eyes, all beneath that Breton cap. I thought of the posy of
flowers he'd brought, the herbs and vegetables. I'd seen him a few
times after we first met – at a talk he'd organised, in a cafe in Dingle.
And I'd read his book about sailing to Iceland, *In the Wake of St Brendan*. I'd been struck in particular by the mercurial relationship he
had with the sea (probably because, in part, I recognized it). He
recalled his reaction when first being invited to join the boat: 'I leapt
in the air and punched the kitchen ceiling with clenched fist. My
heart swelled and I gave a great shout of joy. I leapt again and high-
fived the air with my palm, roaring at the top of my voice: "God's
help is but a step away!"'

But he wrote too of the opposite – the worry, the isolation, 'the
black cloud of misery that used to come upon me whenever I went
on any journey by land or sea. From time to time I would be seized
by a fearsome fit of loneliness, bereft of my people, my family, my
neighbours and the beauty and culture of my home place. This
nightmarish affliction would penetrate the roots of my mind and
the depths of my being.'

I pictured him and the crew rowing and rowing, for weeks on
end, and the partying and music-making as they made their way
south and then west towards Compostela. I pictured the moment
the *naomhóg* began to go over, and imagined a part of him – the

storyteller, the poet – thinking: *What are the words to tell this?* But it was the one story he was never be able to share.

And I remembered the blessing he recited as he left *Tsambika*:

> As I cross the deep ocean,
> O king of patience, take me by the hand.
> And if the seas grow too steep,
> Holy Mary, look down upon me, do not leave me.

The rain was beginning again. I pressed on into empty waters, the bows pointing into nothingness. The chart plotter had been playing up, the screen flickering on and off. I reverted to a compass course. Long seas bulked out of the gloom, slipped under the hull and rolled back into the gloom. The wind was dying, and the sails started to flop. Idly, the genoa wrapped itself around the forestay, slid off and, with a loud crack, kicked against the block. A comb of spray rose from the sheet. The boom swung to the centre, then back – and half a gallon of water sluiced out of the sail on to my shoulder. Rain was flowing from every surface, building into streams which quick-flowed along the toe-rail to spill through the scuppers. The sea around me looked more heartless than ever.

Over the next couple of hours, the cloud lifted to reveal a cast of shapes standing on that watery stage. The Small Isles: Muck and Eigg, and in the mid-afternoon Rum, with its western screes plunging into the water. Beneath grey skies a single cloud sat over the island. I puzzled for a while over its resemblance – a beret or a halo, or a burger bun? It started to swell and rise, as if sucking all the moisture from the slopes.

In the Sound of Canna, the tide was stirring the water. Puffins whirred off the surface at my approach, with their strange headlong flight. Sanday rose low to the north, with Canna behind it; on the other shore, Rum was all high cliff and rock. I watched the streak of a waterfall run down its side, a narrow vein of run-off. A patch of sunlight was brushing the slopes and, down at the bottom, it caught something bright: white superstructure and a hull – a large trawler smashed against the rocks. I remembered the warning issued by Stornoway Coastguard for some days now: *Beware debris off the north of Rum.*

It was raining hard when I pushed into the harbour of Canna, a natural horseshoe of sheltered water. The anchor chain rattled out over the bow-roller. I listened to the late forecast on the radio – *Strong winds, clear skies . . .* The cloud and rain had long gone. I opened the forehatch and lay looking at the night sky. Stars in the infinity of space . . . seals on Sanday, making a sound like a slowed-down soundtrack. My eyelids closed. The day's seas were still shifting behind them – images of wreckage below the Rum cliffs, the skewed angle of that trawler, and an upturned *naomhóg* washed ashore on an Iberian beach.

MA DH'FHOSGAIL, DUIN! – IF YOU OPENED IT, SHUT IT!

I shut it – gently swung the wicket gate until the latch clicked. I entered a tunnel of escallonia. Overhead the foliage had long ago met to form a thick canopy. It closed out the day's sun; down at ground level, ancient boughs snaked through the shadows. I crushed a leaf and sniffed it. Even so late in the season, there was that escallonia smell. It took me back at once to the hidden spaces of the Cornish garden where we'd spent summer holidays – the same high bushes with their pink flowers and sticky leaves, the syrupy tang.

When I came out of the tunnel, it was into sunlight and another world. The wind heaved through the sycamore tops; the waves on the shore were a distant hiss, but here in the shelter of the garden all

was still and warm. Daisy-spotted lawn stretched out from a grav-
elled path. At the top of the path stood the front of Canna House,
with its dark stone walls and pale granite quoins, a squared-off,
lairdly look.

The windows were shuttered but the front door was ajar. I
had arranged to meet the archivist and, stepping inside, I called,
'Hello?' No response. In the vestibule was a wooden settle, and I
sat to replace my sea-boots with docksiders. The paraphernalia of
summer recreation was propped in the corner – a shrimping net
and croquet mallets, assorted walking sticks. Through the window,
I could see back into the garden, where a wheelbarrow, half full
of plucked weeds, stood beside a herbaceous border; a rake leaned
up against a tree. It was as if the entire household had been somehow spirited away and the place frozen on a June afternoon a
generation ago.

I had been here, two decades ago. It was February. My friend
Iain – Professor of Modern History, expert on all things Hebridean
– had called at Christmas and said he was planning a trip to Canna
to see Margaret Fay Shaw and did I want to come.

'She's ninety-three,' he explained. 'You won't regret it. There's no
one quite like Margaret.'

He was right, on both counts. I arranged to write a feature article
about her and her work. We spent five days on the island – days
full of long meals in the Canna House kitchen with Margaret and
Magda, the family archivist, and striding the cliffs until dusk, or
exploring the archive, then stretching out evenings in the drawing
room with stories and readings aloud, and Margaret's tiny figure at
the piano, her bent fingers flitting over the keyboard to play pieces
by Chopin or Mozart or Schubert. After playing, she would turn on
the stool, reach for her cigarettes and, with a hint of long-ago Pitts-
burgh drawl, begin to talk.

Margaret Fay Shaw had been born in 1903 to an industrial family in Pennsylvania. She was the youngest of five sisters. Her father had a steel mill. In her autobiography, she remembers the air of prosperity, the books, the aunts and uncles, the dream-like winter sleigh rides. But then her mother died when she was seven, and her father a few years later. The prosperity melted away. With her sisters, she moved to a small flat in a small town.

From an early age, Margaret showed a striking ability to play music by ear. At eighteen, she was accepted by a musical academy in New York. To help pay her way, she found a job ushering box-holders at Carnegie Hall. She remembered keeping open the little window in the box door to hear performances that then stayed with her for her whole life. Toscanini was the conductor at the time and 'anyone who has ever heard Toscanini knows you never hear his equal'. She practised six hours a day, allowed herself to think that she might, just might, make it as a concert pianist. Then she contracted a virus. It affected her joints. There followed a round of specialists and treatments and operations, and the realization that playing the piano professionally was now impossible. She was in her early twenties, and her planned life had been cut short. But there was another life; she had her own set of far-away islands.

'What would you like to do?' asked her doctor.

'I have been on a bicycle tour of the Hebrides,' she told him. 'I would like to go back there, to live and to collect songs.'

For five years, she lodged in an earthen-floored house on South Uist with Peigi and Mairi MacRae, a pair of Gaelic-speaking, and Gaelic-singing, sisters. In winter, they all sat round the peat fire. The MacRaes taught Margaret Gaelic and they sang, and other islanders came in and sang and told stories. In the summer, there was work during the long, light-filled days, and always song. Milking songs, spinning songs, waulking songs.

In 1935, Margaret met the folklorist John Lorne Campbell, who shared her commitment to collecting what remained of island life. They married and spent their first summer living aboard John's thirty-eight-foot lug-sailed cruiser, hopping from one Hebridean harbour to another. Even Margaret found the boat cramped. They moved into a corrugated-iron building on the island of Barra. It had no running water. When one of her uncles sent her some money 'for essentials', Margaret went to Glasgow, selected a Steinway baby grand and had it shipped back to Barra on a fishing boat. A few years later, John came into a small inheritance and stretched it to breaking to buy the island of Canna. He and Margaret moved into the house and Margaret installed her piano in the drawing room. It has been there ever since.

What drew Margaret Fay Shaw to these islands, out on the opposite side of the Atlantic, and what made her stay? Her ancestry, in part – four generations back, the Shaws had emigrated from Scotland. The physical nature of the Hebrides was always important to her – 'colour and form of indescribable beauty whenever there is the least clarity'. And the people – 'the loveliest people in the whole universe', for their unceasing toils, their fortitude on sea and land, their love of merriment and dancing and jokes. But above all, the music.

It was not enough just to listen and observe. She recorded. She collected songs on reels of EMI magnetic tape. She copied down the Gaelic in notebooks, going over the spelling and grammar with native speakers, like the South Uist bard Angus John Campbell. She tried to capture the airs in flight, to trap their soaring melodies in the earthly system of the modal scale. It wasn't easy. 'Time meant nothing to us, as we worked at what we all enjoyed. When one song was declared to have been correctly taken down, someone would suggest another . . . often people present would remember other verses, and I have known a song to begin with one verse and end with eleven.'

She travelled to the furthest islands. She asked to be dropped off on recently deserted Mingulay, and spent days there living off gulls' eggs and oatcakes rolled out with a whisky bottle. She took her cine-camera to the nesting sites where the squawk of chicks 'sounded exactly like the children on the East Side of New York'.

Wherever there were people, she took down lore and stories as well as song – instances of second sight, anecdotes, proverbs (*muc shàmhach as mutha dh'icheas* – 'the quiet pig eats most'), riddles (*thàid an làir ghlas a Shashunn gun a cas a fhliuchadh* – 'the grey mare will go to England without wetting a foot' – answer: a letter), and folk cures ('BLISTER – rub a slug on it'). She travelled to Inis Meáin, Ireland's equivalent of South Uist, with the same concentration of old stories and language and song, caught in the same twilight moment. In May 1930, she was on the ship to St Kilda with the officials bearing the news that the last thirty-six inhabitants were to be evacuated – 'most of them wanted to go'. She heaved her ten-pound Graflex camera to the top of the great cliffs of Conachair, where the St Kildans used to lower themselves on horsehair ropes to collect gulls' eggs.

And from everywhere she went, and everywhere she lived during those years, came the same stark impression: that it was over. For all the depth of tradition, the generations behind every marriage *feis*, the centuries in every song, the oceans in every story, everything was on the cusp of extinction. It only made the urge to collect even stronger.

I kept up with Margaret through her late nineties. Age affected her physically, but on the phone her voice was always strong. I once asked her the secret of longevity. Back came the drawl: 'Don't take any person too damned seriously, particularly yourself. Have fun. Don't listen to anyone else's advice.'

In 2003, she celebrated her hundredth birthday. A party of islanders came over from South Uist in an old Faroese boat. On board was a piper, an accordion player, a South Uist salmon, bags of South Uist potatoes and some traditional struthan cake.

'Oh, we had a damned good party,' she told me, chuckling at the memory. 'We were singing and dancing, and telling stories for hours and hours.'

The following year, she took the ferry to Mallaig for the last time, and died in a nursing home in Fort William.

I spent the rest of that day in Canna House, most of it in the old billiard room. Fiona the archivist brought books and papers and albums which piled up on the table around me. She was working on the sound archive in the corner and as I browsed and read, the room filled with the crystalline notes of Gaelic a cappella, the tap-tap rhythm of weaving songs, or the clipped tones of 1950s' radio – 'This is the BBC Home Service . . . On winter days and winter nights in Canna House, music fills every room . . .'

I read again of the story of John and Margaret on Canna, their pedigree cattle-breeding, the butterfly-collecting. I read of their gentle and inclusive stewardship. For more than forty years, the islanders would come up to Canna House every Saturday to play billiards. And here, against the wall, next to a stuffed capercaillie, was the cue-stand and scoreboard; the table-top I was working at, I now realized, covered the leather-rimmed pockets and green baize. Filed away with everything else were records of all the scores from those sessions. It was the ethos of the house: everything that happens must be written down, nothing is ephemeral.

I watched some of Margaret's footage of the island and islanders, and turned the pages of photo albums to share in sepia picnics and family groups, in fishing trips, in building the Canna pier and seeing the house in snow. Each picture produced a stab of nostalgic regret. For what? This was not my past. It is the trick of these islands and their vanished lives – they make you share their loss, a loss that feels universal.

Later I wandered through other parts of the house – the dining room, with its archaeological finds lying on the floor; the library; the kitchen, where we'd eaten and talked all those years ago. The drawing room had been preserved exactly as I remembered it – piano and owl-lamp and the bookended books and the cat cushions, Margaret's ash tray. Upstairs was now 'unsafe' because of the rotting floor-boards – but there too were more collections. The entire house was an archive. In published books and journals, in piles of story, sound recordings, photos, card indexes, boxes marked '2B sorted', in Gaelic manuscripts, Gaelic song and Gaelic scholarship, recordings of long-dead individuals from the Gaelic-speaking islands of Scotland and Nova Scotia, in Margaret's photographs, the house was filled not just with the meticulous hoardings of two people, but with the trace-memories of an entire civilization. If St Brendan came ashore now on Canna, he would find it an Island of Memory. He would walk up the escallonia tunnel to Canna House and enter one of those portals popular in Irish myth, and be transported to another time.

It was late afternoon when I passed back through the escallonia tunnel, back to the present.

The wind had built through the day and I could see *Tsambika* pulling hard at the anchor. The shore was too close; I needed to move her for the night. But the Zodiac was on the pier and the ferry was approaching. I'd have to wait.

Loch Nibheis of Glasgow slowed as she came in, swivelling and backing up, lowering the stern-gate. There was a rattling as it hit the slipway. A line of pack-carrying, case-wheeling passengers walked up it onto the quay. A similar line of visitors and islanders uncoiled itself and headed on board. Beetling in after them was a Manitou forklift, reappearing with a pallet of fence posts. The quay was a mass of greetings and goodbyes, and I couldn't avoid a bitter-sweet thought of home – these sons and daughters and parents coming together after weeks away, or being pulled apart.

The ferry shrank into the distance. The last of the arrivals left along the track, on foot or in battered old 4x4s that rolled and pitched through the potholes like old liberty-boats. I was alone on the quay. Before launching the Zodiac, I crossed to the ferry waiting room, where there was an exhibition. A flat-screen TV flickered with old images. Beside it was a lifebuoy and a series of spirals, painted by children, continuous lines leading inwards to the middle. The exhibition title was written around the lifebuoy: 'Tha mise aig meadhan mo shaoghail – I am at the centre of my world'.

What did that mean? Was it just solipsism? Or a reassuring corrective for all those still living out here on the periphery? It made me uneasy. The soundtrack of the film was now a hissy recording of Margaret playing Chopin's Nocturnes. Black-and-white cine images accompanied it – a lone boat crossing the bay, two men bringing it into shore and unloading sheep, sun sparkling on water, Canna House and the escallonia, and three smiling children sitting on a wall. I was suddenly overwhelmed by a feeling I couldn't quite explain, and my eyes filled with tears:

> Tha mise aig meadhan mo shaoghail,
> I am at the centre of my world.

20

I woke to sunlight playing on the hatch-casing above my head, on the familiar contours of the forecabin. I lay for a while, as I had done on so many mornings, following the intricacies of the woodwork, the white-painted ribs and frames with their regular spacing of twin fastenings, and the knees and the deck shelf above, and everything tapering up towards the chain locker beyond my feet, and into the bows where, like pilgrimage roads, the timbers of the hull led to the single point of the stemhead.

I listened. The faintest of creaking. I thought of the countless pieces of wood themselves, the lignin no longer propping up vascular vessels of xylem and phloem so that sugars could pass downwards from the canopy, and minerals and moisture could pass up from the roots, and how it was all felled and sawn and measured and joined until it was one solid piece again, a vessel now to keep out the water, to bend to the wind as its parts once did in the forest. The Vikings thought of their ships as living. The long clinker-built hulls would flex, and those aboard thought of them as sentient beasts – dragons or birds or sea-serpents.

Hardly a right angle, hardly a regular form, none of the set-square conformity of fixed architecture. What did Arthur Ransome say? 'Houses are badly built boats so firmly aground you cannot think of moving them. They are definitely inferior things, belonging to the vegetable not the animal world, rooted and stationary.' A building must fit its site, but a boat has no site, so its design is simply a variation on some earlier design. Alan Buchanan at his drawing board created the particular lines of *Tsambika* by modifying the smaller Trojan class and the larger Saxon class, and they themselves grew out of other yachts, which had been modified from the shape of old shore-boats and skiffs, quay punts, cogs and caravels, an ageless continuity of seagoing craft and seafaring – because the shape of the sea is always the same. Or rather it's always different, but in the same way.

And now, today's task – the passage to Skye, four or five hours. Setting out from another harbour into an unknown sea, towards an unknown shore, and then on through more unknown waterways to the north. I suddenly felt an immense fatigue – the weight of the miles behind dragging down those to come. Why was I continuing? The days were growing colder, the nights longer . . . In such moments, it was the boat itself that urged me on.

The early sun proved brief. Within an hour, the true face of the morning showed itself – thickening cloud, a dampness in the air that moistened every surface. The BBC forecast rubbed it in: '. . . *a very warm September day with unbroken sunshine . . . Except for the far north-west of Scotland, where weather fronts will bring cloud all day . . .*'

Shortly after eight, I hauled up the anchor. I motored out past the quay and the cliffs beside it. Ahead was a milky screen of mist. The shore of Sanday had become a soft-pencil outline. I now couldn't see the buoy for the skerries, the Sgeir a' Phuirt. That worried me. The whiteness ahead was doing strange things to my orientation. I looked at the chart plotter. It had been dodgy recently, but now it had reached a new level of defunct. The screen was a psychedelic sunset, horizontal pinks and purples and greens: pretty, but useless. I took out my phone to open the Navionics app, but when I zoomed in on Canna, it zoomed out, and the red pointer of my position sat like a giant foot over the whole of the Hebrides. The touch screen was too wet. My fingers were too wet. Everything was too wet.

I'd filled in the tide predictions. I'd carefully worked out a compass course for the Sound of Sleat – but the course started outside the skerries. For now, I had nothing but visuals to give me my position. And the visuals were fading fast. I fumbled the arm of the autohelm into its slot, jumped down below, and from the chart worked out a course to clear everything. Up on deck, I steered east-north-east, glancing at the only reliable thing in that white void: the digits of the depth sounder. Soon they were twenties and thirties, and then the cloud began to lift and I could see the seas spreading out from the boat. I was clear of Canna, heading for the north coast of Rum, a slow emerging of its slatted geology, its layers of sandstone and the sheen of wet scree. Within a few minutes, the southern end of Skye came into view, and then the mainland.

There were still long pieces of coastline missing, smudged out by traces of low cloud. But I could relax. I took a fix on the Point of Sleat, some ten miles off, in case the fog came back, slotted the autohelm back in, put on coffee, and grabbed from the shelves below the slim booklet which I'd been reading last night.

After a visit to Canna's public shower (in a farm shed), I'd taken my oilskins and boots next door, into the mini-museum of the old dairy to finish dressing. Propped outside was a whale-rib; inside was a rough floor and the sort of things that would have been chucked in the nettles a couple of generations ago – mixing bowls, a butter churn, several butter hands. Fixed to the wall were also some photocopied pages from a translation of one of the greatest of all Gaelic poems – the eighteenth-century sea epic *The Birlinn of Clanranald* by Alasdair Mac Mhaighstir Alasdair.

It is said that Alasdair wrote at least part of the poem under an upturned boat on Canna's shore. He was bailie on the island in the dark years after the 1745 Jacobite rising. It is powerful stuff: 566 lines of resonance and metrics. 'The verse is hard, terse and business-like,' comments the Gaelicist Derick Thomson, 'the clean rhythm of the lines like the movement of cold sea-water along the side of a boat.'

Reading it again, in Alan Riach's stirring translation, hunched in the cockpit and cold to the core after the dampness of the morning, I was infected with the joy of the opening lines:

May the great lord god of movement
carry us safe
on all the choral waters of this world.

Those choral waters! On one level, the poem is the account of a journey by birlinn, or galley, from South Uist down to Carrickfergus in Ulster. A crew of burly clansmen leave Uist on an unnamed mission to their kin in Ireland. When they're clear of the harbour, in the offing,

Big Malcolm the Stalwart stands up,
thick-set and heavy and swaying, son of Old Ranald the
Ocean.

He calls for the *iorram*, the rowing song. And you can see him – body tilting with the motion of the boat, beginning the song, and you can hear the booming unison of the oarsmen's response (but wouldn't you like to glimpse too, just for what he *looks like*, his father, 'Old Ranald the Ocean'?)

They row.

Stretch, bend, and now, pull all the way back
on the smooth-handled oars.

The birlinn speeds south through the islands – 'Oak boards and tar, nails made of iron, ocean rising.' The narrative builds to the climax of a storm which hits them to the north of Islay, an intense and violent storm:

Blind in the smart of it
spindrift and rain
constant assault
thundering onslaught.

The stanzas go beyond the standard terror of a storm at sea, pressing their images deep into the imagination. Much is made of the moment of its writing, after the Battle of Culloden – 'post-Apocalypse, post-Armageddon', as Alan Riach puts it in his introduction. The clans have been crushed and the story's purpose is in part to remind the reader of the old world and all that great continent of life and letters and craft and song, all that has been lost. And the best way to do that was through the inherent nostalgia of a boat.

The birlinn was a type of craft used widely on the west coasts of Scotland and Ireland. It had a single sail and up to eighteen oars, and was handy for quick beaching and quick manoeuvring, for raiding, and for the capricious winds and sudden downdraughts of sea lochs. It was in birlinns that mercenaries travelled down to Mayo to support Granuaile – Grace O'Malley; they were in the fleets of the Lords of the Isles. And, from the late sixteenth century, the Privy Council in England called for their destruction. Get rid of their boats and you'll curb their mutinous ways. By the time of Mac

Mhaighstir Alasdair, there had been no birlinns for over a century.

A large part of the poem deals with the crew – the oarsmen, the helmsman, the bowman, those on the sheets and halyards and back-stays, the lookout and the watcher for seas, the man to bail and the six men in reserve. Each of the tasks is described with relish by the poet, in its technical detail, in the skill and strength required and the way each contributes to the imperative of survival. Underlying every line of the poem – every man at his given post, every stage of the voyage, the very thrust of it all – is the boat itself. Lengths of fixed timber, clinkered strakes, the slim hull assembled by a ship-wright to a design that he did not initiate but knew by heart. The birlinn in the story is more than a ship. It is a traditional tale in itself, a poem. It is all those craft – the Ark, the *Pequod*, the *Mayflower*, the *Titanic*, Odysseus's unnamed craft – that carry on board a cargo of myth, and whose passage across the hostile sea is the wild track of our lives – the course of our ideals and hopes, our past and our future.

The sails were flapping. I jumped up and heaved on the main-sheet. The wind had veered. I hauled in the genoa and the boat picked up speed. The Point of Sleat lay a few cables to the north – grey broken stone and a ruff of surf beneath it. I flicked off the autopilot to take control again, holding the tiller, feeling history in the weight of the helm. *Tsambika*'s bows were cleaving a colourless sea, pointing up towards the great taper of the sound, towards the Kyle of Lochalsh and the mountains of Wester Ross.

'I saw you coming. I saw you coming in round the head.'

From eight miles away, from his window above Loch Slapin, John Purser had spotted my lone sail. Now we were driving up from the village of Armadale, through the treeless expanse of Skye, to his home. The route was all story. He was pointing at a sign for an old shieling – 'Lot of islanders owed their conception to shielings' – and then at a hill – 'Just up there beyond the burn' – to a boulder that, if you hit it, sounded like a gong, and the bell heather which had been late to bloom this year, and the geo-narrative in the rocks of the Cuillins above – when I happened to mention something I'd read by the historian Hugh Trevor-Roper.

The car slowed. John's knuckles tightened on the wheel. Behind his frown, I could see he was weighing something up: 'If you mention that name again, I will throw you out of the car, right here on the hill. I don't care.'

I'd been given John Purser's name by Alan Riach, translator of *The Birlinn of Clanranald*. Crofter, scholar, composer, poet, Purser is also one of Scotland's leading musicologists. He studied under Sir Michael Tippett and Dr Hans Gál. His own words appear in steel on the exposed beams of Edinburgh's Library of Scottish Poetry – *A nation is forged in the hearth of poetry*. Scotland's discrete body of literature and music have been his life's work. So his objection to Trevor-Roper was natural. Trevor-Roper's essay 'The Invention of Tradition: The Highland Tradition of Scotland' makes the case that much of what we think of as Scottish is pure fabrication: the ancient political structures of the nation were dreamed up by George Buchanan, the literary tradition by James Macpherson, and the kilt was the eighteenth-century invention of an English Quaker.

When Purser could bring himself to talk of it, he recalled how 'that man' had also written *The Invention of Scotland*, which was republished in time for the independence referendum, to bolster the unionist cause. He picked easy holes in the evidence. But the most interesting part of Trevor-Roper's thesis is not where it leads but where it begins – with Scotland and Ireland's capacity to generate mythology. Trevor-Roper notes, with only a little overstatement, that the English developed their myths not from Anglo-Saxon traditions but from the Celts. 'It was from Celtic Britain that Shakespeare and Spenser drew their native heroes. It was in the Celtic cycle of Arthur and his court that Milton sought, and Malory and Tennyson found, inspiration. It was in Celtic Scotland and Celtic Ireland that Romanticism recreated its mythology.'

We got over our tricky start. I survived the journey, and we spent the evening together talking. We talked, and talked. John was quick and heated in his judgements, with a farmer's physical presence and the eagerness of a man who gets things done quickly and well. He reminded me in spirit, somehow, of *The Birlinn* – a hearty blend of the tough, the practical and the tender. There was nothing that did not interest him, about which he did not have an opinion. Pictish art (an underrated glory), Jack B. Yeats (an underrated writer and painter), parenting ('there comes a time, in their teens, when you just get in their way'). We ate his home-reared beef and drank his home-brewed beer. At one point, he took from the shelf a tiny marble object. He'd carved it himself. 'Someone gave me this piece of Connemara marble. These veins – here – they suggested the lines of a boat – see what it is?'

In the padded cradle of his palm was a small piece of stone. He'd inserted into it a slender mast with a gaff-rigged mainsail and jib.

I saw: 'It's a Galway hooker!'

But it was strange that when you looked at it, it wasn't actually the shape of a hull at all – the bow was too high, the quarter and stern too stocky. But, like a good caricature, it somehow distilled the very essence of boat.

In the morning, I came down and John was in bare feet, standing at the stove and stirring the porridge. He wore pale cotton trousers, a Leatherman at his belt. He was already talking. When we'd finished talking at breakfast, we carried on talking in his library.

266

Here was the physical extension of his own thoughts – the books, the files, the sound equipment. A mound of old peat ash stood in the hearth; the carpet in front was pocked with spark-burns. John filled a swivel chair at his desk, a screen glowed behind him and a strip of Ogham letters ran below the keyboard. He turned back and forth to illustrate what he said with books and quotes and recordings. And when there were no recordings, he sang . . . He sang of a lark. He sang in Gaelic, a traditional song, and his voice rose like a lark's, reaching higher and higher. 'The story it tells is of a lark's nest being plundered – but the real point is the sound. That repetition – *biodach, biodach* – in an otherwise varied flow.'

I told him that on Canna I'd listened to Margaret Fay Shaw's recording of Annie Johnston's bird rhymes. 'She was doing an oystercatcher. I have to say – it didn't sound *that* much like an oystercatcher, but there was the same playful bird-like sound to her voice.'

'In the School of Scottish Studies is a set of recordings of old Gaelic bird imitations, and in those recordings, you're hard pushed to tell where the language ends and the music and birdsong begins.' He added: 'The word for "music" in Irish and Gaelic is *ceol*, and its etymology is linked to birdsong.'

We spoke of the notion that human speech is just flattened song, that song preceded it, and of the idea that birds sing, in part, for the pleasure of it.

'One of my favourite passages of old Irish story,' I told him, 'is the beginning of the *Voyage of Bran*, when Bran hears a woman singing and he's put into a trance-like sleep. Music is the spur to the whole story – the entire voyage.'

'That would be *súantraige*, "sleeping music". In early Irish music, there was a threefold division. The other two were *goltraige*, or "weeping music", and *geantraige*, "laughing music".'

Music also offers transcendence, and in Ireland and Gaelic

Scotland, transcendence has meant the link between this world and the otherworld. Often it was the faint strains of music that signalled the presence of the *sìth*, or came drifting out from the Irish *raths*. Music was a force of nature, more powerful than any single musician. The Dagda's harp disarmed the Fomorian warriors with laughter, while the harpists of Fráech once performed with such beautiful sadness that twelve men died.

In all of what John said, and in what he played and sang, there was not just the intrinsic appeal of the music, of Gaelic song ('it's all in the purity of the vowel sounds'), but also the unstated authority of its age. On these coasts, music is a constant – constantly present, constantly redolent, echoing back through the songs gathered by Margaret Fay Shaw and John Lorne Campbell of Canna, and by Alexander Carmichael before them, back beyond the coming of Christianity to the great music-filled expanse of Hibernian prehistory.

A few miles from John's croft is a cave. The Uamh an Ard Achadh ('Cave of the High Pasture') is an inaccessible place. It's a liminal place too, offering entry to the otherworld – situated near where the Durness limestone meets the prevailing granite. Down in the chamber, buried in layers of mud and ash, was recently discovered a small piece of charred oak. The wood had been worked in a very particular manner, with one side arched and notches cut into the other. John had been closely involved with interpreting the find and soon realized what it was: the bridge of a stringed instrument, probably a lyre. Carbon analysis of the ash in which it was found dated it at around 500 BC – a thousand years earlier than anything comparable in western Europe.

The sound would not have been loud, and probably needed the chamber of the cave to amplify it. The site has also yielded deposits of human bones, including foetal remains, along with large numbers

268

of excarnated pig bones. The picture it suggests is startling: generations of people from the Iron Age and earlier, gathering from far beyond the Isle of Skye at this remote place – to feast, to drink, to commemorate and worship, to be transported for a while in a cave full of music.

As we left the room, John placed in my hand a long, horn-like object. 'Feel the weight of that. Reproduction of a Bronze Age instrument. We think of those people waging war, that their minds were always on defence, or the next raid. But that's an awful lot of spearheads. Seems they were just as keen to make music.'

Back at Armadale, I rowed out to *Tsambika*. I peeled off the cellophane from the CD John had given me, of his own compositions. I posted it in the boat's player, and viola and clarsach and cello filled the cockpit. I stood and looked across to the mainland. The colours of the distant hills grew sharper, the drifting clouds whiter.

The CD cover was a collage of an Admiralty chart of the Hebrides. Set on it, sailing westward, was the boat John had carved from Connemara marble. The album's title, he explained in the sleeve notes, was based on 'something that I have been doing since childhood days in Scotland and Ireland'. It was called *Dreaming of Islands*.

The late sun was out of sight behind the hills, but I could see its goldwork on the mountains to the east. It was much too good an evening to stay put. I hoisted the mainsail, let the genoa take wing and, in a fresh south-easterly, sailed on up the coast to Ornsay. I gained a few more miles to the north.

21

TWO SOUNDS IN THE CHILL of dawn. The scutter of a blackbird ashore – then closer, *tap-tap* on the hull. And suddenly – *krak-KRAK* . . .

Buoy trouble.

I threw on some clothes, started the engine, pulled in the mooring line. With the helm against my leg, I untangled the straps of my life jacket, clipped it on and headed out into the morning. A low wave curled away from the bows, a long chromium V. Patches of wind lay scattered across the water. Overhead the clouds were not thick but mottled, allowing a tortoiseshell brightness to leak through them. Off to starboard, I could see Beinn Sgirtheall and Beinn a'Chappuill, and beyond them the lines of further peaks, fading into the dawn. Fifty miles of nothing. Each mountain wore its age as a kind of stillness, giving the strange sensation of gazing at a picture. But no picture could hold such depth, such splendour.

The channel narrowed ahead. The island of Skye was closing in on the mainland. Steep gullies were now at hand on both sides. Some were wooded down their length, vertical corridors of birch and rowan and alder. Others were too tight for trees and the gap between their cliffs was just a slit in the side of the hill. I saw the white of a waterfall tumbling over the high scarp; at the foot of the slope, it ran out over a mound of its own detritus, widened and lost itself in the sea. In one place, a Sitka plantation had been clear-felled – the ground looked like a battlefield.

The conditions weren't challenging; I missed the wind. Motor-sailing through the narrows, I came out into the Kyle of Lochalsh and headed west for Skye Bridge. Coming in under it, I could see a Co-op lorry climbing the span and heard its rattle, sixty feet above the mast.

The wind dropped altogether as I came in round the top of Scalpay. The water lay flat and inert, reflecting on its surface the blue and white of the clouds above. It felt as if the boat were drifting through the sky. I could see down through the sun's shafting rays, through the dust of phytoplankton, to where three jellyfish were flying in parallel with me, propelled by their pulsing skirts. The Sound of Raasay opened out suddenly to the north, to open sea – and there in the duck-egg blue horizon was the chill of the north.

In the mid-afternoon I reached the entrance to Portree harbour. High cliffs rose several hundred feet to one side; at their base, looking very small, was a tourist boat. I could see a line of heads along the landward rail, each one tilted upwards, as if a celebrity was about to make a balcony appearance. I ran my binoculars across the rock face but could spot nothing of interest.

Inside the harbour, I cruised back and forth, choosing a mooring. Many were empty now, the boats taken ashore for the winter. There was a slender wooden sloop with a Norwegian ensign, and I came in close to admire the sheer of the hull and the gleam of the varnished spars.

A woman's head popped up from the cockpit. Before I was able to shout, 'Beautiful boat!' she shouted, 'Beautiful boat!' So I thanked her, lest we be sucked into a loop of wooden-boat smuggery.

'We are not seeing so many wooden boats round here,' she called. 'All plastic . . . Tupperware!'

Above her in the stern, still and solid as the rigging, stood a man with a grey beard and all-seeing blue eyes. I hadn't noticed him.

'It is not easy sailing on your own?' He spoke without moving.

'I'm learning!'

'We too, we are always saying, What have we learned today?'

I asked if they were headed back to Norway.

'We are leaving the boat in Scotland for the winter. We are sailing south. The weather not being so good.'

I headed away. Was I the only boat still heading north?

Portree has a small fishing fleet and Skye's main hospital and college, but its primary purpose in the summer months is tourism. Now, in September, the shop windows still displayed 'Skye-scented candles' and 'Peatcense – Breath of Scotland'. In the saloon of the Tongadale Hotel, a group of Americans was eating fish and chips and talking about castles. At the bar stood a couple of men whose pinkish faces spoke, like mine, of a day spent out on the water. I was after a new shackle. One of them said I should go to the lifeboat station.

'Aye,' said his mate. 'They'll sort you out.'

One of the men, it turned out, was skipper of the tourist boat I'd seen below the cliffs.

'We were looking for sea eagles.'

'Sea eagles!' spluttered the other. 'They're not sea eagles. Those guys just whistle and down the buggers come. They're just big bloody budgies.'

I was running out of time. As the days grew shorter, the good days grew fewer. No more than fifty or sixty miles of water now lay between me and the Summer Isles. With decent weather, that would be three or four hops along the coast. But the weather was not decent. That evening, I scanned ahead through a week of barometric charts and saw the isobars rebuild. Two days of storms and an easing of sorts, but then a veering to the east and north-east. None of it was favourable.

The wind howled that night, and beneath the howling the boat was filled with bumps and taps and strains. I was up and down checking the lines and the bulky launch that was fish-tailing at its mooring just in front of me. I rose to a day full of skidding clouds and a sleepless ache behind my brow. A shore day.

I was glad to spend it on Skye. Of all the Hebrides, it is the one where the gauze between this world and the otherworld appears to be thinnest. It has its Fairy Bridge and Fairy Knoll and Fairy Glen and the Cave of the Fairies and sightings of *cro sìth* ('fairy cows') that live beneath the sea and graze on seaweed. It has more than its fair share of brownies and *glaistigs* and *urisg*, the solitary spirits that are found around the Cuillins and are said by those who encounter them to evoke pity more than fear. Second sight was always common on Skye, and one seer's eyes would swivel so far up in his head they had to be pulled back down by an assistant. It was to Skye that the warriors of Irish antiquity travelled to learn the mystical skills essential for heroic adventuring. In the Ulster Cycle, Cú Chulainn did a formative stint on Skye.

As the largest of Scotland's inner isles, it may simply be aggregation that has led to Skye's abundance in such lore. But it's not just size. In the last few centuries, the sheer scale of human loss has filled the landscape with ghosts – the evictions following the Jacobite risings, the famines, the clearances. I wondered too if it was something in the cumulative presence of the land itself, the legacy of volcanic turbulence, the shapes left in time-whittled gabbro, and the coming and going of cloud around them – the name 'Skye' comes from the Norse for 'mist', and the Gaelic name, Eilean Cheo, means the same.

I took a bus across the island to Dunvegan Castle to see 'one of the most fascinating relics of faerie in the country'. Am Bratach Sìth, 'the fairy flag', is a shred of cloth that was once part of a clan battle-banner that helped ensure many glorious victories. Several centuries ago, runs one version of the story, when the heir to the MacLeod chief was a baby, he kicked off his bedding. A *sìth* woman came and wrapped him in a shawl of fine silk. When his nurse returned, she found the room full of the sound of the Fairy Lullaby. Another version of the cloth's origin has a MacLeod chief spending time in the *sìth* kingdom, married to a *sìth* woman. When he has to return, she gives him the shawl.

On the wall of the castle's drawing room, framed behind glass, I found what was left of Am Bratach Sìth. The silk was in tatters. It was as much absence as substance. As I peered more closely, so the pattern of threads and holes began to look less like silk than the map of an island – one on these coasts, with hundreds of tiny pools in the boggy interior, and its rim broken by watery incursions.

A. J. B. Wace was a consultant from the Victoria and Albert Museum who inspected the cloth in the 1930s. He saw at once that it was Middle Eastern in origin, and did a little research. A forebear of the MacLeods was known to have a bought a 'famous banner' while on one of the early crusades. The cloth itself, Wace explained to the twenty-seventh chief, Sir Reginald MacLeod, was even older – probably woven between the fourth and seventh centuries, in Syria or on Rhodes (the island of Tsambika). He added, with some excitement, that it might well have been preserved because it was a relic, the shroud of an early Byzantine saint.

'Mr Wace,' replied Sir Reginald, 'you may believe that, but I know it was given to my ancestor by the fairies.'

*

The next morning, still stormbound, I went walking in the Quiraing. In William Mackenzie's 1930 *Skye Traditions, Reflections and Memories* is a description of this high rocky area to the north of Portree: 'Truly a wonderful assemblage of fantastic nature, bewildering in its confusion, instilling an awesome feeling, expectant of encountering some ghostly phantom, gliding noiselessly through one of the many apertures.'

Most of the day I spent among its rocky colonnades. You'd have to be very low in spirit not to feel a little spooked in that place. Nowhere I'd been to in the past months better combined the physical and the metaphysical, the real and the imaginary. Mist spilled down its gullies. Veils of cloud ghouled about the heights – covering and uncovering the Needle, and the flat-topped rock known as the Prison, and the once-haunted chasm where 'a smith threw a piece of iron through this cleft and so laid the ghost'.

Iron too did for another of the area's ghosts, the Colann-gun-Cheann, the 'Headless Body'. Originally from these hills, Colann-gun-Cheann was identified as evil and driven out to the mainland, to Arisaig. There they again discovered his true nature and cut off his head. But the head still flew around attacking travellers. Someone caught it and impaled it on a sword. They banished it with his body, back here to the foggy heights of Trotternish.

It was in the late nineteenth century that J. G. Campbell collected and published the Colann-gun-Cheann story. He added variants from around the Hebrides and a number of similar tales from elsewhere, including the incident when Sir William Wallace met the headless body of a man whom he himself had once decapitated.

A more recent edition of Campbell's compendious collection has been published as *The Gaelic Otherworld*, edited by Ronald Black. His commentary alone runs to more than 300 pages. Black finds further examples of headlessness – a place on Islay named

Glac Gille Gun Cheann, 'Hollow of the Headless Boy', and a poem in which the Fianna, that heroic corps of Irish warriors, find themselves in 'a ghastly house occupied by a three-headed woman and a headless man who has a single eye protruding from his breast, with nine bodies ranged along one side of the room and nine heads on the other'.

Headless hauntings, *sìth* and *selkies*, second sight (*dà shealladh* – the 'two sights'), changelings, hobgoblins, king otters and water horses have always existed in the shadows of these shores. Ronald Black notes that for several hundred years 'academics in both England and Scotland . . . have recognized the Highlands and islands as an area in which the occult was extraordinarily close to the surface of people's lives.'

In the past century or so, with the decline of religious belief, much of the context of these stories has been removed. Rational theories have neatly despatched them as, variously: the expression of collective anxiety, the product of dreams, psychic constructs to contain pathology, social constructs to normalize behaviour, ways of explaining the inexplicable, of visualizing the invisible.

But go into any Highland bookshop and you will still find stacks of titles exploring the more bizarre of those outmoded beliefs. The thirst for such stories remains. They are the weird fruit of the collective consciousness, ripened over centuries, and it is their strangeness that helps give them such lasting flavour. J. G. Campbell himself talks of their 'tinge of the ludicrous'. Like jokes, like metaphor, it is the most tenuous or far-fetched that are the most effective. *Credo quia absurdam* – 'I believe because it is absurd' – was the phrase made famous by Thomas Browne to express the paradox.

The more colourful traditions of these coasts can be celebrated for many reasons, but above all for their high jinks – those bizarre scenes, the dream-like places and the labyrinth of narrative laid with the slenderest thread of logic. It is a miracle that they have survived, but they have, everywhere. They've survived because they remind us of the human urge to elaborate what we see. Why? To give it meaning? Or simply to remind us of the more subtle ways in which the imagination is constantly at work, colouring every moment, everything we see? The imagination enables us to see beyond what is in front of us. It is what keeps us alive. Ted Hughes thought it 'the most essential bit of machinery we have if we are going to live the lives of human beings'. A generation before him, fellow poet Wallace Stevens likewise singled it out: 'The imagination is the only genius . . . It enables us to live our own lives.' It is, he wrote, 'the necessary angel'.

The cloud had dropped over the Quiraing, thickening into fog. The wind was driving it in. I found myself walking in white. From time to time it would open up – with a sudden snapshot of cliff or edge, or a section of gale-flecked waters far below. Then the cloud would close again, leaving me to wonder whether it had really been there at all. I lost the path. I found my way back by way of contours, as I would have done using the depth sounder on the boat.

It took no more than fifteen minutes standing by the road with a thumb out before I got lucky. Doubly so – a car pulled up, and in it was a Kurdish doctor and his Lithuanian girlfriend. They both worked in a hospital near Mosul. They'd discovered, during the dark days of the conflict with Islamic State, that they shared a love for Scotland, and a love for the Isle of Skye in particular. Neither had ever been, but they both knew the same stories of its ghosts and fairies, and now here they were, in their hired car, staring at its misty slopes through the double arc of the windscreen wipers.

'Pity about the weather,' I said.

'No, no!' The Lithuanian woman was smiling. 'This is *exactly* how we thought of it.'

*

The gale blew itself out overnight, but the wind was still fresh when I set sail in the morning. Above grey waters, the great scarp of Trotternish stretched ahead for fifteen miles or more. I felt I was following the edge of some ancient citadel, my white sails tiny outside it, the green slopes and dark cliffs of the Quiraing rising high above the masthead. Beyond the cliffs, the sky was an autumnal blue. October was just days away.

The landscape was growing larger and less peopled. I was heading for the island of South Rona (population: two). From a distance, its shores offered no sign of any anchorage. I could see silent swells rising and breaking on blocks of glaciated gneiss. The waves gave little sense of the power in them until they struck the rock and sent columns of spray shooting upwards. I sailed in closer and spotted a small gap. Tucked in behind the islet of Eilean Garbh was the dog-leg of a channel. The seas were smaller inside, but there were scuffs of broken water where rocks hid beneath the surface. Weaving between them, I crept in and reached an inner pool. Into its quiet waters I dropped the anchor and fed out the chain.

The open sea was out of sight, cut off by a number of heathery headlands and islands. The haven is known as Acairseid Mhor, or 'big harbour'. But that name covers an older, less neutral one – Port nan Robaireann ('port of the robbers'). The sixteenth-century account of Sir Donald Munro, High Dean of the Isles, describes it as 'good for fostering of thieves, robbers, and reivers, who wait upon the plundering and pillaging of poor people'.

On the other side of Rona was a cave that was also a church. I rowed ashore and walked up over the ridge of the island to the east-facing slope, and scrambled down to a place where the cliff dropped to a shadowy void. It was a textbook cave, a fairy-tale cave, a cave drawn for a children's story. Inside was the smell of fungal spores and, on the mud, rows of small boulders arranged as pews.

There was an altar too, a rock at the entrance and a natural font filled with run-off. On the floor, someone had arranged a group of stones into a cruciform.

The story goes that the cave was adopted by the islanders for worship while a proper church was being built in 1912. It was still in occasional use. But I couldn't help thinking of the church elements as bolt-on, the appropriation of something older. Above the entrance, the sandstone was a very distinctive pink and orange and black, running down in stripes that twisted and fused like dye drops in water. Was it that geological curio that helped sanctify the place long ago? The English name, Church Cave, overlays an earlier one, a name from the age of heroes and giants: Uamh na Gaisgeach, 'Cave of the Warrior'.

In the Irish *Book of the Dun Cow* is the tale of Tuán meic Chairill. St Finnian meets a hermit called Tuán, who has lived so long that he is able to recall the very first invasion of Ireland. How have you managed so many years? asks the saint. Tuán explains. Whenever he feels himself fading, he goes to a certain cave and, having fasted, falls into a deep sleep. In that sleep, he dreams of all his previous selves – a stag, a boar, a hawk, a salmon. It is as a salmon that he is then caught by a woman who eats him and thereby conceives him again. That is his secret. Like Amergin, like the youth who meets St Columba on the shores of Lough Foyle, Tuán is speaking of the mobility of the soul, its gift for migrating between bodies, between this world and the otherworld. The story should have been anathema to those early Christians who recorded it. But there was too much time in it, too much power to ignore. So it is with places like Uamh na Gaisgeach.

I took a circuitous route back. In the early evening I found myself in a clearing in a birch wood. It had been weeks since I'd been among trees; I thought of my own down south. To one side rose a twenty-foot rock face. On top, beneath more squat birches and rowans, ran a thick layer of turf. Grass flopped from it like a fringe. It felt like the sort of place *sith* might appear.

'Islets in an ocean of green' was how James Frazer described the groves of ancient Europe in *The Golden Bough* – those green spaces which had played such a central role in traditional belief. The forest was then as limitless as the ocean. Where the canopy was open could be found precious islands of light and colour, ready-made sites of worship. Now in our deforested world, it is not the clearings but the woods themselves that are the islands.

I remained there as the light dimmed. There was a moment when everything suddenly took on a vibrant intensity – the papery white of the birch boles, the moss on the boughs' upper sides, the ferns where they met the main trunk, the brown seed heads of asphodel in the moss. It was the coming darkness that made it all look so bright.

Back on board, I spread out the chart. For the hundredth time I checked the waters ahead. How close I was now! I didn't feel close. Headwinds were pushing the Summer Isles away; time was running out. But it wasn't just that. The islands had been abstract for all this time, a place without co-ordinates. Now they were all about pilotage and weather windows and angles of approach and holding ground. I was finding it hard to square the two versions.

I heard a noise ashore and went up on deck. In the half-darkness it took me a while to make out what it was: an otter being dive-bombed by a herring gull. The otter had a fish in its claws and was trying to eat it, but every time it brought it in to the rocks, the gull swooped and the otter was forced back into the water. I don't know how they resolved it, but only that they did, because soon there was no more screeching and no splashing, and only the lonely hiss of the wind.

22

LEAVING SOUTH RONA IN THE early morning, I cleared the end of the island and sailed on north. The wind was good to begin with, but then it backed against me, increasing as it did so. In the end, I had to put in several tacks even to fetch Gairloch. No chance of any further progress. I spent the night in the cove at Badachro, and woke to find my bows pointing inland. Easterlies. Was that any better than northerlies? For now, yes.

In autumnal sun, I raised the sails – for the last time? – and scooted down the loch before a steady breeze. Lengths of stratus tangled with contrails in a milky sky. I took the inside passage past Longa Island and hardened sheets to reach up the Melvaig peninsula. The wind built, the gunwale dipped. I held the helm tight and propped one leg against the leeward coaming. Filled with the morning and the promise of completion, I contemplated the west. Out there in the haze was nothing but sea and sky; then, like barely audible notes, darker shapes on the horizon – the island of Lewis and Harris. The water was a deep blue and the hull drove through it like a blade. It was as exhilarating a sail as I'd had all trip.

I'd seen the forecast. I knew what was coming. But when the wind's abeam and the seas are small, you become a willing hostage to the immediate. What was I thinking? By the time I was off the smooth head of Rubha Reidh ('smooth head' in Gaelic), I was struggling. Rounding the point, the seas and the wind struck at about the same time – hard and hostile and sudden from a place a little north of east, exactly the bearing of the Summer Isles. I tightened sheets. Water poured along the lee deck. I put in a reef and shortened the genoa, but the wind was fresh and growing fresher, gusting twenty-eight knots and more.

We were on a roller coaster, but one without rails. The waves were fast and steep. They were hitting the bow and raising it, or breaking full to douse the deck. Everything was under strain. When I came about, the sound of the flapping sails was explosive. One of the genoa sheets caught on a mast-set cleat and I clipped on to edge forward and free it. The canvas was thrashing – the whole boat was shaking. As I re-entered the cockpit, the hull fell off a sea and I fell too, pulled up short by my harness, contemplating my own distorted face in the chrome drum of a winch.

A couple more hours, a few more tacks, and the Summer Isles were still out of sight in the haze. The anchorage there would be exposed. I cut my losses. I bore away, deferring the final stretch, leaving the islands still far upwind, and headed south-west towards the entrance of Loch Ewe. Off the wind, the crazy movement settled and *Tsambika* surged down the short seas, liberated and easy in her roll.

Loch Ewe looked like the loneliest place on earth. Its waters were streaked white by the wind, its hills were grey and long. Not another boat, not a harbour in sight. I felt I'd never find anywhere quiet enough to stop. It was several miles into the loch before I came to a wide bay and dropped anchor. Tight to the chain, the bows pointed at the scattered dwellings of Aultbea.

I sat it out the next day. There was nothing else I could do. It was blowing harder. In the evening, the rain set in. I inflated the Zodiac, motored in to the quay and, in full oilskins, walked round to the pub. They didn't get many yachtsmen in, they said, didn't encourage them. 'They wash their clothes in the basins.'

It was dark when I left. The rain was still heavy, driving in hard from the east, sweeping out unseen into the loch. I passed scattered bungalows, their windows flashing with screen-light. In the driveways stood cars and pickups and basketball hoops, and trampolines on neat squares of lawn; a B & B sign squeaked back and forth in the wind. Then, set back from the road, an abandoned house. A privet grew high and wild in front of it; rainwater gushed from its unguttered roof. Its two storeys rose head and shoulders above the other buildings; unlit and untended, hovered over by the ghost of generations past. Out on the end of the quay, I stared into the black. I listened to the *shush* of water below, and suddenly – a feeling of hollowness as wide as the ocean.

I woke to the same noise as yesterday, the same as so many days: rigging and stays whining in the wind. I lay, assessing it. If I could raise the anchor, I'd go. The gale had eased, but the weather was due to come in again, and then set in for a week at least. Today was my last chance.

Up on the foredeck, I put a hand to the chain. The links were solid. I went aft and started the engine, shunted the boat forward, then hurried back. I managed to heave a couple of metres before the wind drove the hull against it again. It needed a lot of toing and froing before I bundled the hook in under the rail, and started to pick off the kelp.

Untied, unhelmed, the boat skipped away on the wind. I sat on the coachroof and caught my breath. I didn't mind the drift; I had plenty of sea-room and here in the loch the water was flat. I stowed the chain and sluiced down the foredeck. It felt anarchic to leave the hull so free, almost a pity when I pushed down the tiller and felt the rudder bite. Now the bows pointed out towards the open sea. Ominous lumps of white water were already visible along the horizon.

The wind funnelled into the entrance, building the swells into something mountainous and wild. For an hour I hammered into them, watching the bows rise high to climb their peaks, then slam down behind. Beating would have prolonged the ordeal, so I had the engine on and the main up. Visibility was better today. I watched the water open out beyond Greenstone Point, and beyond that to the grey skyline of Sutherland.

They were in there, somewhere – close enough, low enough against the mainland to merge with it from this distance. So I could see the Summer Isles, but couldn't yet distinguish them. Anyway, my attention was busy with the mountains above – that weird assembly of Torridonian sandstone that defines the north-west Highlands. Stac Pollaidh, close to the shore, smallest of the peaks, a forty-minute scoot up from the road. Cùl Mòr and Cùl Beag, afternoon hikes, with their open summits and views of the Minch. Then Suilven, strangest of them all, looking like some celestial locomotive. Bridget and I had been up it a number of times; you had to walk in for three hours before even reaching its base. The climb up its side was less of a challenge than it looked, and when you reached the saddle, something that amazed and puzzled us each time – a beautifully built, drystone wall.

Beyond Suilven, diminished a little by distance, stood Ben More Assynt. The biggest of all those peaks, two of its summits rise over 3,000 feet. It was where Bridget had died. I couldn't help looking at it now with prejudice, seeing in its grey shoulders a brutality, like a figure standing in the dock.

What had happened that day? The police had given us map co-ordinates, but when I checked them on the Ordnance Survey, they didn't make sense. They were some way off to the south, some

286

distance from the route down. She had basic safety equipment – a canvas bag we always took with us, with survival blanket, compass, first aid. But nothing could have saved her from the fall. Her camera was found with her, and when the film was processed, it answered one of my questions. She had made it to the summit. There were the victory shots, from the top – the views back down the Oykel, and out towards the Minch, the Summer Isles pretty much invisible in the wide-angle frame.

At the funeral, I talked to one of the rescue team – a young mother who worked for Bridget and Francis from time to time. She said that when the team first spotted her, at the foot of a steep cleft, her black Labrador, Canna, was sitting beside her. But what she remembered most about that night was bringing the body down in the helicopter, and being met by Francis. 'He'd been waiting all evening for her to come back. He was in quite a state – you can imagine. But he came up to each one of us and shook our hands, thanking us. Only then did he go on to identify Bridget. I'll never forget that.' There were tears in her eyes.

Francis had always been a somewhat distant figure in my child-hood. Only when he and Bridget moved to Sutherland, and I spent time with him there, did I come to know him properly. He was a true countryman, as familiar with trees and wild flowers, with the comings and goings of migrating birds, as with anything in the human field. The shift of seasons affected him with an emotional force that grew more powerful with every passing year. He engaged with his surroundings from a position stripped bare of presumption – yet his humility was more than a personal quality. It was a way of being in the world, and when you were with him, it seemed there couldn't possibly be any other way. I grew to admire him as I have few others.

Francis had had his own imagined island. His childhood holidays were spent on the Hebridean island of Tiree; after school he went up for longer, becoming semi-feral for a while, wandering around the island barefoot, shooting his own food. Later he'd taken his own family there each summer. It was the memory of Tiree that had helped draw him north again.

After Bridget died, Francis carried on living alone in Sutherland. Whenever I visited him, he showed something of the old enthusiasm – for the river and its fish, for the trees he'd planted, the hen harrier that ranged the sedge grass, for his friends there – all the other scattered residents further down the strath. But there was an absence now, made more acute by the great emptiness of Sutherland itself. I often remembered that June evening when I'd arrived on my motorbike, and saw them both up beside the track, raking and scything in the late sun, and it broke my heart.

Francis was buried alongside Bridget in a cemetery just beyond the eastern skyline here, a high-walled graveyard of Highland austerity, set on its own above the river Oykel. Once I asked him why, when he had the choice, he had chosen to come to Sutherland rather than to live on Tiree. He paused, trying to recall what had been so obvious at the time. 'I don't think you can ever really go back, not like that.'

The morning's wind did not ease. It grew in strength. Now it was heading me. I had to put in a couple of tacks. The seas became smaller, but the breeze was more flukey near the mainland, more severe in its gusts. The helm fought against my hands. It was becoming hard to hold.

Not far short of Tanera Mòr, I went up in the bows to prepare the anchor. I didn't put on the autohelm; it wouldn't hold the course in this wind. The sails flapped. I knelt and reached for the two small lanyards which kept the anchor tight to the deck, fastenings I'd done up just a few hours earlier. The genoa was going wild over my head. The boat was convulsing. I could see the island between the life-lines – a grey presence hidden and revealed behind the beating sail. I took the two-ply cord in my fingers. As I did so, I knew that I had no intention of untying it, that I would not draw out the chain in two-metre sections on the deck and heave the anchor over the side, that in these conditions the haven of Tigh an Quay – so quiet in Fraser Darling's photo, and in Daniell's print – was too exposed. I had come up on the foredeck simply to confirm what I had already decided. The forecast was terrible. I would not be landing on the Summer Isles.

Back in the cockpit, I took the mainsheet and flicked it from its jamming cleat. The boom swung away. I heaved on the helm. With the wind abeam, the boat picked up speed, heading down towards the entrance to Loch Broom and the harbour at Ullapool. I was overwhelmed by a great tide of liberation.

Despite its title, Brian Friel's play *Wonderful Tennessee* takes place entirely on a pier in Donegal. Three couples wait for a boatman to ferry them out to an island. The island is named as Oileán Draoíchta, 'Island of Mysteries', but it is based on the pilgrimage island of Inish-keel. The group talk and sing as they wait. They flirt, argue about religion, ruminate about happiness, drink whisky, reminisce, tell improbable stories, discuss mutual friends, and misunderstand each other. In short, they get on with living. But all the while the island hovers offshore. The boatman never comes. Friel's working title for the play was *The Imagined Place*.

I could now identify two types of island on my route up from Dingle: those I'd reached and those I hadn't. The ones I'd been to were thick with incident, with people and stories and places. Those I hadn't reached were shapes in the haze, smooth and distant, as still as anything on the surface of this earth. In his *immram*, Bran reached his island, but he and his crew were warned there that they could never again set foot on Irish soil. One man tried. When Nechtán place his foot on the shore, he crumbled to dust.

I passed close in to one of the outlying islands. It was a miniature island with a miniature pale beach. Two oystercatchers busied themselves on the sand, peep-peeping, their red beaks probing. An acre or so of grass grew on top. The boulders above the shoreline looked like mountains. For a moment, I lost the scale of it. Was the island a yard long, or a mile?

I tried to grasp it, but it was all moving away too quickly. *Tsambika* was doing what she was designed to do – to go with the wind. The power that filled the sails, that tilted the decks, that was channelled through her bows and parted the waters ahead, was the power of the ever-spinning world.

The Summer Isles were already shrinking astern.

Off Inishdooey

Oil introductory

NOTES

The stanza from *Immram Brain* is translated both in Meyer (1895), p. 18, and in Murphy (1931), p. 95. The version here I have adapted from Murphy. *Locksley Hall* was written by Alfred Tennyson in 1835, and first published in 1842. The lines from *Wonderful Tennessee* are in Friel (1993), pp. 28–9.

1

David Brewster's letters to Walter Scott – *Letters in Natural Magic* – addressed the interest that both men shared in strange natural phenomena. Scott had already explored some of these in *Letters in Demonology and Witchcraft* (1830), but Brewster brought to the subject his own emphasis on the technical aspects of optics. The letters were first published in 1832 by John Murray in London and J. & J. Harper in New York. I consulted a later edition, Brewster (1883), pp. 203–15.

Bibliograhical details of the manuscripts and recensions of *Echtrae Chonnlai* can be found at https://www.vanhamel.nl/codecs/Echtrae_Chonnlai. The story of *Echtra Cormaic i Tír Tairngiri*, 'Cormac's Adventure in the Land of Promise', trans. Whitley Stokes, can be seen at http://sejh.pagesperso-orange.fr/keltia/version-en/echtraCormacB.html.

'I would suggest that . . . expressed in narrative' is from Carey (1989), p. 31.

The Atlantic Ocean's mythical islands have been written about extensively, and my principal sources have been *Tales of the Enchanted Islands of the Atlantic* by Thomas Higginson (1899), *Legendary Islands of the Atlantic: A Study in Medieval Geography* by William Babcock (1922), and *Phantom Islands of the Atlantic* by Donald Johnson (1997); more general studies of islands, their semiotics and history are equally extensive, but I have found the work of John Gillis (2004, 2012) particularly probing; see also Edmond and Smith (2003).

The most complete account of the long-standing myth of Hy-Brasil is in Freitag (2013). See also Lynch (2010). For T. J. Westropp's account of seeing Hy-Brasil himself, Westropp (1912–13), pp. 223–60.

Columbus's perceptions of the earth, the classical and Biblical tenets he held, are discussed in Gillis (2004) pp. 56–61.

Mythical geography being 'the only geography man could never be without' is from Eliade (1963) p. 433. Oscar Wilde's famous quote is taken from his libertarian manifesto *The Soul of Man under Socialism*, first published in *The Fortnightly Review* in 1891. It was later republished in book form, in many editions, see Wilde (1912), p. 40.

For the Roman *alter orbis*, see Byrne (2016), p. 183, and also an address given at St Nicholas Greek Orthodox Church, Southampton, 14 July 2012 http://britishorthodox.org/glastonburyreview/issue-122-alter-orbis/. 'It would seem that the notion of the otherworld . . . travel and discovery': see Byrne (2016), p. 183.

Madeleine Bunting puts the Fraser Darlings' project on the Summer Isles into a wider historical context. She links it with others who, at about the same time, found in the Scottish islands the physical context with which to explore their scepticism about the modern world – Compton Mackenzie, George Orwell, Gavin Maxwell, John Lorne Campbell, Hugh MacDiarmid, etc.; see Bunting (2016), pp. 46–53. For the account of Frank Fraser Darling's 'relatively slight accident' of his broken leg, see Fraser Darling (1943), pp. 123–7; for Bobbie's temporary paralysis, ibid., p. 175; and the pursuing of 'the *idea*' of living on the island, ibid., p. 222.

2

'The sea connects the real world to the supernatural . . . like hell' is from Hilliers (1993) p. 67. The Three Waves of Erin are listed in Westropp (1912–13). '*Tonn*' is 'wave' in Irish and the Tonn Rudraige can be found in Dundrum Bay, County Down; Tonn Clíodhna is associated with Glandore Harbour in Cork, while the Tonn Tuath rises at the mouth of the River Bann in Derry. In *Acallam na Senórach*, Dooley (1999), pp. 97–8, is the story of Lí Bán, who drowned in the Wave of Flood off the Ulster coast and haunted it with the 'resounding music of the *síd*'; she appeared to Caílte, who recited a beautiful poem, asking where such a wave could come from, and mentioning each of the great waves of Ireland.

The story of St Columba reading the sound of the waves is in Stokes (1905), p. 9 ff. 'Colloquy of the Two Sages', *Immacallam in dá Thuarad*, which tells of young Néde, son of the *Ollamh* – chief poet – of Ireland. He is studying in Scotland when the wave announces news of his father's death and tells him that the new *Ollamh* is a man named Ferchertne. Néde puts on a beard of grass and goes to see Ferchertne, to challenge him, and the two of them confront each other with a wonderfully esoteric exchange; see Stokes (1905), p. 9.

The story of Amergin is told in the *Lebor Gabála Érenn*, 'The Book of the Taking of Ireland' (see Macalister, 1941), commonly referred to simply as the 'Book of Invasions'. Amergin was one of the leaders of the Milesians, who came to do battle with the existing inhabitants of Ireland, the Tuatha Dé Danann. Initially the Milesians remained out 'beyond the ninth wave', but when they broke through and landed, Amergin was the first ashore – and his initial act was to utter the strange lines now known as the *Song of Amergin*. The Milesians, who defeated the Tuatha Dé Danann, are the mythical ancestors of the Irish. Amergin's lines have been much translated and there are versions by Lady Gregory, H. d'Arbois de Jubainville, Robert Graves (very loose), R. A. S. Macalister, Paddy Bushe, among others. The version here is a synthesis, combining those elements that – to me – best convey the verses' mystical rhetoric.

Dinnseanchas survives in both verse and prose versions. Edward Gwynn translated and glossed the metrical versions between 1903 and 1935 (Royal Irish Academy Todd Lecture Series), while the prose versions were translated by Whitley Stokes, 1894–1895 (*Revue Celtique*). The Irish tradition itself points to a much wider human tendency: to use the features of the outer, physical world to reflect the inner. *Dinnseanchas* stories occur in many of the Irish medieval cycles, in particular in the *Acallam na Senórach* – from which the quote comes; see Dooley (1999), p. 71.

In her essay on the work of Thomas Kinsella (Obert, 2009), Julia Obert explores how the importance of *dinnseanchas* was established and maintained, suggesting that it arose with the coming of Christianity in order to preserve something of the indigenous traditions, and that it was sustained, in part, in opposition to the English preference for precise map-making. Nuala Ní Dhomhnaill is quoted in this essay, ibid., p. 71.

The popular derivation of the name *naómhog* is that it means 'little saint' or 'little holy one', from *noíb*, 'holy, saint'. But it is more likely to have its origin in the Old Irish *nó*, *noe*, 'a boat', generally a small one, propelled by oars (private correspondence with Dónall Mac Giolla Easpaig). A possible link exists too with the Basque *nao*, a larger fishing boat or whaler. On the islands of Inishkea, off Co. Mayo, was a holy stone called the '*Naomhóg*', with its root in *noíb* (see Chapter 13). The coincidence of spelling – the boat and sanctity – suggests that some elision of meaning has taken place over the years, and some saintly quality has been added to the boats. Danny Sheehy named his boat *Naomhóig Na Tinte*, '*naomhóg* of the tents'. The story of Danny Sheehy's sea journey to Santiago de Compostela is told in the 2018 documentary *The Camino Voyage* (director Dónal Ó Céilleachair).

The distinction between *immrama* and *echtrai* is generally accepted to be hazy, and there is some overlap, but the *immrama* tend to take place in a loosely Christian or monastic context, while *echtrai* are journeys to the pagan otherworld. '*Echtrae* is a derivative of the preposition *echtar*, "outside", by means of the feminine abstract suffix -*e* and as such basically means "outsideness", in effect being or going outside or away from home'; from *The Echtrae as an Early Irish Literary Genre*, Leonie Duignan, PhD thesis, NUI Maynooth, 2010, p. 1.

Ernest Renan's essay was written in 1854 (though not published in English until the 1890s), and was one of the spurs to Matthew Arnold's four famous Oxford lectures (first published in 1867 as *On the Study of Celtic Literature*, London, Smith & Elder). The works of these two men did more than anything else to create the myth of the Celt; see Renan (1896), p. 9. The 'Celtic Revival' and 'Celtic Twilight' are interchangeable to an extent, referring to a late-nineteenth and early-twentieth-century movement that was strongest in Ireland, and mainly literary in focus – but it became popularized much more widely in Britain and Europe; many of its ideas and motifs are still with us. W. B. Yeats's counter to narrow Celticism comes from an essay published first in the arts journal *Cosmopolis* in 1898, and republished in *Writings on Irish Folklore, Legend and Myth*; see Yeats (1993), p. 190. In the context of everything that has been written about Celtic matters, the elaboration and the debunking, Yeats's perspective is a refreshing reminder of all that is most true, most appealing and most bogus about the figure of 'the Celt'. 'Have not all races . . . to rock and hill?' is from Yeats (1999), vol. III, p. 167.

For the results of the extensive genetic analysis of northern European populations, and its thirty-nine authors, see Haak et al. (2015).

Carl Marstrander was a Norwegian champion pole-vaulter and his feat of clearing Tomás Ó Crohan's roof is recounted in Kiberd (2001), p. 521. 'Like taking off one's clothes . . . some mountain-pool' and 'that world of the lost childhood . . . eternally young' are from Ó Faoláin (1943), p. 144. Tomás Ó Crohan's comment on King George is in Ó Crohan (1978), p. 29. The scene in Ó Crohan's house is recorded in Flower (1978), pp. 132–4. Peig Sayers in the heather is in Sayers (1962), p. 130. Her lament for youth and the losses life imposes are the opening lines of her memoir, ibid., p. 1. The account of the death of her son Tom is in ibid., p. xiii. The flight of the earls from Ulster in 1607 is generally seen as the end of the old Gaelic order, the exile of the last of the Irish ruling aristocracy. Pierce Ferriter's connection with the Blaskets is in Flower (1978), pp. 84–91, while the fascinating story of the bards of south-west Munster, and their end, is the subject of Daniel Corkery's *The Hidden Ireland* (1956). For the Blasket islander's thoughts on 'young people', see Synge (2009), p. 92.

'One can scarcely find it credible . . . rich store of oral lore': Bo Almqvist on An File is from O'Guiheen (1982), p. xvii. An extensive account of Maria Simonds-Gooding's life and work – including a Q & A with Colm Tóibín – can be found in the catalogue of her 2014 exhibition, *Maria Simonds-Gooding: A Retrospective*, Royal Hibernian Academy, Dublin (2014). The translation of O'Guiheen's verse on the *An Lia Fáil* picture is by Aogán Ó Muircheartaigh.

4

For pilotage of Blasket Sound see Wilcox (2009), pp. 48–9. I also used the Irish Cruising Club *Sailing Directions* (Kean 2016). For the fate of Armada ships in Blasket Sound, see Douglas (2010). In *Moby Dick*, Chapter XXXII, Herman Melville discusses cetaceans. He refers generically to dolphins and porpoises as the 'Huzza Porpoise' as it is hard, he believes, to withhold giving 'three cheers' on seeing them. 'They are the lads . . . *a lucky omen*' is from Melville (1988), p. 145. The hypersonic senses of dolphins is from Casey (2015), pp. 22–3. For the Magharee Islands, see Wilcox (2009), p. 40.

Fionn mac Cumhaill's horse race, etc.: see O'Donoghue (1895), p. 45. 'Over the loud-voiced waves . . . relentless ocean' is from ibid, p28. A number of different versions of St Brendan's voyage survive, and I have drawn particularly on the Anglo-Norman one, see Mackley (2013) and Waters (1928), but have consulted others, including the translation from the Irish by O'Donoghue (1895), and also McNamara (2013). Details of Saint Brendan's life come also from the *The Book of Lismore*, see O'Donoghue (1895), pp. 1–103. *The Otherworld Voyage in Early Irish Literature*, a collection of essays edited by Jonathan Wooding (2000), provides an excellent companion not only to Saint Brendan's voyage but also to the other surviving *immrama* and *echtrai*.

Tim Severin's account of his voyage across the Atlantic, in a boat built using only technology available in Brendan's time, is Severin (2005).

5

'Rise up by the strength of this charm . . . ashes be made of you' – the *dinnseanchas* of Slieve Mish comes from *Acallam na Senórach*, Dooley (1999), pp. 177–8. The flying church is in Flower (1978), pp. 134–5. The phenomenon of ships in the sky is explored in Carey (1992) and found to be widespread in medieval Ireland, 'including in the Annals of Ulster, of Tigernach, of Clonmacnoise, of the Four Masters, as well as in annalistic material in some manuscripts of *Lebor Gabála*', ibid., p. 16. The Clonmacnoise version occurs in *Anecdota from Irish Manuscripts*, vol. III, see Bergin et al. (1910), pp. 8–9, but there are details – the anchor being cast and a man swimming down through the air – that suggest derivation from earlier texts. The story travelled far. A thirteenth-century British version was told by Gervase of Tilbury in his book of marvels, the *Otia Imperialia*. It crops up in an old Norse text, the thirteenth-century *Konungs skuggsjá*; see Meyer (1910), p. 12. In Texas, in 1897, a similar report occurs in the *Houston Post* – of an anchor hanging from an airship, and of a man from above cutting it; the anchor was put on display in a blacksmith shop: Carey (1992), pp. 20–21. Seamus Heaney drew on the same monastic story for his poem 'Lightenings', viii, Heaney (2014) p. 32 – a work which was used as 'an example of a crystallisation of much of Heaney's imaginative world: history and sensuality, myths and the day-to-day' in his Nobel Prize citation. Which all goes to prove that, if certain strange stories strike a chord, they will not stay confined to one place and one time.

The lines from the *Voyage of Bran* are in Meyer (1895), p. 18. 'Here all things are possible . . . attributes can be isolated and transferred' is from Carey (1989), p. 31.

For the Law of Similarity, see Frazer (1923), p. 11. The Thomas Gibbons quote comes from his *Boxing the Compass*, and James Fenimore Cooper's from *The Red Rover* (1855), both from Bassett (1885), p. 8 – an excellent overview of the whole world of mariners and their numerous superstitions. 'The western world contains not a more hallowed island,' is from James Kenney's *The Sources for the Early History of Ireland: Ecclesiastical*, quoted in Kingshill and Westwood, (2015), pp. 462–4. For a discussion of *Amra Senáin*, see Breatnach (1989), pp. 7–28. For Danny Sheehy's leather-encased stones, see Sheehy (2017), pp. 103–105.

6

Tim Robinson's two Aran books, and his three on Connemara, as well as his meticulous maps, represent an intense scrutiny of a small piece of physical territory. Their importance beyond the Galway coast comes from the example of unpeeling those layers of story and memory that exist beneath all places. 'The unsummable totality of human perspectives' is from Robinson (1986), p. 3, and the story of St Gregory of the Golden-mouth and Gregory's Sound is told in ibid., pp. 21–3.

'No one even knows but God the number of saints buried there' ('*nemo scit numerum sanctorum qui sepulti sunt ibi, nisi solus Deus*') is from the twelfth-century life of St Ailbe, quoted in O'Connell (1994), p. 137. The evidence suggests Aran as one of the largest of the many monastic communities that populated Ireland's western islands in the early Christian centuries. Roderic O'Flaherty was the colourful author of two large works in the seventeenth century – *Ogygia: Or, A Chronological Account of Irish Events* and *A Chorographical Description of West Or H-Iar Connaught*. 'The Isles of Aran are fameous . . . and miraculous virtues there wrought' is from O'Flaherty (1684), pp. 72–6. For *The Speckled Bird* by W. B. Yeats, see Sheeran (1994), p. 299.

'More than anything I have ever seen . . . out of the disturbing sea' is from Symons (1918), p. 326. For Yeats's famous remark to Synge, see Synge (1992), p. xxi. The coincidence of Lady Gregory and J. M. Synge being on Aran was recalled by Lady Gregory: 'I was jealous of not being alone on the island among the fishers and the seaweed gatherers. I did not speak to the stranger nor was he inclined to speak to me. He also looked upon me as an intruder', quoted by Colm Tóibín in https://www.theguardian. com/stage/2005/jul/09/theatre.edinburghfestival2005.

Patrick Pearse visited Aran in August 1898 and wrote up his impressions as *Fáinne an Lae*; see Ó hEithir (1991), p. 93. For Mary Banim's *Here and There through Ireland*, see ibid., p. 73. For the genetic anomaly of the Aran islanders, see the paper in *Annals of Human Biology*, Relethford (1983). James Joyce wrote a number of pieces, in Italian, for *Il Piccolo della Sera*, including, in September 1912, an account of his brief trip to Aran; see Joyce (2000), p. 204.

For Antonin Artaud's adventures in Ireland and his peyote-taking – 'terrifying moments of . . . lucidity' – see Peter Collier's very full article in the *Irish Times*, 14 August 1997, https://www.irishtimes.com/culture/ artaud-on-aran-1.96677. Artaud's adventures in Ireland can also be traced through his letters; see Artaud (2018).

Tim Robinson's two *Stones of Aran* books are Robinson (1986, 1995). 'Step carries us across geologies . . . of personal associations,' is from Robinson (1986), p. 12; Aran as '*the* exemplary terrain upon which to dream of that work', ibid., p. 13. As well as his books, Robinson's maps have vastly enhanced my experience of exploring the Aran Islands; see *Oileáin Árainn*, Folding Landscapes, Roundstone, Co. Galway. His three books on Connemara are *Listening to the Wind* (2007), *The Last Pool of Darkness* (2008) and *A Little Gaelic Kingdom* (2011).

'The Aran Excursion . . . that has ever yet taken place' is from Martin Haverty's first-hand account of Wilde's Ethnological Excursion to Aran, which was first published in the *Freeman's Journal* (est. 1763), Ireland's oldest nationalist newspaper. All subsequent details of the expedition and the cliff-top banquet come from the same source; see Haverty (2018). 'The entire Revival fashioned the western island . . . living myth': see Foster (1977), p. 267.

7

The rabbit playing the flute is in Synge (1992), p. 106. An excellent source for the various boats of the Irish coast – the *currach* and *naomhóg*, the Galway hooker (*húicéir*) and *púcán* – is MacCárthaigh (2008). For J. M. Synge's joy on arriving on Inis Meáin by *currach*, see Synge (1992), p. 12, and for Robin Flower's similar joy at the Blaskets, see Flower (1978), p. 6.

Frank Fraser Darling's thoughts on nostalgia are in Chapter 1 of *Island Farm*, Fraser Darling (1943). The pernicious aspects of nostalgia were discussed compellingly by Mohsin Hamid in 'On the Dangers of Nostalgia', *Guardian*, 25 February 2017, https://www.theguardian.com/books/2017/feb/25/mohsin-hamid-danger-nostalgia-brighter-future, in which he argues the case for narrative over nostalgia. Likewise Elif Sharak warns of the worldwide threat from 'imperial nostalgia': 'It's Not Just Europe – Toxic Imperial Nostalgia Has Infected the World', *Guardian*, 10 December 2018, https://www.theguardian.com/commentisfree/2018/dec/10/nostalgia-for-empires-lost-seductive-dangerous. The more positive aspects of nostalgia, and the academic study of it, were introduced to me in a piece by John Tierney, *New York Times*, 8 July 8 2013: 'What Is Nostalgia Good For? Quite a Bit, Research Shows', https://www.nytimes.com/2013/07/09/science/what-is-nostalgia-good-for-quite-a-bit-research-shows.html. The analysis of Johannes Hofer, originally published in 1688, is in Hofer (1934), pp. 376–91. Krystine Batcho provides a detailed overview of nostalgia from Hofer onwards, Batcho (2013b). A growing body of academic literature and experimental psychology is exploring the behavioural aspects of nostalgia. 'An acute yearning for a union with the preoedipal mother . . .' is from Kaplan (1987), p. 466. For the benefits of nostalgia, see Batcho (2013a), also Zhou et al. (2008).

For Hesiod's view of life in the past, 'And they lived like gods . . . beyond the reach of all evils, see Hesiod (1914), ll. 109–20. For the 'trees were forever in fruit . . . the beard of the jaguar' see *The Mythology of All Races*, vol. 11, p. 262 by Hartley Burr Alexander (Boston 1920), quoted in Heinberg (1989), pp. 52–3. The description of Atlantis ('whatever fragrant things there are in the earth . . . thrived in that land') is in the speech of Critias; see Plato (1871). For 'an emotion that is partly local . . . supreme beauty of the world', see Synge (1992), p. 69. 'Imagination = nostalgia for the past, the absent . . . art without imagination is as life without hope', is from Connolly (1944), p. 52. Thanks to Matthew Connolly for help with sourcing this.

8

The story of the dulse-collectors on Na Sceirdí rocks was told by a *seanchaí*, Seán MacGiollanáth, in *Annála Beaga Ó Iorrais Aithneach* (Dublin 1941), translated and quoted in Robinson (2007), p. 124. A dramatic first-hand account of the *Arosa* rescue mission is told in Courtney (2008), pp. 328–36. 'These rocks sometimes appear . . . people running to and fro' is from O'Flaherty (1684). 'More rain, more rest . . .' is cited in Clark (1999), p. 41.

9

St Féichín was a seventh-century saint whose cult is associated with several islands – Omey Island and Inis Meáin as well as High Island. He came west in about AD 650 in search of *an díseart*, the austere context offered by the islands of Ireland's west coast. The lines about his extreme asceticism are by Seán Ó Riordáin (*docuiredh a asna truagh / le carcair cruaidh gan edach*; 'He used to lay his wretched body / In the stony cell without raiment'), quoted in Herity (1977), p. 65. Thanks to Deirdre Roberts at Mercier Press, Cork, for permission to quote these lines, and to Micheál Ó Conghail at Cló Iar-Chonnacht for the Irish original.

For Cornish miners on High Island, see Sheehy (2017), p. 27. 'I wrote continuously . . . except on the ground' is from Murphy (2002), p. 288. 'A stone altar seen . . . not only the builder but the building' is from Murphy's diary, 3 August 1970, ibid., p. 288. 'To make our tourists feel . . . a gold-threaded anchor-badge' is from ibid., p. 195. For 'Combustion . . . we create', see Sebald (1999), p. 170.

For a very thorough study of Cromwell's Barracks, and of Inishbofin's seventeenth-century history in general, see Walsh (1989/90). An account of the priests imprisoned there being 'tortured with great cruelty' is from John Lynch's *Cambrensis Eversus* (1662), quoted in ibid., p. 39.

Richard Murphy's memoir, *The Kick: A Life among Writers*, contains a colourful account of his years spent on the west coast of Ireland, living at Rosroe, arriving on Inishbofin, running the *Ave Maria*, and of all the various literary guests he hosted. It was assembled from his diaries; see Murphy (2002). For Theodore Roethke standing on the quay at Cleggan 'like a defeated prize-fighter . . . sweating alcohol', see ibid., p. 200. The lines on the plaque in Day's Bar are taken from Roethke's late poem 'The Far Field' (posthumously published in 1964), an astonishing series of images and meditations. For Richard Murphy's first trip to Inishbofin in a 'haunted, leaking boat . . . rite of passage that changed my life', see Concannon (1997), p. x. The visit of Mary Ure and Robert Shaw is in Murphy (2002), pp. 211–12. Sylvia Plath 'inhaling the sea air ecstatically' is from ibid., p. 224. The mythical origin of Inishbofin and the story of the white cow is told widely; see Westropp (1912–13), pp. 250–51.

'Desperately . . . no squalling babies': see Plath to Murphy, 21 July 1962, Plath (2018), p. 801; 'you would be a very lovely person . . .': ibid., p. 801. Murphy's reaction to Plath is from Murphy (2002), pp. 226–8. 'My health depends on me leaving England . . . Sincerely, Sylvia' is from Plath to Murphy, 21 September 1962, Plath (2018), pp. 825–6. Five weeks before her suicide, Sylvia Plath wrote to her psychoanalyst in the US, Dr Ruth Beuscher: 'At first I had thought of burying myself & the babies in Western Ireland for the winter – where I had discovered a wonderful town on the sea with an Irish poet sailing the old Galway Hookers and cooking on turf . . .', 2 January 1963, ibid., p. 951. Murphy's last meeting with Plath is recorded in Murphy (2002), p. 229. A few days after her death, Ted Hughes asked Murphy to meet him at Sylvia's flat, and told him what he knew of her suicide and about the 'pile of recent poems' he'd found, ibid., p. 229. Murphy's account of Roethke's first stay on Inishbofin is in ibid., pp. 199–207. Roethke died from a heart attack in the swimming pool: see Seager (1968), pp. 285–6; he was fifty-five years old.

10

For a comprehensive account of the Cleggan Disaster, extensively illustrated and including details of how the same storm killed others on the Inishkeas and in Lacken Bay, see Feeney (2001). An excellent photo-essay, interviews and a short biography of Pascal Whelan were put together by Kevin Griffin (2013). Whelan died in his caravan in February 2017.

The abandoning of Inishark in October 1960 was witnessed by Dixon Scott of the *Daily Mirror*; see http://www.inishbofin.com/death-of-inishark/.

11

A report on the provenancing analysis of porcine material from sites near Stonehenge can be seen at Madgwick et al. (2019). Pork as the meat of the otherworld is in Ó hÓgáin (1999), p. 108. Strontium and calcium trace-element analysis has revealed that boar was as important in the diet of Iron Age Celts as literary and artistic references suggest; see Rowlett (1994). For the *Torc Sona*, or 'happy hog', see Campbell (2008), p. 53, and pp. 332–33 for links between the *Torc Sona* and the corn-spirit. The 'Scottish Pork Taboo' and 'Swine Cults' are discussed in consecutive chapters in Mackenzie (1935), pp. 41–74. Walter Scott includes a footnote in Chapter XXVII of *The Fortunes of Nigel*; see ibid., p. 42. The earliest surviving version of the story of *Macc Da Thó's Pig* is in the *Book of Leinster* (c. 1160), though there are references to it in earlier texts. For a translation, and a discussion of its possible satirical elements, see Gantz (1981), pp. 179–87.

An impressive selection of Celtic archaeological finds featuring the figure of the boar can be seen at *Sons of Moccus: The Cult of the Wild Boar in Celtic Europe* https://balkancelts.wordpress.com/2014/06/21/cult-of-the-wild-boar/. 'I shall deal with the sow . . . the same to me whether I live or die', is from Dooley (1999), p. 68. The origin of the name 'Orkney' is based on a coincidence of words in Norse and Irish: the name is generally thought to have been taken from the Norse *orcn*, or 'seal', but the Norsemen are believed to have simply adopted its existing name from *arc*, or 'young pig' – from http://www.orkneyjar.com/placenames/orkney. htm and private correspondence with Dónall Mac Giolla Easpaig.

12

The figure of Granuaile, female pirate and sea-rover, has generated a great deal of speculative writing over the years. I have used Anne Chambers's sober and well-sourced *Granuaile* (2009). An illustrated study of the state papers relating to Granuaile's visit to Queen Elizabeth I, translated by Anne Chambers, can be found at http://www.iisresource.org/Documents/0A4_Grace_Elizabeth.pdf.

The results of the Clare Island research were published, in sixty-seven parts, as *A Biological Survey of Clare Island in the County of Mayo, Ireland,*

and of the Adjoining District, Parts 1–68 (Part 8 was never published), by Hodges, Figgis & Co. for the Royal Irish Academy, 1911–15.

For Robert Lloyd Praeger, see Lysaght (1998), and also Patricia Byrne's article in the *Dictionary of Irish Biography*, McGuire and Quinn (2018). 'Fifty miles or so . . . on a toothbrush and a collar': see Praeger (2014), p. iv. 'The western islanders . . . constituted a genealogical link with pre-conquest Ireland': see Foster (1977), p. 265. For the Praegers' dramatic sight of Clare Island, see Prager (2014), p. 185, and for 'I recall the more leisurely . . . at the bottom of all true science', ibid., p. 384. I am grateful to Patrick O'Toole for permission to reproduce lines from his song 'Clare Island'.

The *Jane Black*'s story can be found in the Ships List for Quebec, 1842 http://www.theshipslist.com/ships/Arrivals/1842a.shtml.

For an account of the *Francis Spaight*, see Simpson (1994), pp. 129–34. Jack London wrote a semi-fictionalized account of the incident in a short story, 'Francis Spaight', published in his collection *When God Laughs, and Other Stories*, Mills and Boon, London (1911).

13

For Paul Henry and the dangerous pigs of the Inishkeas, see Dornan (2000), pp. 138–42. Robert Lloyd Praeger deliberately does not name where he saw the phalarope, but it was somewhere near Belmullet; see Praeger (2014), pp. 199–200. It was for him and his wife 'the most interesting ornithological adventure that has befallen us'. The geomorphological history of the islands, their sinking and splitting, is told in Dornan (2000).

Françoise Henry's first trip to the Inishkeas is recorded in her own words, in her diary for 11 April 1937: 'like devils . . . they are headed for America'; see Henry (2012), p. 36; 'her face is made stunning . . . black lashes', ibid., p. 39; 'To the west . . . embossed on the surface of the waves', ibid., p. 39. 'This dying island . . . The rabbits undermine it' is from her diary entry of 11 August 1946, ibid., p. 117.

The discovery and excavation of the dye factory is described in Henry (1952). For a general discussion of the production and use of purple dye in the ancient world, see Ziderman (1990), pp. 98–101. The migration of words for 'purple' and the link with Phoenicia is presented in Astour

(1965), pp. 346–50. For Pliny's description of the production of purple dye, see Pliny the Elder, *Natural History*, IX, pp. 127–40. 'Which the intensity of the sun . . . it is the more beautiful': see Bede (1990), p. 44–5. For William Cole, see Henry (1952), p. 175. 'One of the most fastidious and subtle systems of decoration the world has ever seen': see Henry (1965), p. 190. For Margaret Stokes on *The Book of Kells* – 'the epitome of Irish art' – see Stokes (1887), p. 13. James Joyce's fascination with the *The Book of Kells* and his letter to Arthur Power are discussed in *The Book of Kells: Exploring a Medieval Masterpiece*, Trinity College, Dublin https://www.futurelearn.com/courses/book-of-kells/1/steps/387037. 'This multiform and changing world . . . haunts the mind of the Irish poets': see Henry (1965), p. 193.

'Whose idea . . . low dungeon' is from Mandelstam (1989), p. 58.

For Fleming's Castle, see Dornan (2000), p. 245; a rendering of the story of the *Naomhóg* is in ibid., pp. 245–51. The 'gross superstition . . . of the inhabitants' was the view of Rev. T. A. Armstrong, ibid., p. 246. T. H. White's obsessive interest in the *Naomhóg* is recorded in White (1959). 'I was off at full tilt . . . the veritable Land of Youth', ibid., p. 104. 'If I had had paper . . . eternal things', ibid., p. 77. 'I chased that *Naomhóg* for five months . . . a half-baked archaeologist', ibid., p. 97. The 'ascetics' pillows' is from Henry (1945), p. 147. 'Bathing on summer days . . . I never went to the islands again' is from White (1959), pp. 134–5.

14

For the story of the Children of Lir, and its many forms, see Ó hÓgáin (2006), pp. 309–11.

The *Konungs skuggsjá* is translated in Meyer (1910), p. 6.

'The gyres! The gyres! Old Rocky Face, look forth' is from Yeats (2010), p. 293. He tells the incident of his youthful soaking in Donegal Bay in Yeats (1916), p. 20. 'You most of all, silent and fierce old man / . . . the daily spectacle / That stirred my fancy' is from Yeats (2010), p. 101. Sailing with his English friend is told in Yeats (1916), pp. 67–8; 'the world was full of monsters and marvels', ibid., p. 59; and 'I have walked . . . my fancy', ibid., pp. 59–60. In his essay 'Yeats, Nietzsche and the Conquest of the Sea', Nicholas Midgley quotes Yeats as saying 'there is for every man some one scene, some one adventure, some one picture that is the image of his secret life', going on to suggest that for Yeats himself it was the sea voyage; see Midgley (1995), p. 30.

Jack Yeats's painting *Memory Harbour* is used as a frontispiece in W. B. Yeats's *Reveries over Childhood and Youth*, Yeats (1916). 'I feel melancholy ... better verses': ibid., p. 59.

Links between Irish monasticism and Egypt have been widely, though not conclusively, discussed. I have used Cunliffe (2001), pp. 471–7; see also Ghazarian (2006). For Demetrius of Tarsus, see Burn (1969), p. 2.

The obituary of Monsignor Pádraig Ó Fiannachta is in the *Irish Times*, 16 August 2016, https://www.irishtimes.com/life-and-style/people/msgr-patrick-fenton-pádraig-ó-fiannachta-scholar-linguist-and-poet-1.2748206.

15

'What wonderful happiness ... in secluded monasteries' is from Merton (1990) p. 316. Navigation of Aran Sound is described in Kean (2014), pp. 328–30. For Burton Conyngham, I consulted two main sources: Forsythe (2012), and Kelly (1985). Cormac Gillespie's maritime lexicon is Gillespie (1992). The 'Ungenerous Payment' quatrain is 'cited as an example of *deibide baise fri tóin* ("slap-on the-buttocks *deibide*")' – Murphy (1956), p. 215. The version here appears in an eleventh-century manuscript, but is dated originally to the ninth century. A later version, from the fifteenth century, occurs in several manuscripts, but does not differ hugely from the earlier one. For the story of the Stag Rocks and the petrification of the three brothers, Mic Ó gCorra, see Ó hEochaidh and Ó Laoire (1989).

16

Details of Derek Hill's life on Tory Island can be found in Arnold (2010) and Gowrie (1987). I have drawn also on conversations with Anton Meehan, and a visit to his old home, Glebe House and Gallery, near Letterkenny, where his work is on display (https://glebegallery.ie). 'The earth and the sea ... than the gods': see d'Arbois de Jubainville (1903), p. 220.

A number of theories are in circulation to explain the name Tory. *Tór ri*, 'tower of the king', and *Thor ey*, 'isle of Thor', are both cited in Fox (1978), pp. 1–3. One widespread misconception is that the name Tory derives from *toraigh*, meaning 'thief' or 'robber' – though *toraigh* has a short o.

Tory Island has a different toponymic root: '*Toraigh* is the oblique case of original O.Ir. *Torach*, a name that signifies a place abounding in steep rocky heights or sea-stacks' – from private correspondence with Dónall Mac Giolla Easpaig.

Patsy Dan Rodgers, King of Tory Island, died on 19 October 2018. His obituary can be found at https://www.irishtimes.com/life-and-style/people/patsy-dan-rodgers-obituary-painter-king-and-irish-speaker-1.3683474.

The figure of Balor occurs frequently along these coasts and there are many variants to his story. For the textual basis, see Ó hÓgáin (2006), pp. 28–30, and also the entry for Lugh, ibid., pp. 312–13. An account of Balor's death at the hands of Lugh is found in *Cath Tánaiste Maige Tuired* ('The Second Battle of Mag Tuired'), filling out the reference to the battle in *Lebor Gabála Érenn*. Discussion of the universal aspects of the Balor myth can be found in Ward (2011), pp. 46–7 and p. 54; Krappe (1927), p. 18–22; and Sheeran and Witoszek (1990).

17

'Delightful I think it . . . face of the sea' is from Jackson (1935), p. 9. 'Comparing these poems . . . an old man who has been familiar with it for a lifetime': see Jackson (1971), p. 61. The 'tang and clarity of a pristine world . . . in any other European language' is from Heaney (1980), p. 181. 'The voice of the wind . . . lovely music': see Jackson (1935), p. 5; 'The smooth sea . . . cover the world', ibid., p. 23; 'Gleaning of purple lichen . . . trout leaping', ibid., p. 16; 'The woodland thicket . . . sings to me', ibid., p. 3.

'To seek out and watch and love Nature . . . a unique position in the history of the world': see Meyer (1911), p. xii. 'Its makers possessed a secret . . . the abstract and discursive': see Murphy (1931), p. 99. 'A genuine delight mingled with terror' is from Jackson (1935), p. 91. 'The ocean is full, the sea is in flood / Lovely is the home of ships' is from ibid., p. 31. For the marginalia in Cassiodorus's commentary, see Meyer (1912) – with thanks to Will Hobson for help with translation from the German.

'My tidings for you . . . my tidings': I have largely used Kuno Meyer's translation; see Meyer (1911), p. 56. None of the translations – Meyer's, Jackson's nor Murphy's – quite conveys the brevity and rhyming scheme of the Irish original:

Scél lem dúib:
dordaid dam;
snigid gaim;
ro fáith sam.

Gáeth ard úar
Ísel grían;
Gair a r-rith
Ruirthech rían

Rorúad rath;
Ro cleth cruth;
Ro gab gnáth
Giugrann guth

Ro gab úacht
Etti én;
Aigre ré
É mo scél.

For Brian McDonald talking about his life and work in Greencastle, there is a podcast: https://www.irishlifeandlore.com/product/
brian-mcdonald-born-1950-greencastle.

Two versions of the *Lough Foyle Colloquy* were translated and published,
with notes, in Carey (2002), pp. 53–87. For the poem of the woman with
the silver branch, see *Voyage of Bran*, Meyer (1895) I, pp. 2–28.

18

For M222, see 'Who Do You Think You Are?', Part 4, *Scotsman*, 2 March
2011. 'A metasedimentary and igneous rock succession . . . and Early
Cambrian', is from 'Dalradian', Geological Society, https://www.geolsoc.
org.uk/Groups-and-Networks/Commissions/Stratigraphy-Commission/
Brief-Summary-of-British-Stratigraphy/Dalradian.'The Fairies . . . of rock
or earth' is from Campbell (2008), pp. 1–2. W. B. Yeats's piece in the *Scots
Observer*, 1899, is republished in Yeats (1993), pp. 26–9. For the story of the
blind man and the vanishing island, see MacDonald (1994/5), pp. 32, 45.

The William Daniell print of the Summer Isles which hung in the house on the Summer Isles is in Fraser Darling (1943), p. 40. William Daniell's prints and an account of his journey appear in Ayton (1978). For the dust-filled skies of 1816, listen to the discussion on BBC Radio 4: '1816, Year Without a Summer', *In Our Time*, 21 April 2016, https://www.bbc.co.uk/programmes/b077j4yv. For Colman Ela, see Plummer (1922), vol. 2, p. 168, also available online: https://celt.ucc.ie/published/T201000G/text010.html.

Clann 'ic Codrum nan ron is in Campbell (2008), p. 156. The Donegal origins of *selkies* are explained in Thomson (1980), p. 185; the stabbing of the red-haired man, ibid., p. 186; the seal outside the chapel, ibid., p. 123; the Belmullet fair, ibid., pp. 128–9. The belief that seals were fallen angels is discussed by Ronald Black in Campbell (2008), p. xxxi, and examples are given by Campbell, ibid., p. 156. For Seamus Heaney on the 'old trope . . . angels and the animals', see Thomson (2012), p. xii.

'Of bodies changed to other forms I tell' is from Ovid (1986), Book I, l. 1, and 'adopt / in their migrations ever-varying forms', ibid., Book XV, ll. 173–4. 'Ovid locates and captures . . . and is transformed': see Hughes (1997), p. x. The verse from the Cornish *Ordinalia* is '*Myreugh worth an vorvoran / hanter pysk ha hanter den / y vos dev ha den yn wlan / the'n keth tra-na crygyans ren*', ll. 2403–6; see Norris (1859), vol. I, p. 415.

19

Martin Martin's description of Corryvreckan is from Martin (1716), pp. 236–7, and is also included with other early accounts of the straits between Jura and Scarba on the website of the Royal Scottish Geographical Society, https://rsgs.org/collections-corner-corryvreckan/. For Horace Beck's story of Corryvreckan, see Kingshill and Westwood (2015), pp. 272–3.

'I leapt in the air . . . "God's help is but a step away!"' is from Sheehy (2017), p. 1.

There is a very moving tribute to Danny Sheehy by Albaola, the Sea Factory of the Basques, where he overwintered his *naomhóg* en route to Santiago de Compostela: https://www.youtube.com/watch?v=7YcfaX4U6Pg

John Lorne Campbell's *Canna: The Story of a Hebridean Island* is a meticulous study of the island from the time of St Columba to 1981. The story of Margaret Fay Shaw is reassembled from private conversations with her in 1999, from her own work, her autobiography – *From the Alleghenies to the Hebrides* – and her *Folksongs and Folklore of South Uist*. Her time as an usher at Carnegie Hall in New York is in Shaw (2018), p. 34; the infection in her fingers, ibid., p. 57. The years she spent with the MacRaes is in Shaw (1999), pp. 1–18; her marriage in Shaw (2018), p. 106; the buying of the Steinway, ibid., p. 113.

'Time meant nothing to us ... and end with eleven' is from Shaw (1999), p. 17; 'sounded exactly like the children on the East Side of New York': see Shaw (2018), p. 102. See Shaw (1999) for the pig proverb, p. 37; the letter riddle, p. 46; the slug cure, p. 47.

20

For the Vikings' animistic view of their boats, see Marit Synnøve Vea at http://avaldsnes.info/en/viking/vikingskip/. Arthur Ransome's thoughts on houses and boats come from Ransome (2015), p. 71. For an overview of Alan Buchanan's work as a yacht designer, see John Leather's article in *Classic Boat* at http://buchananownersassociation.org/CB_Buchanan_article_p1.html.

'The verse is hard, terse ... along the side of a boat' is from Thomson (1974), p. 173. I have used Alan Riach's excellent rendering of *The Birlinn of Clanranald*, Mac Mhaighstir Alasdair (2015). For the story of birlinns, and the Privy Council's commissions calling for their destruction, see MacCoinnich (2015), p. 297.

John Purser's steel words on the exposed beams of the Library of Scottish Poetry are reproduced in Purser (2014), p. 215. Hugh Trevor-Roper's essay 'The Invention of Tradition: The Highland Tradition of Scotland' was published in Hobsbawn and Ranger (1983), pp. 15–43. The later edition of Trevor-Roper's *The Invention of Scotland* is Trevor-Roper (2014). The three modes of music are shown in action in *Lebor Gabála Érenn*, Chapter VII, section XI, d'Arbois de Jubainville (1903), p. 107. The story of the Harp of the Dagda is told in *Lebor Gabála Érenn*, Chapter VII, section XI, ibid., p. 107. The story of the harpists who played with such sadness that twelve men died is told in *Táin Bó Fraích* ('The Cattle Raid of the Fráech'), https://celt.ucc.ie/published/G301006.html.

A fully referenced overview of the excavations at Uamh an Ard Achadh, headed by Simon Birch and Martin Wildgoose (2004–10), is available at Canmore, National Record of the Historic Environment, Edinburgh, https://canmore.org.uk/site/273776/skye-uamh-an-ard-achadh. See also Purser (2019). For a comparison of porcine finds at feasting sites in the Stonehenge area, see Madgwick et al. (2019), http://advances.sciencemag.org/content/5/3/eaau6078.

John Purser's CD, *Dreaming of Islands* (JWP010), is issued by Sabhal Mòr Ostaig, Isle of Skye.

21

The story of Am Bratach Sìth can be found in Macgregor (1937), pp. 20–22, and on the website of Dunvegan Castle https://www.dunvegan-castle.com/castle/fairy-flag/.

The description of the Quiraing is in Mackenzie (1930), p. 33. The Colann-gun-Cheann story is in Campbell (2008), pp. 276–7, 515–18, and the Glac Gille Gun Cheann, 'a ghastly house ... on the other', is from ibid., pp. 515–16. 'Academics in both England and Scotland ... extraordinarily close to the surface of people's lives', is from Ronald Black's Introduction, ibid., pp. xxii–xxiii. 'The tinge of the ludicrous' is from ibid., p. 27. 'The most essential bit of machinery ... human beings': see Hughes (1970). 'The imagination is the only genius' is from Stevens (1960), p. 139; 'It enables us to live our own lives', ibid., p. 150.

For the island of South Rona, see Haswell-Smith (1996), pp. 136–9. For Garbh Eilean, 'Rough Island' – not to be confused with Eilean Garbh off the south of the island, nor with Eilean Garbh, the name of one of the Shiant Isles – see ibid., p. 136. 'Good for fostering of thieves, robbers, and reivers, who wait upon the plundering and pillaging of poor people' (in the original: 'guyed for fostering of theives, ruggairs, and reivairs, till a nail, upon the peilling and spulzeing of poure pepill'): from *A Description of the Western Isles of Scotland Called Hybrides* (1549), by Sir Donald Munro, p. 113, https://www.undiscoveredscotland.co.uk/usebooks/monro-westernislands/index.html.

For Uamh na Gaisgeach, or Church Cave, see Haswell-Smith (1996), p. 138. The text, translation and commentary on 'Scél Tuáin meic Chairill' can be found in Carey (1984).

22

Brian Friel's play, *Wonderful Tennessee*, opened at the Abbey Theatre, Dublin, on 30 June 1993. It is published in Friel (1993).

BIBLIOGRAPHY

For the voyage, the titles crammed into *Tsambika*'s saloon shelves were made up of old favourites, books picked up along the way, large-format volumes of pilotage, and sailing manuals. *Marine Diesel Engines: Care and Maintenance* sat alongside Chekhov's *About Love and Other Stories*, Adlard Coles's *Heavy-Weather Sailing* with Whitman's *Leaves of Grass*, *One Hand for Yourself and One for the Ship: The Essentials of Single-Handed Sailing* by Tristan Jones with *At Swim-Two-Birds* by Flann O'Brien. Back in Cornwall, where the disparate elements of the journey were pulled together, my shelves are rather more accommodating, with the added advantage of not scattering their contents on the floor whenever the wind gets up.

Below are those sources referred to directly in the text and the Notes. References in the Notes can be matched to the sources below by the author and publication date.

Arnold, Bruce, *Derek Hill*, Quartet Books, London 2010

Artaud, Antonin, *Artaud 1937 Apocalypse: Letters from Ireland*, trans. and ed. Stephen Barber, Infinity Land Press, London 2018

Astour, Michael C., 'The Origin of the Terms "Canaan", "Phoenicia", and "Purple"', *Journal of Near Eastern Studies*, vol. 24, no. 4, Part 2, pp. 346–50, University of Chicago Press 1965

Ayton, Richard, *A Voyage Round Great Britain: Undertaken Between the Years 1813 and 1823 And Commencing from The Land's End, Cornwall, With a Series of Views Illustrative of the Character and Prominent Features of the Coast, Drawn and Engraved by William Daniell*, 8 vols, reprinted Tate Gallery, London 1978

Babcock, William, *Legendary Islands of the Atlantic: A Study in Medieval Geography* American Geographical Society, New York 1922

Bassett, F. S., *Legends and Superstitions of the Sea and of Sailors in all Lands and at all Times*, Belford, Clarke & Co, Chicago and New York 1885

Batcho, Krystine, 'Nostalgia: Retreat or Support in Difficult Times?', *American Journal of Psychology*, vol. 16, no. 3, pp. 355–67, University of Illinois Press 2013a

—'Nostalgia: The Bittersweet History of a Psychological Concept', *History of Psychology*, vol. 16, no. 3, pp. 165–76, Association of Psychological Science, Washington DC 2013b

Bede, *Ecclesiastical History of the English People*, Penguin Classics, London 1990

Bergin, O. J., R. I. Best, Kuno Meyer, J. G. O'Keeffe (eds), *Anecdota from Irish Manuscripts*, Hodges, Figgis & Co. Ltd., Dublin 1910

Breatnach, Liam, 'An Edition of *Amra Senáin*', in Donnchadh Ó Corráin, Liam Breatnach, Kim McCone (eds.), *Sages, Saints and Storytellers: Celtic Studies in Honour of Professor James Carney*, Maynooth Mongraphs 2, An Sagart, Maynooth 1989

Brewster, David, *Letters in Natural Magic*, John Murray, London 1883

Bunting, Madeleine, *Love of Country: A Hebridean Journey*, Granta Books, London 2016

Burn, A. R., 'Holy Men on Islands in Pre-Christian Britain', *Glasgow Archaeological Journal*, vol. 1, pp. 2–6, Edinburgh University Press 1969

Byrne, Aisling, *Fantasy and History in Medieval Literature*, Oxford University Press 2016

Campbell, John Gregorson, *The Gaelic Otherworld*, ed. Ronald Black, Birlinn, Edinburgh 2008

Carey, John, 'Scél Tuáin meic Chairill', *Ériu*, vol. 35, pp. 93–111, Dublin 1984

—'Time, Space, and the Otherworld', *Proceedings of the Harvard Celtic Colloquium*, vol. 7, pp. 1–27, Department of Celtic Languages and Literatures, Harvard University, 1987

—'Otherworlds and Verbal Worlds in Middle Irish Narrative', *Proceedings of the Harvard Celtic Colloquium*, vol. 9, pp. 31–42, Harvard 1989

—'Aerial Ships and Underwater Monasteries: The Evolution of a Monastic Marvel', *Proceedings of the Harvard Celtic Colloquium*, vol. 12, pp. 16–28, Harvard 1992

—'The Lough Foyle Colloquy Texts', *Ériu*, vol. 52, pp. 53–87, Dublin 2002

Casey, Susan, *Voices in the Ocean: A Journey into the Wild and Haunting World of Dolphins*, Oneworld, London 2015

Chambers, Anne, *Granuaile: Grace O'Malley, Ireland's Pirate Queen c.1530–1603*, Gill and Macmillan, Dublin 2009

Clark, Wallace, *Sailing around Ireland*, Wallace Clark Book Sales 1999

Concannon, Kieran, *Inishbofin through Time and Tide*, preface by Richard Murphy, Inishbofin Development Company 1997

Connolly, Cyril, *The Unquiet Grave*, Horizon, London 1944

Corkery, Daniel, *The Hidden Ireland: A Study of Gaelic Munster in the Eighteenth Century*, M. H. Gill & Son, Dublin 1956

Courtney, David, *Nine Lives*, Mercier Press, Dublin 2008

Cunliffe, Barry, *Facing the Ocean: The Atlantic and its Peoples*, Oxford University Press 2001

Cunningham, Bernadette, *The Annals of the Four Masters: Irish History, Kingship and Society in the Early Seventeenth Century*, Four Courts Press, Dublin 2010

d'Arbois de Jubainville, H., *The Irish Mythological Cycle and Celtic Mythology*, trans., with additional notes, Richard Irvine Best, O'Donoghue and Co. and M. H. Gill and Son, Dublin 1903

Dooley, Ann, and Harry Roe (trans.), *Tales of the Elders of Ireland: A New Translation of* Acallam na Senórach, Oxford World's Classics 1999

Dornan, Brian, *Mayo's Lost Islands: The Inishkeas*, Four Courts Press, Dublin 2000

Douglas, Ken, *The Downfall of the Spanish Armada in Ireland*, Gill and Macmillan, Dublin 2010

Edmond, Rod, and Vanessa Smith (eds.), *Islands in History and Representation*, Routledge, London 2003

Eliade, Mircea, *Patterns in Comparative Religion*, New American Library, New York 1963

Feeney, Marie, *The Cleggan Bay Disaster: An Account of the Savage Storm in October 1927 that Devastated the Connemara Communities of Inishbofin and Rossadilisk*, Penumbra Press, Glencolumbkille, Co. Donegal 2001

Flower, Robin, *The Western Island or The Great Blasket*, Oxford University Press 1978

Forsythe, Wes, 'Improving Landlords and Planned Settlements in Eighteenth-Century Ireland: William Burton Conyngham and the

Fishing Station on Inis Mhic an Doirn, Co. Donegal', *Proceedings of the Royal Irish Academy: Archaeology, Culture, History, Literature*, vol. 112C, pp. 301–32, Dublin 2012

Foster, John Wilson, 'Certain Set Apart: The Western Island in the Irish Renaissance', *Studies: An Irish Quarterly Review*, vol. 66, no. 264, pp. 261–74, Irish Province of the Society of Jesus, Dublin 1977

Fox, Robin, *The Tory Islanders: A People of the Celtic Fringe*, Cambridge University Press 1978

Fraser Darling, Frank, *Island Farm*, G. Bell & Son, London 1943

Frazer, James, *The Golden Bough: A Study in Magic and Religion*, Macmillan, London 1923

Freitag, Barbara, *Hy Brasil: The Metamorphosis of an Island: From Cartographic Error to Celtic Elysium*, Rodopi, Amsterdam 2013

Friel, Brian, *Wonderful Tennessee*, Gallery Books, Oldcastle, Co. Meath 1993

Gantz, Jeffrey (trans. and ed.), *Early Myths and Sagas*, Penguin, London 1981

Ghazarian, Jacob, *The Mediterranean Legacy in Early Celtic Christianity*, Bennett & Bloom, London 2006

Gillespie, Cormac, *Maritime Matters in Ulster Irish*, MA thesis, Queen's University, Belfast 1992

Gillis, John R., *Islands of the Mind: How the Imagination Created the Atlantic World*, Palgrave Macmillan, New York 2004

— *The Human Shore: Seacoasts in History*, University of Chicago Press, London 2012

Gowrie, Grey, *Derek Hill: An Appreciation*, Quartet Books, London 1987

Griffin, Kevin, *Omey Island: 'Last Man Standing'*, Lost Cat, London 2013

Haswell-Smith, Hamish, *Scottish Islands: A Comprehensive Guide to every Scottish Island*, Canongate, Edinburgh 1996

Haak, W., et al., 'Massive Migration from the Steppe is a Source for Indo-European Languages in Europe', *Nature*, vol. 522, pp. 207–11, June 2015; also at https://www.biorxiv.org/content/10.1101/013433v1. article-info, Cold Spring Harbour Laboratory, New York 2015

Haverty, Martin, *The Aran Isles: Or a Report of the Excursion of the Ethnological Section of the British Association from Dublin to the Western*

Islands of Aran in September 1857, CELT (Corpus of Electronic Texts),
    University College, Cork 2018, www.ucc.ie/celt

Heaney, Seamus, *Preoccupations 1968–1978*, Faber & Faber, London 1980

—*New Selected Poems 1988–2013*, Faber & Faber, London 2014

Heinberg, Richard, *Memories and Visions of Paradise: Exploring the*
    Universal Myth of a Lost Golden Age, Aquarian Press, Los Angeles 1989

Henry, Françoise, 'Remains of the Early Christian Period on Inishkea
    North, Co. Mayo', *Journal of the Royal Society of Antiquaries of Ireland*,
    vol. 75, no. 3, pp. 127–55, Royal Society of Antiquaries of Ireland,
    Dublin 1945

—'A Wooden Hut on Inishkea North, Co. Mayo (Site 3, House A)', *Journal*
    of the Royal Society of Antiquaries of Ireland, vol. 82, no. 2, pp. 163–78,
    Royal Society of Antiquaries of Ireland, Dublin 1952

—*Irish Art in the Early Christian Period to 800 AD*, Methuen, London 1965

—*Françoise Henry in Co. Mayo: The Inishkea Journals*, ed. Janet T.
    Marquardt, Four Courts Press, Dublin 2012

Herity, Michael, 'The High Island Hermitage', *Irish University Review*,
    vol. 7, no. 1, 'Richard Murphy: Special Issue', pp. 52–69, Edinburgh
    University Press 1977

Hesiod, *Work and Days*, trans. Hugh G. Evelyn-White, 1914, www.sacred-
    texts.com/cla/hesiod/works.htm

Higginson, Thomas, *Tales of the Enchanted Islands of the Atlantic*,
    Macmillan, New York 1899

Hilliers, Barbara, 'Voyages between Heaven and Hell: Navigating the Early
    Irish Immram Tales', *Proceedings of the Harvard Celtic Colloquium*, vol.
    13, pp. 66–81, Department of Celtic Languages & Literatures, Harvard
    University 1993

Hobsbawn, Eric, and Terence Ranger (eds.), *The Invention of Tradition*,
    Cambridge University Press 1983

Hofer, J., 'Medical Dissertation on Nostalgia', trans. C. K. Anspach,
    Bulletin of the History of Medicine, 2, pp. 376–91, Johns Hopkins
    University Press, Baltimore 1934

Hughes, Ted, *Tales from Ovid*, Faber & Faber, London 1997

—'Myth and Education', *Children's Literature in Education*, vol. 1, Issue 1,
    pp. 55–70, https://link.springer.com/article/10.1007/BF01140656
    1970

Jackson, K. H., *Studies in Early Celtic Nature Poetry*, Cambridge University Press 1935

—*A Celtic Miscellany: Translations from Celtic Literature*, Penguin Classics, London 1971

Johnson, Donald, *Phantom Islands of the Atlantic*, Souvenir Press, London 1997

Joyce, James, *Occasional, Critical, and Political Writing*, ed. Kevin Barry, Oxford University Press 2000

Kaplan, H. A., 'The Psychopathology of Nostalgia', *Psychoanalytic Review*, 74, pp. 465–86, Guilford Press, New York 1987

Kean, Norman, *Sailing Directions for the South and West Coasts of Ireland* (fourteenth edition), ICC Kilbrittain, Co. Cork 2014

Kelly, James, 'William Burton Conyngham and the North-West Fishery of the Eighteenth Century', *Journal of the Royal Society of Antiquaries of Ireland*, vol. 115, pp. 64–85, Dublin 1985

Kiberd, Declan, *Irish Classics*, Harvard University Press 2001

Kingshill, Sophia, and Jennifer Westwood, *The Fabled Coast: Legends and Traditions from around the Shores of Britain and Ireland*, Random House, London 2015

Krappe, Alexander, *Balor with the Evil Eye: Studies in Celtic and French Literature*, University of Michigan 1927

Lynch, Sean, 'Preliminary Sketches for the Reappearance of HyBrazil', *Utopian Studies*, vol. 21, no. 1, pp. 5–15, Penn State University 2010

Lysaght, Seán, *Robert Lloyd Praeger: The Life of a Naturalist*, Four Courts Press, Dublin 1998

Mac Mhaighstir Alasdair, Alasdair, *The Birlinn of Clanranald*, trans., with Introduction, Alan Riach, Kettilonia, Angus 2015

Macalister, R. A. S. (trans. and ed.), *Lebor Gabála Érenn: The Book of the Taking of Ireland*, Irish Texts Society, Dublin 1941

MacCárthaigh, Críostóir, *Traditional Boats of Ireland: History, Folklore and Construction*, Collins Press, Cork 2008

MacCoinnich, Aonghas, *Plantation and Civility in the North Atlantic World: The Case of the Northern Hebrides, 1570–1639*, Brill, Leiden 2015

MacDonald, Donald, 'Migratory Legends of the Supernatural in Scotland: A General Survey', *Béaloideas*, vol. 62/63, 'Glórtha ón Osnádúr: Páipéir a cuireadh i láthair ag an Siompósium Nordach-Ceilteach / Sounds from the Supernatural: Papers Presented at the Nordic-Celtic Legend Symposium', pp. 29–78, An Cumann Le Béaloideas Éireann/Folklore of Ireland Society, Dublin 1994/5

MacGregor, Alasdair Alpin, *The Peat-Fire Flame: Folk-tales and Traditions from the Highland & Islands*, Moray Press, Edinburgh 1937

Mackenzie, Donald, *Scottish Folk-lore and Folk Life: Studies in Race, Culture and Tradition*, Blackie & Son, London and Glasgow 1935

Mackenzie, William, *Skye Traditions, Reflections and Memories*, Alex Maclaren & Sons, Glasgow 1930

Mackley, J. S., *The Anglo-Norman Voyage of Saint Brendan* (bilingual version), Isengrin Publishing, Northampton 2013

Madgwick, R. et al., 'Multi-Isotope Analysis Reveals that Feasts in the Stonehenge Environs and Across Wessex Drew People and Animals from Throughout Britain', *Science Advances*, vol. 5, no. 3, Washington DC, 2019

Mandelstam, Osip, *Journey to Armenia* (trans. Clarence Brown), Redstone Press, London 1989

Manning, Conleth, and Karena Morton, *Clare Island, Co. Mayo: The Abbey and Its Paintings*, Archaeology Ireland, Heritage Guide no. 46, Wordwell Books, Dublin 2009

Martin, Martin, *Description of the Western Islands of Scotland* (second edition), Bell, London 1716

McGuire, James, and James Quinn (eds.), *Dictionary of Irish Biography* (11 vols), Cambridge University Press 2018

McNamara, Gerard (trans.), *The Voyage of Saint Brendan the Navigator*, CreateSpace Independent Publishing Platform, 2013

Melville, Herman, *Moby Dick*, Oxford University Press 1988

Merton, Thomas, *The Seven Storey Mountain*, SPCK, London 1990

Meyer, Kuno, *The Voyage of Bran, Son of Febal, to the Land of the Living*, 2 vols, David Nutt, London 1895

—'The Irish Mirabilia in the Norse "Speculum Regale"', *Ériu*, vol. 4, Royal Irish Academy, Dublin 1910

—*Selections from Ancient Irish Poetry*, Constable, London 1911

—'Neu aufgefundene altirische Glossen', *Zeitschrift für Celtische Philologie*, 8, pp. 173–77, University of Bonn 1912

Midgley, Nicholas, 'Yeats, Nietzsche and the Conquest of the Sea', *The Harp (Journal of Irish Studies)*, vol. 10, pp. 30–39, https://www.jstor.org/stable/20533352, 1995

Murphy, Gerard (trans. and ed.), *Early Irish Lyrics: Eighth to Telfth Century*, Oxford 1956

—'The Origin of Irish Nature Poetry', *Studies: An Irish Quarterly Review*, vol. 20, no. 77, pp. 87–102, 1931

Murphy, Richard, *The Kick: A Life among Writers*, Granta Books, London 2002

Norris, Edwin (trans. and ed.), *The Ancient Cornish Drama*, 2 vols, Oxford University Press 1859

Ó Crohan, Tomás, *The Islandman*, trans. Robin Flower, Oxford University Press 1978

Ó Faoláin, Séan, *An Irish Journey*, Longmans, Green, New York 1943

Ó hEithir, Breandán, and Ruairí Ó hEithir (eds), *An Aran Reader*, Lilliput Press, Dublin 1991

Ó hEochaidh, S., and L. Ó Laoire, 'An Diabhal i Seanchas Thír Chonaill', *Béaloideas*, no. 57, pp. 37–86, Dublin 1989

Ó hÓgáin, Dáithí, *The Lore of Ireland: An Encyclopedia of Myth, Legend and Romance*, Boydell Press, Cork 2006

—*The Sacred Isle: Belief and Religion in Pre-Christian Ireland*, Collins Press, Cork 1999

O'Connell, J. W., 'St Enda of Aran: Tracing an Early Irish Saint', in *The Book of Aran: The Aran Islands, Co. Galway*, ed. John Waddell, J. W. O'Connell, Anne Korff, Tír Eolas, Kinvara, Co. Galway 1994

O'Donoghue, Denis, *Brendaniana: St Brendan the Voyager in Story and Legend*, Browne & Nolan, Dublin 1895

O'Flaherty, Roderic, *A Chorographical Description of West Or H-Iar Connaught*, Irish Archaeological Society, Dublin 1684, https://archive.org/details/achorographicaloooflgoog/

O'Guiheen, Michaél, *A Pity Youth Does Not Last: Reminiscences of the Last of the Great Blasket Island's Poets and Storytellers*, trans. Tim Enright, Oxford University Press 1982

Obert, Julia, 'Space and the Trace: Thomas Kinsella's Postcolonial Placelore', *New Hibernia Review / Iris Éireannach Nua*, vol. 13, no.

4, pp. 77–93, University of St Thomas (Center for Irish Studies), Houston, Texas 2009

Ovid, *Metamorphoses*, trans. A. D. Melville, ed. E. J. Kenney, Oxford University Press 1986

Plath, Sylvia, *Letters of Sylvia Plath*, vol. II: *1956–1963*, Faber & Faber, London 2018

Plato, *Critias*, trans. Benjamin Jowett, Scribner's, New York, 1871, http://www.sacred-texts.com/cla/plato/critias.htm

Plummer, Christopher, *Bethada Náem nÉrenn: Lives of Irish Saints*, 2 vols, Clarendon Press, Oxford 1922

Praeger, Robert Lloyd, *The Way that I Went*, Collins Press, Cork 2014

Purser, John, *Scotland's Music: A History of the Traditional and Classical Music of Scotland from Earliest Times to the Present Day*, Mainstream, Edinburgh 1992

—*There is No Night: New and Selected Poems*, Kennedy & Boyd, Edinburgh 2014

—'A Lyre Bridge of the Early Iron Age from High Pasture Cave, Scotland', *Studien zur Musikarchäologie*, XI, pp. 265–80, Rahden 2019

Ransome, Arthur, *Racundra's First Cruise*, Fernhurst Books, Leamington Spa 2015

Relethford, J. H., 'Genetic structure and population history of Ireland: a comparison of blood group and anthropometric analyses', *Annals of Human Biology*, vol. 10, no. 4, pp. 321–34, Taylor & Francis 1983

Renan, Ernest, *The Poetry of the Celtic Races, and Other Essays*, Walter Scott Publishing Co., London 1896

Robinson, Tim, *Stones of Aran: Pilgrimage*, Penguin, London 1986

—*Stones of Aran: Labyrinth*, Lilliput Press, Dublin 1995

—*Connemara: Listening to the Wind*, Penguin, London 2007

Rowlett, Ralph, 'Did Iron Age Celts Really Hunt Wild Boar (*Sus Scrofa*)?', *Proceedings of the Harvard Celtic Colloquium*, vol. 14, pp. 195–210, Harvard University 1994

Saramago, José, *The Stone Raft*, Vintage, London 2000

Sayers, Peig, *An Old Woman's Reflections: The Life of a Blasket Island Storyteller*, trans. Séamus Ennis, Oxford University Press 1962

Seager, Allan, *The Glass House: The Life of Theodore Roethke*, McGraw-Hill, New York 1968

Sebald, W. G., *The Rings of Saturn*, Harvill Press, London 1999

Severin, Tim, *The Brendan Voyage: The Seafaring Classic That Followed St Brendan to America*, Gill Books, Dublin 2005

Shaw, Margaret Fay, *Folksongs and Folklore of South Uist*, Birlinn, Edinburgh 1999

—*From the Alleghenies to the Hebrides: An Autobiography*, Birlinn, Edinburgh 2018

Sheehy, Danny (Domhnall Mac Síthigh), *In the Wake of St Brendan: From Dingle to Iceland 2011* (originally *Iomramh Bhréanainn MMXI*), trans. Camilla Dinkel, An Sagart, An Díseart, An Daingean, Dingle 2017

Sheeran, Patrick, 'Aran, Paris and the Fin-de-Siècle' in *The Book of Aran: The Aran Islands, Co. Galway*, ed. John Waddell, J. W. O'Connell, Anne Korff, Tír Eolas, Kinvara, Co. Galway 1994

—and Nina Witoszek, 'Myths of Irishness: The Fomorian Connection', *Irish University Review*, vol. 20, no. 2, pp. 239–50, Edinburgh University Press 1990

Simpson, Brian, *Cannibalism and Common Law: A Victorian Yachting Tragedy*, Hambledon Press, London 1994

Stevens, Wallace, *The Necessary Angel: Essays on Reality and the Imagination*, Faber & Faber, London 1960

Stokes, Margaret, *Early Christian Art in Ireland*, Chapman & Hall, London 1887

Stokes, Whitley, 'The Colloquy of the Two Sages, *Immacallam in dá Thuarad*', *Revue Celtique*, vol. XXVI, Paris 1905

—and E. Windisch, *Irische Text mit Übersetzungen und Wörterbuch*, Von S. Hirzel, Leipzig 1891

Stommel, Henry, *Lost Islands: The Story of Lost Islands that have Vanished from Nautical Charts*, University of British Columbia Press, Vancouver 1984

Symons, Arthur, *Cities and Sea Coasts and Islands*, Collins, London 1918

Synge, J. M., *The Aran Islands*, ed. Tim Robinson, Penguin, London 1992

—*Travels in Wicklow, West Kerry and Connemara*, Serif, London 2009

Thomson, David, *The People of the Sea: A Journey in Search of the Seal Legend*, Paladin, London 1980; with an introduction by Seamus Heaney, Canongate, Edinburgh 2012

Thomson, Derick, *An Introduction to Gaelic Poetry*, Gollancz, London 1974

Trevor-Roper, Hugh, *The Invention of Scotland: Myth and History*, Yale University Press, London 2014

Walsh, Paul, 'Cromwell's Barrack: A Commonwealth Garrison Fort on Inishbofin, Co. Galway', *Journal of the Galway Archaeological and Historical Society*, vol. 42, pp. 30–71, Galway Archaeological and Historical Society 1989/90

Ward, Alan, *The Myths of the Gods: Structures in Irish Mythology*, CreateSpace Publishing, 2011

Waters, E. G. R. (ed.), *The Anglo-Norman Voyage of St Brendan by Benedeit: A Poem of the Early Twelfth Century*, Oxford University Press 1928

Westropp, T. J., 'A Biological Survey of Clare Island in the County of Mayo, Ireland, and of the Adjoining District (Sections 1–3)', *Proceedings of the Royal Irish Academy: Archaeology, Culture, History, Literature*, vol. 31, Royal Irish Academy, Dublin 1911–15

—'Brasil and the Legendary Islands of the North Atlantic: Their History and Fable. A Contribution to the "Atlantis" Problem', *Proceedings of the Royal Irish Academy*, vol. 30, pp. 223–60, Royal Irish Academy, Dublin 1912–13

White, T. H., *The Godstone and the Blackymor*, Jonathan Cape, London 1959

Wilcox, Robert, *Southern Ireland: Cruising Companion*, Wiley Nautical, Chichester 2009

Wilde, Oscar, *The Soul of Man under Socialism*, Arthur L. Humphreys, London 1912

Wooding, Jonathan, (ed.), *The Otherworld Voyage in Early Irish Literature: An Anthology of Criticism*, Four Courts Press, Dublin 2000

Yeats, W. B., *Reveries over Childhood and Youth*, Macmillan, New York 1916

—*Writings on Irish Folklore, Legend and Myth*, Penguin Classics, London 1993

—*The Collected Works of W. B. Yeats*, vol. 3: *Autobiographies*, Simon & Schuster, London 1999

—*The Collected Poems of W. B. Yeats*, Palgrave Macmillan, London 2010

Zhou, Xinyue, Constantine Sedikides, Tim Wildschut, Ding-Guo Gao, 'Counteracting Loneliness: On the Restorative Function of Nostalgia', *Psychological Science*, vol. 19, no. 10, Association of Psychological Science, Washington DC 2008

Ziderman, I. Irving, 'BA Guide to Artifacts: Seashells and Ancient Purple Dyeing', *The Biblical Archaeologist*, vol. 53, no. 2, pp. 98–101, University of Chicago Press 1990

ACKNOWLEDGEMENTS

Single-handed sailors are not always as independent as their status suggests. I found support when it was needed, offered with a mixture of enthusiasm by those who love the sea, and concern by those who respect it (the one rarely existing without the other). In each port-of-call, harbour masters and local mariners were happy to share vital pieces of information. Progress was made a lot easier, and a lot more fun, with the help and hospitality of Gary Adams, Annie Breslin, Conan Breslin, Tommy Burke, Fiona Bushe, Paddy Bushe, Dermot Concannon, Pat Concannon, Adrian Connell, Olly Cotterell, Lance Dutton, Aoife Dutton, Catherine Fitzgerald, Paul Fjelrad, Manus Gallagher, Cormac Gillespie, young Cormac Gillespie, Liam Holden, Brian Mcdonald, Philip Mcdonald, Fiona Mackenzie, Anton Meehan, Hugh Musgrave, Nicola Musgrave, Donnchadh Ó Baoill, Catherine Peat, John Purser, Hugh Raven, Jane Raven, Patsy Dan Rodgers, Ian Shanahan, Richard Sheehy, Danny Sheehy, Maria Simonds-Gooding, Ian Thomson, Paula Vine, Peter Vine, Jackie Ward, Damian Ward, Dominic West, Anthony Wills, Maggie Young and Stephen Young.

My thanks to all those who, in the hunt for *Tsambika*, showed me their various vessels, in various conditions, in various ports around the UK and Ireland. To Barney Sandeman of Sandeman Yachts, and Richard and Peter Gregson of Wooden Ships; to Andrew Massey, and to *Tsambika*'s previous owners, whose spirit remains in her – the Trebilcock family, Souter Harris and David Newman.

From the boatyards along the Roseland side of the Fal estuary – Freshwater, Polvarth, Tolverne and particularly Pasco's – *Tsambika* received preparatory attention from Craig Brown, Gawain Bysouth, Graham Churchill, Chris de Glanville, Jonathan Leach, Jack Leckie, David Llewellyn, Hugh Noott, Colin Pugh, Roger Smith and Liam Stacpoole. In Cornwall, I have benefitted for years from the good company and skill of Peter Bryant, Bill Handley, Lynda Handley, Steve Miles and all who crew with me on the Falmouth Working Boat *Florence*. Thanks also over the years to the boats and their skippers who have taken me on board – including *Ratona, Dyarchy, Inca, Raua, Emily Grace, Liberty, Whitbread*.

The conception of this book goes back many years. Mike Fishwick at HarperCollins was an early supporter, before being handed an entirely different manuscript. To the staff of Acadamh na hOllscolaíochta Gaeilge, An Cheathrú Rua for teaching me something of the Irish language. To all those friends and contacts who have helped, consciously and unconsciously, along the way – David Bucknell, Roland Chambers, Matthew Connolly, Mike Croft, Tarlach de Blacam, Mick Delap, Richard Hoare, Oliver Hoare, Will Hobson, Miles Hoskin, Jeremy Letcher, Sam Llewellyn, Jane Mulvagh, Andrew McNeillie, Brian Perman, Sophie Poklewski-Koziell, Iain Robertson-Smith, Tim Robinson, Magda Sagarzazu, Margaret Fay Shaw, Fiona Stafford, Charles Thomas, Colin Thubron, Jane Turnbull, Tom Varcoe, Arabella Windham.

During the writing of these pages – a lone adventure as challenging and rewarding as going to sea – I have had support from many of those I've worked with before. It was the last book I did with Gillon Aitken, legendary agent and friend (who refused all attempts to get him to join me on the water). He died in 2016. Anna Webber took over and has proved adept at adding to her role as friend that of professional agent – thanks to her and Georgie Le Grice and Zoe Ross and all at United Agents. I am grateful too for help with the manuscript from Cormac Gillespie and Dónall Mac Giolla Easpaig ('the brother'), Alan Riach, John Purser and Sinéad O Callaghan. Laura Barber proved once again a wizard with the editing pencil, everything one could wish for in an editor, likewise Daphne Tagg. Many thanks to Emily Faccini for the maps, to the good spirits and patience of Christine Lo, Angela Rose, Pru Rowlandson and to all at Granta.

And, as always, a loving thank you to Charlotte, Clio and Arthur for tolerating sustained absences at sea, writerly absences at home and for the buoyant part they play in my life, in ways I cannot begin to explain.

INDEX